Multicultural Education in Western Societies

Edited by

JAMES A. BANKS
and
JAMES LYNCH

To: Sara
With Best wishes
and warm regards,
Jim Banks
December 15 / 1986
Seattle

HOLT, RINEHART AND WINSTON
London · New York · Sydney · Toronto

Holt, Rinehart and Winston Ltd: 1 St Anne's Road,
Eastbourne, East Sussex BN21 3UN

British Library Cataloguing in Publication Data
Multicultural education in Western societies.
  1. Minorities—Education
  I. Banks, James A.   II. Lynch, James
  370.11′5   LC3719
ISBN 0-03-910676-4

Typeset by Oxford Print Associates Ltd.
Printed and bound in Great Britain by Mackays of Chatham Ltd.

Last digit is print number: 9 8 7 6 5 4 3 2 1

MULTICULTURAL EDUCATION IN WESTERN SOCIETIES

Contents

Notes on Contributors

James A. Banks is Professor and Chairman, Curriculum and Instruction, University of Washington, Seattle. A past president of the National Council for the Social Studies and a former school teacher, he has held fellowships from the National Academy of Education, the Rockefeller Foundation and the Kellogg Foundation. Professor Banks has studied and worked in multicultural education in several nations, including Mexico, Australia, the Netherlands, France and the United Kingdom. His books include *March Toward Freedom: A History of Black Americans; We Americans: Our History and People; Teaching Strategies for the Social Studies*, third edition; and *Multiethnic Education: Theory and Practice*.

Brian M. Bullivant is a Reader in Education, Faculty of Education, Monash University. A former school teacher in Britain and Australia, he is Associate Editor of the *Journal of Intercultural Studies*. He has served as the Senior Research Officer-in-Charge of the National Information Centre for Social Science Education and as Co-Director, Social Science Materials Development Project at the Australian Council for Educational Research, Melbourne. His books include *The Way of Tradition: Life in an Orthodox Jewish School; Race, Ethnicity and Curriculum; The Pluralist Dilemma in Education: Six Case Studies;* and *Pluralism: Cultural Maintenance and Evolution*.

Maurice Craft is Professor, Pro-Vice-Chancellor and Chairman of the School of Education at the University of Nottingham. He was formerly Goldsmiths' Professor of Education at London University, and before that Professor and Chairman of the Centre for the Study of Urban Education at Latrobe University, Melbourne, Australia. He was Chairman of the Commission for Racial Equality's National Advisory Group on Teacher Education from 1980 to 1984. His publications include *Education and Cultural Pluralism; Training Teachers of Ethnic Minority Community Languages* (with Madeleine Atkins); *Teaching in a Multicultural Society*; and *Linking Home and School* (co-editor).

Geneva Gay is Professor of Education and Assistant Dean of the School of Humanities, Social Sciences and Education at Purdue University. She is a former high school social studies teacher and Assistant Professor of Education and Director of Ethnic Studies at the University of Texas in Austin. Currently a Kellogg National Fellow, Professor Gay has contributed many papers to journals and books. Among the books to which she has contributed are *Teaching Ethnic Studies: Concepts and Strategies; Pluralism and the American Teacher, Considered Action for Curriculum Improvement; Introduction to Education*; and *The Social Studies*, the 80th Yearbook of the National Society for the Study of Education.

James Lynch is Professor of Education and Dean of the Faculty of Education, Sunderland Polytechnic. Professor Lynch is a former school teacher and has been a Visiting Professor at the University of Frankfurt and Head of the School of Education, Newcastle College of Advanced Education, Newcastle, New South Wales, Australia. He specialises in teacher education and is interested in a theory and pedagogy of emancipatory education appropriate to multicultural societies. His publications include *Parents and Teachers, Lifelong Education and the Preparation of Educational Personnel; Education for Community; Teaching in the Multi-Cultural School; The Multicultural Curriculum*; *Change in Teacher Education* (co-editor); and *Multicultural Education: Principles and Practice*.

Kogila A. Moodley is on the Faculty of Education at the University of British Columbia and is also the Coordinator of the Multicultural Teacher Education Program. A former high school teacher in South Africa, she is a member of the Board of Directors of the Canadian Ethnic Studies Association. She has contributed papers on issues related to race and ethnic relations to several books, including *Change in Contemporary South Africa; The Liberal Dilemma in South Africa*; and *Ethnicity, Power and Politics in Canada*. She is the editor and co-author of *Race Relations and Multicultural Education*.

Preface

Western democratic societies share an egalitarian ideology which maintains that a major goal of the state is to protect human rights and promote equality and the structural inclusion of all racial, ethnic and cultural groups into the fabric of society. Despite the fact that a democratic ideology is institutionalised within Western nation-states, they are characterised by widespread inequality and by racial, ethnic and class stratification. This gross discrepancy between democratic ideals and societal realities, and the rising expectations of victimised racial and ethnic groups, have created ethnic protest and revival movements within each of the Western nations since the 1960s. This series of ethnic revitalisation movements has caused leaders and dominant groups in these societies to reflect seriously about issues of inequality and to take actions, often merely symbolic ones, to make societal realities more consistent with declared democratic ideals.

A major goal of the ethnic revitalisation movements was to change social, economic and political institutions so that they more accurately reflected the values, goals and aspirations of structurally excluded ethnic, cultural, linguistic and religious groups. Ethnic reformers and their allies have used much of their energy trying to change and influence educational institutions because they believe that educational institutions have been one of their main oppressors and therefore can play a pivotal role in their liberation.

The ethnic revival movements have taken various forms at different times in each nation. In response to these movements, educational institutions in the major Western nations have taken steps to implement reforms that reflect ethnic diversity and promote equality, while maintaining an overall commitment to social cohesion and political stability. These educational initiatives have created lively and sometimes embittered and prolonged controversy because little agreement exists within each nation about what should be the proper role of state schools in the ethnic education of both majority and minority students. The views range from those who endorse a strong cultural pluralist position and argue that the state school should promote the ethnic allegiances and cultures of students, to those who believe that state schools should remain neutral on questions and issues related to race, ethnicity, language and religion.

Some citizens believe that the major role of the state school should be to socialise students so that they attain the universalistic values and culture of the nation-state. They contend that if state schools promote allegiances to ethnic groups and cultures, this will create a degree of ethnic and social polarisation that will be inimical to the universalistic culture of the nation-state. Some reformers believe that the school can play a key role in promoting educational equality and helping students to attain the knowledge, attitudes and skills needed to make their societies and the world more humane. On the other hand, most radical scholars and reformers maintain that the school is one of the major institutions that perpetuate inequality and that it is therefore incapable of promoting societal reform and greater educational equality.

The major purpose of this book is to examine the various ideological positions, concepts and paradigms that have emerged in a selected group of Western nations in which multicultural education has developed over the last decades and to propose tentative guidelines for practising educators who have responsibilities for developing curricula and programmes related to ethnic and cultural diversity. The previous work of the editors in several different nations has convinced them that the various perspectives from each nation can enrich and illuminate the practices of others, and that these multiple perspectives, appropriately analysed and presented, can provide effective guidelines for educational reform and curricular change.

This book is divided into three major parts. Part I consists of a chapter which formulates a typology that describes the phases of ethnic revitalisation movements, the paradigmatic responses that educators have made and are making to these movements, and the limitations which characterise educational reforms that are based on single-factor paradigms. In the final part of Chapter 1, the author advances the view that educational reforms must be based on multi-factor paradigms and a holistic approach in order to increase educational equality and help all students to acquire the knowledge, skills and attitudes needed to live successfully in a multicultural society and world.

Part II consists of chapters that describe examples of the paradigms and concepts delineated in Chapter 1. Scholars who have studied and observed the evolution of multicultural education within their respective nations or geographical regions describe the status and problems of conceptualising and implementing multicultural education, government policies and programmes, evolving practices, and the debates and controversies related to education and ethnic diversity that are taking place in these societies. A salient theme in these chapters is the difficulty that each nation-state is having in attempting to formulate educational policies that simultaneously respect the cultural integrity of students from diverse groups, help students to attain the knowledge and skills needed to live productive lives in the national civic and highly technological culture, and help students to develop a commitment to the overarching ideals and ethos of the nation-state.

The final part of this book consists of two chapters devoted respectively to a consideration of the rationale and components of an effective multicultural teacher-education programme, and a summary of the major issues raised in the book, together with an outline agenda for policy and action. This part of the book is designed to treat the important and enduring issues in multicultural education that are not comprehensively discussed in the previous chapters and to summarise the major concepts, issues, paradigms and problems discussed in the book.

We are keenly aware of the fact that the ethnic revitalisation movements that emerged in the 1960s and 1970s echoed throughout the world and were not limited to the developed Western nations. The development of educational policy and programmes related to ethnic and racial diversity in the Third World is not only an immensely important topic but an inherently interesting one. An examination of such policies and practices in the developing nations would certainly deepen our understanding of multicultural education in the Western nations and help us to formulate more powerful generalisations about the formation of educational policy and practice related to cultural and ethnic diversity. Despite the insights that the inclusion of the development of multicultural education in the Third World would have brought to this book, the scope of this book is limited – for several reasons – to a consideration of multicultural education in selected Western societies.

We limited the scope of this book in part because we felt that trying to do more within a short volume would be overly ambitious and impractical. We also limited our focus because the problems of educating ethnic and cultural minorities in the developing nations raise a series of fruitful and difficult questions over and above those raised in the Western nations. These questions, because of their complexity, merit a depth of exploration and analysis that is beyond the possibilities of this modestly ambitious volume. To give just one example, while each of the developed Western nations has shaped a national identity with relatively well-defined boundaries, many of the Third World nations are still in the process of shaping a nation-state and a national identity. The quest for ethnic identity and entitlements has very different meanings in a nation that has a well-developed national identity and in one that is in the process of formulating a national ethos and identity.

We hope that this book will help practising educators, policy makers, curriculum developers, head teachers and others to conceptualise, plan, implement, evaluate and improve programmes designed to increase the achievement of ethnic minority students and to help all students acquire the knowledge, attitudes and skills needed to live creative and satisfying lives in a culturally diverse society and world. We have designed this book for introductory courses in multicultural education, for foundation courses in education, for graduate courses in comparative education, and for inservice teacher education courses at various levels.

We are deeply grateful to the contributing authors who took invaluable time from exceedingly busy schedules, not only to write their chapters but to revise them to make them more consistent with the goals of this book. We should also like to thank Cherry A. Banks for preparing the index. Editing this book has deepened our sensitivity to the plight of ethnic and cultural minorities in Western societies and has reaffirmed our commitment to strive to create a world in which cultural freedom becomes a possibility for all individuals and groups.

JAMES A. BANKS
Seattle, Washington

JAMES LYNCH
Ilkley, West Yorkshire

PART I

Concepts, Paradigms and Issues

The chapter that constitutes this part of the book describes some of the basic concepts, paradigms and issues in multicultural education, which are illustrated more comprehensively in the chapters in Parts II and III. The author discusses the nature of ethnic and cultural diversity in Western societies, the democratic ideologies that are institutionalized within these nations, and the ethnic revitalization movements that emerged within them because of the wide discrepancies between their liberal ideologies and the institutionalized discrimination and structural exclusion of ethnic and cultural groups.

The author conceptualizes ethnic revitalization as consisting of four major phases: a precondition phase, a first or early phase, a later phase, and a final phase. He then describes the prototypical responses that educational institutions have made and are making to ethnic revitalization movements, which he calls paradigms. He describes ten major paradigms: ethnic additive, self-concept development, cultural deprivation, language, racism, radical, genetic, cultural pluralism, cultural difference, and assimilationism. The author explains how single-factor paradigms – which try to explain why ethnic and cultural minority students achieve poorly in school – dominate the field of multicultural education. He explains why multi-factor paradigms must be used to guide educational reform and practice if educational institutions are to promote equality and help all students to develop the knowledge, attitudes and skills needed to function effectively in a culturally diverse society and world.

Chapter 1

Multicultural Education: Development, Paradigms and Goals

JAMES A. BANKS

ETHNIC AND CULTURAL DIVERSITY IN WESTERN SOCIETIES

When the ethnic revitalization movements emerged in the 1960s, the Western nations were characterized by tremendous ethnic, cultural and racial diversity. This diversity resulted from several historical developments. The nations in Western Europe had longstanding linguistic and cultural minorities, such as the Basques in France and Spain, the Germans in Denmark, the Danes in Germany, and the Welsh and Scots in the United Kingdom. The nation-states that were created by the European explorers and settlers, such as the United States, Canada and Australia, were populated by an array of ethnic and cultural groups from Europe. The ethnic and cultural diversity within these new nations was enriched by the native people that the European settlers displaced, by blacks from Africa, and by the large numbers of immigrants and refugees from nations throughout the world who flocked to these nations to realize their religious, political and economic dreams.

THE ASSIMILATIONIST AND LIBERAL VISION OF SOCIETY

While the Western nations were characterized by tremendous cultural and ethnic diversity in the period after the Second World War, they were dominated by an assimilationist ideology. A major national goal in each of the newer Western nations was to create a nation-state in which one culture – the Anglo-Saxon or Anglo-Celtic – was dominant. The diverse ethnic and cultural groups that made up these nations were expected to forsake their original cultures in order to become effective citizens of their nation-states. The older nation-states in Western Europe, such as the United

Kingdom, France and Germany, were also dominated by an assimilationist ideology. Their goal was to maintain their national identities and the cultural hegemony of existing dominant groups.

The assimilationist ideology that dominated the Western nations was undergirded by the liberal expectancy and a liberal ideology that envisioned a nation-state in which individuals from all ethnic, cultural and racial groups are able to participate fully. However, the liberal believes that in order for this kind of equitable, modernized society to emerge and blossom, individuals must be freed of their ethnic and cultural attachments. Ethnic attachments and traditionalism, argues the liberal, are inconsistent with modernization and a technological culture. Traditional cultures promote historic prejudices, we–they attitudes, and cultural conflict (Porter, 1975). They also lead to the Balkanization of the nation-state. Traditionalism and cultural pluralism also stress group rights over the rights of the individual, and regard the group rather than the individual as primary (Patterson, 1977). In a modernized, equitable society, individual rights are paramount; group rights are secondary.

Liberals are also critical of traditionalism because, they maintain, it promotes inequality, racial and ethnic awareness, group favoritism, and ethnic stratification. As long as attachments to cultural and ethnic groups are salient and emphasized, argues the liberal assimilationist, they will serve as the basis for jobs and educational discrimination as well as other forms of exclusion that are inconsistent with democratic ideals and values. The solution to this problem, argues the liberal modernist, is a common national culture into which all individuals may be assimilated and public policies that are neutral on questions of race and ethnicity.

THE RISE OF ETHNIC REVITALIZATION MOVEMENTS

The liberal assimilationist vision dominated Western societies when the ethnic revitalization movements emerged in the 1960s. These movements were triggered by the civil rights movements led by blacks in the United States. The movement begun by American blacks echoed throughout the world. The French and Indians in Canada, the West Indians and Asians in Britain, the Indonesians and Surinamese in the Netherlands, and the Aborigines in Australia joined the string of ethnic movements, expressed their rage and anger, and demanded that the institutions within their nation-states become more responsive to their needs, hopes and dreams.

The scope and intensity of the ethnic protest movements during the 1960s and 1970s revealed that the liberal ideology that dominated Western social science and national policies had serious shortcomings and neither adequately explained nor predicted the course of ethnic events and the status of ethnic groups. Western social scientists studying race relations in the period after the Second World War viewed assimilation of ethnic groups in Western nations as the proper and inevitable goal. They were heavily influenced by the writings of Robert E. Park (1950), the US sociologist. Park believed that the four basic processes of social interaction were contact, conflict, accommodation, and assimilation.

It was not only national policy makers and social scientists who endorsed an assimilationist ideology during this period in Western societies. Most ethnic groups themselves, and their leaders, accepted assimilation into their national societies as a desirable goal and worked hard to achieve it. There are some important exceptions to this generalization, including the Welsh in the UK, the French in Canada, the Garvey movement in the United States, and other isolated separatist movements in Western nations that began prior to the Second World War. However, until the 1960s, most ethnic groups in the Western nations worked to attain cultural assimilation and structural integration into their societies.

Ethnic groups tried to become assimilated into their national societies in large part because of powerful economic and political incentives. The strong appeal of attaining social mobility within the industrialized nation-states such as the United States, Canada and Australia motivated many citizens of these nations to rid themselves of most aspects of their ethnic cultures and to become skeptical and ashamed of folk cultures and traditionalism. There has been historically, and continues to be, a cogent push toward assimilation in Western nations because of the strong appeal of social and economic mobility in these societies.

In many respects, the strong assimilationist and liberal ideology that has dominated the Western nations such as the United States, Canada and Australia has been successful. These nations were originally peopled by cultural and ethnic groups with divergent values, beliefs and ethos. Today, however, each of these nations is unified by an overarching set of ideals and an ethos shared by groups with disparate origins. With the exception of Canada, separatist movements have not been an important aspect of the history of the newer Western nations that are dominated by Anglo culture and institutions.

Given the impressive success of the assimilationist and liberal conception and ideology, why are the Western nations today faced with problems related to ethnic and cultural pluralism? This question has no simple answer, but a number of hypotheses can be formulated. The ethnic and racial problems in the Western nations developed in part because specific ethnic groups, because of their physical and cultural characteristics, were denied the opportunity to attain the attributes and behaviors that were needed to assimilate in the mainstream society. While blacks and Indians in the United States were expected to assimilate culturally, they were frequently denied the opportunity to attain an education, to vote, and to participate in the political process. The Canadian Indians had a similar experience, as did the Australian Aborigines. The Western nations created expectations and goals for excluded ethnic groups but often made it impossible for these groups to attain them.

Ethnic protest movements also arose in Western societies because ethnic groups that experienced discrimination and racism, such as the blacks in the United States and the Indians in Canada, internalized the egalitarian and democratic ideologies that were institutionalized within the Western nations and believed that it was possible for these ideals to be realized. While the conditions of these groups improved in the period after the Second World War, they still did not have many of the benefits enjoyed by the dominant groups in their societies. In the post-war period, their governments took steps to eliminate some of the most blatant forms of discrimination and to improve their social and economic status. However, these improved conditions created rising expectations and hope, and stimulated the rise of ethnic protest and revitalization movements.

Rising expectations outpaced the improvement within the social, economic and political systems. Widespread discrimination, racism and structural exclusion experienced by ethnic groups served as a vehicle for political mobilization. As the ethnic revitalization movements matured they acquired cultural, political and economic dimensions. Ethnic groups demanded jobs, political participation, and the legitimization, recognition and incorporation of their cultures and languages into the general culture and the state school system. The disillusionment and shattered dreams that resulted from the historic quest for assimilation caused ethnic groups to demand structural inclusion but the maintenance of important aspects of their cultures and symbols.

The failure of Western nation-states to further close the gap between their democratic ideals and societal realities, and the existence of discrimination and racism, do not sufficiently explain the rise of ethnic revitalization movements in the 1960s. The strong cultural and symbolic components of many of these movements suggest that they emerged in part to help individual members of ethnic groups to acquire the sense of community, moral authority and meaning in life that highly modernized societies often leave unfulfilled. Writes Apter (1977, p. 75): '[Modernization] leaves what might be called a primordial space, a space people try to fill when they believe they have lost something fundamental and try to recreate it.' As Apter points out, the liberal assimilationist conception of the relationship between tradition and modernity is not so much wrong as it is incomplete, flawed and oversimplified. It does not take into account the spiritual and community needs that ethnic cultures often help individuals to satisfy. The push toward assimilation in modern Western societies is counterbalanced by the trenchant pull of primordialism, traditionalism and the quest for community.

ETHNIC REVITALIZATION: A PHASE TYPOLOGY

Ethnic revitalization movements have arisen in most of the major Western nations. However, the various nations are in different phases of ethnic revitalization and consequently have varying types of educational responses or paradigms. I will describe a typology that attempts to outline the major phases of the development of ethnic revitalization movements in Western societies.[1] The typology is a preliminary ideal-type construct in the Weberian sense and constitutes a set of hypotheses based on the existing and emerging theory and research and on the author's study of ethnic behavior in several Western nations. However, it is drawn largely from ethnic events in the United States and the United Kingdom and therefore might not be generalizable to other nations. Educators in other nations must determine the extent to which the typology is valid in their societies. It is presented to stimulate research and discussion and to help educators better to interpret ethnic events in Western nations.

I am conceptualizing ethnic revitalization as consisting of four major phases: a precondition phase, a first or early phase, a later phase and a final phase (see Table 1.1). As already mentioned the typology is an ideal-type construct, and should be considered as dynamic and multidimensional rather than as static and unilinear. The division between the phases is blurred rather than sharp. One phase does not end abruptly when another begins; the phases blend and overlap. As with any ideal-type typology, the phases approximate reality rather than directly describe it. No actual ethnic movements exemplify each of the four phases.

Ethnic Revitalization: The Precondition Phase

Ethnic revitalization movements usually arise within societies that have a history of imperialism, colonialism and institutionalized racism. Groups with particular ethnic, racial and cultural characteristics are denied equality and structural inclusion in the nation-state. These societies also have a national democratic ideology which states that equality and justice should exist for all individuals and groups within the nation-state. The road to the first phase of revitalization is paved when the nation-state takes steps to close the gap between its democratic ideals and the inequality that is institutionalized within it.

The attempt to improve conditions of victimized groups – usually stimulated by action taken by these groups – creates rising expectations and hope, and causes these groups to perceive their condition as intolerable. The ethnic revitalization movement is born out of the hope and rising expectations created by the nation-state when it attempts to mitigate some of its most blatant forms of institutionalized racism and discrimination.

Ethnic Revitalization: The First Phase

In the first phase of ethnic revitalization, positions are sharply drawn and ardent, single-cause explanations and paradigms predominate, controversy is acrimonious, and debate tends to take the form of 'us and them', i.e. you are either for us or with them. Racism is usually the major issue in the debate during the early stages of ethnic revitalization because it has usually not previously been acknowledged as an important component of the society. It is during the early stages of ethnic revitalization that groups which perceive themselves as oppressed or as victims of racism force the dominant society to acknowledge that racism is institutionalized within it.

During the early phase of ethnic revitalization, ethnic groups, in their efforts to shape new identities and to legitimize their histories and cultures, often glorify those histories and cultures and emphasize the ways in which their people have been oppressed by the dominant group and the mainstream society (Banks, 1977). This early combination of protest and ethnic polarization must be understood within a broad social and political context. Groups which perceive themselves as oppressed and which internalize the dominant society's negative stereotypes and myths about themselves are likely to express strong in-group feelings during the early stages of

Table 1.1 *Phases in the development of ethnic revitalization movements*

The precondition phase	The first phase	The later phase	The final phase
This phase is characterized by the existence of a history of colonialism, imperialism, racism, an institutionalized democratic ideology, and efforts by the nation-state to close the gap between democratic ideals and societal realities. This creates rising expectations among victimized ethnic groups that pave the way for ethnic protest and a revitalization movement.	This phase is characterized by ethnic polarization, an intense identity quest by victimized ethnic groups, and single-cause explanations. An effort is made by ethnic groups to get racism legitimized as a primary explanation of their problems. Both radical reformers and staunch conservatives set forth single-cause explanations for the problems of victimized ethnic groups.	This phase is characterized by meaningful dialogue between victimized and dominant ethnic groups, multiethnic coalitions, reduced ethnic polarization, and the search for multiple-cause explanations for the problems of victimized ethnic groups.	Some of the elements of the reforms formulated in the earlier phases become institutionalized during this phase. Other victimized cultural groups echo their grievances, thereby expanding and dispersing the focus of the ethnic reform movement. Conservative ideologies and policies become institutionalized during this phase, thus paving the way for the development of a new ethnic revitalization movement.

ethnic revitalization. There is also an attempt to shape a new identity. During this phase the group is also likely to reject outside ethnic and racial groups, to romanticize its past, and to view contemporary social and political conditions from particularistic perspectives.

Ethnic Revitalization: The Later Phase

During the later phase of ethnic revitalization, ethnic groups search for multiple rather than single causes for their problems; racism as an explanation becomes legitimized but recognized as only one important cause of the problems of ethnic groups; ethnic rhetoric and polarization lessen; and ethnic groups form coalitions and jointly articulate their grievances.

During the first phase of ethnic revitalization many researchers and intellectuals who feel committed to ethnic equality but who do not agree with radical reformers on many issues do not freely express their views in public forums because they fear being called racists. These individuals begin to express their views and opinions freely during the later phase of ethnic revitalization. This becomes possible because emotions cool during this phase and individuals who disagree can engage in fruitful dialogue without accusations and epithets.

Nation-states facilitate the movement from early to later phases of ethnic revitalization by making symbolic concessions to ethnic groups, such as black studies programs, the hiring of ethnics in highly visible positions, the establishment of affirmative action policies, and the creation of a middle-class ethnic élite that serves as visible proof that 'ethnics can make it'. The ethnic élite play a very important role in moving the nation-state from the early to the later phase of ethnic revitalization. They develop counter-arguments to those of radical reformers, teach balanced and scholarly ethnic studies courses, and search for complex paradigms to explain the causes of the social, economic and political problems of ethnic groups.

Ethnic Revitalization: The Final Phase

During the final phase of ethnic revitalization many of the reforms born during the early and later phases become institutionalized within the schools and other educational institutions. Other groups that perceive themselves as oppressed also begin to echo the grievances of ethnic groups and thus broaden the scope of the reform movement. Women, handicapped people and other subcultural groups articulate their problems and make their special case for entitlements. Conflict tends to develop between these groups and ethnic groups because they compete for the same scarce resources.

Institutions such as the state and federal government, universities and schools begin to view these groups as a collectivity and to respond to their needs with single programs, projects and legislation. When women and handicapped groups began to argue their case for inclusion in the school curriculum in the United States, the schools created *multicultural education*, which combined content and information about these diverse groups into a single program. The United States federal government established affirmative action programs that were designed to help both ethnic minorities and women to gain more access to jobs and education.

The final phase of ethnic revitalization is a process that does not end until diverse ethnic and racial groups experience structural inclusion and equality within the nation-state. Consequently, the final phase of ethnic revitalization has not ended in the United States because ethnic groups are still only partially included in the structure of society. Even when ethnic groups attain inclusion in institutions they do not necessarily experience equality. Many middle-class blacks in the United States are discovering, for example, that when they gain access to mainstream US universities they do not necessarily experience equality within them.

At the same time as the United States is experiencing the final phase of ethnic revitalization, social, political and economic events are developing that are paving the way for a new ethnic revival that may have many of the characteristics of the ethnic movement of the 1960s and 1970s. A conservative government and national atmosphere are creating the alienation, hostility and poverty that give rise to ethnic revival movements.

The current situation in the United States suggests that ethnic revitalization movements are cyclic rather than linear. Once an ethnic revival movement has occurred within a nation-state, social, economic and political conditions tend to arise that give birth to new revivals. As ethnic revitalization movements reach their later and final phases – as in the United States today – events tend to evoke new ones. Ethnic revitalization movements will continue to re-emerge in Western democratic societies until racial and ethnic groups attain structural inclusion and equality in their nation-states and societies.

THE SCHOOLS AND ETHNIC REVITALIZATION MOVEMENTS

Structurally excluded ethnic groups in the various Western nations demanded changes in a range of social, economic and political institutions so that they could participate and exercise power in them. Ethnic demands took the form of marches, protests, demonstrations, and on occasion violence. Institutions began to respond to mute ethnic protest and to narrow the gap between the egalitarian ideals and rhetoric and societal realities.

Much of the response to ethnic protest took place in the schools and universities, in part because these institutions included a range of constituencies (including ethnic groups) and in part because they were seen as powerful symbols and bastions of the status quo that had participated in the oppression of ethnic groups. They were consequently viewed as potentially powerful vehicles that could play a pivotal role in their liberation.

Despite the fact that the school is limited in its ability to improve the social, economic and political conditions of ethnic groups, there is a strong belief among the general public (including ethnic groups) that education plays a powerful role in the life chances of children and youths. Thus ethnic groups acted on their beliefs and aspirations rather than on objective data about the power of the schools to help groups to attain structural inclusion in the institutions of their societies.

RESPONSE PARADIGMS: THE SCHOOLS REACT TO ETHNIC REVITALIZATION MOVEMENTS

When we examine the development of ethnic revitalization movements in Western democratic nations such as the United States, Canada, the United Kingdom and Australia, and the responses that educational institutions have made to them, we can identify and describe specific types and patterns of institutional responses. These patterns and prototypical responses are called *paradigms* in this chapter. These paradigmatic responses do not necessarily occur in a linear or set order in any particular nation, although some of them tend to occur earlier in the development of ethnic revitalization movements than others. *Thus the response paradigms relate in a general way to the phases of ethnic revitalization movements described above.* The ethnic additive and self-concept development paradigms, for example, tend to arise during the first or early phase of an ethnic revitalization movement. Single-explanation paradigms tend to emerge prior to multiple-explanation ones. While single-explanation paradigms usually emerge during the first phase of ethnic revitalization, multiple-explanation paradigms usually do not emerge or become popular until the later phase.

A sophisticated neo-conservative paradigm tends to develop during the final phase of ethnic revitalization, when the groups that are trying to institutionalize pluralism begin to experience success and those who are committed to assimilationism and to defending the status quo begin to fear that the pluralistic reformers might institutionalize a new ideal and create new goals for the nation-state.

I shall describe a number of response paradigms that develop when ethnic revitalization movements emerge (see Table 1.2). These paradigms might develop within a nation at different times or they may co-exist at the same time. Each is likely to exist in some form in a nation that has experienced an ethnic revitalization movement. However, only one or two are likely to be dominant at any particular point in time. The leaders and advocates of particular paradigms compete in order to make their paradigms the most popular in academic, government and school settings. Proponents of paradigms that can attract the most government and private support are likely to become the prevailing voices for multicultural education within a particular time or period.

Sometimes one dominant paradigm replaces another and something akin to what Kuhn (1970) calls a 'scientific revolution' takes place. However, what happens more frequently is that a new paradigm will emerge which challenges an older one but does not replace it. During the late 1960s in the United States the cultural deprivation paradigm was dominant (Bereiter and Engelmann, 1966). It dominated the theory, research and practice related to educating lower-income and minority groups. During the 1970s this paradigm was seriously challenged by the cultural differences paradigm

(Baratz and Baratz, 1970). The cultural difference paradigm did not replace the cultural deprivation paradigm: the two paradigms co-existed. However, the cultural deprivation paradigm lost much of its influence and legitimacy, especially among young, ethnic-minority scholars (Banks, 1984). The cultural deprivation paradigm experienced a renaissance in the early 1980s, when a neo-conservative movement emerged in the United States.

The Ethnic Additive and Self-Concept Development Paradigms

Often the first phase of a school's response to an ethnic revitalization movement consists of the infusion of bits and pieces about ethnic groups into the curriculum, especially into courses in the humanities, the social studies and the language arts. The teaching about ethnic heroes and the celebration of ethnic holidays are salient characteristics of the ethnic additive paradigm.

This paradigm usually emerges as the first one for a variety of reasons. It develops in part because ethnic groups usually demand the inclusion of their heroes, holidays and contributions in the curriculum during the first stage of ethnic revitalization. This paradigm also emerges because teachers usually have little knowledge about victimized ethnic groups during the early phase of ethnic revitalization and find it much easier to add isolated bits of information about ethnic groups to the curriculum and to celebrate ethnic holidays than to integrate ethnic content meaningfully into the curriculum. Thus Black History Week, American Indian Day, and Asian and Afro-Caribbean feasts and festivals become a part of the curriculum.

The ethnic additive paradigm also occurs early because educational institutions tend to respond to the first phase of ethnic revitalization with quickly conceptualized and hurriedly formulated programs that are designed primarily to silence ethnic protest rather than to contribute to equality and the structural inclusion of ethnic groups in society. In each of the major Western nations, many early programs related to ethnic groups were poorly conceptualized and implemented without careful and thoughtful planning. Such programs are usually attacked and eliminated during the later phases of ethnic revitalization when the institutionalization of ethnic programs and reforms begins. Their weakness becomes the primary justification for their elimination. When such programs were attacked and eliminated in the United States in the 1980s, many careful and sensitive observers noted that they had been 'designed to fail'.

Another major goal expressed by educators during the first phase of ethnic revitalization is to raise the self-concepts of ethnic minority youths and to increase their racial pride. This goal develops because leaders of ethnic movements try to shape new and positive ethnic identities and because educators assume that ethnic groups who have experienced discrimination and structural exclusion have negative self-concepts and negative attitudes to their own racial and ethnic groups. Much of the social science research prior to the 1960s reinforced this belief (Clark, 1963); some leaders of ethnic movements also express it. Many educators assume that students need healthy self-concepts in order to do well in school. They also assume that curriculum content which includes ethnic heroes and the celebration of ethnic holidays will enhance the self-concepts and academic achievements of ethnic groups. Stone (1981) has described some of the serious limitations of the self-concept paradigm.

Table 1.2 *Multicultural education paradigms*

Paradigm	Major assumptions	Major goals	School programs and practices
Ethnic additive	Ethnic content can be added to the curriculum without reconceptualizing or restructuring it.	To integrate the curriculum by adding special units, lessons and ethnic holidays to it.	Special ethnic studies units; ethnic studies classes that focus on ethnic foods and holidays; units on ethnic heroes.
Self-concept development	Ethnic content can help increase the self-concept of ethnic minority students. Ethnic minority students have low self-concepts.	To increase the self-concepts and academic achievement of ethnic minority students.	Special units in ethnic studies that emphasize the contributions that ethnic groups have made to the making of the nation; units on ethnic heroes.
Cultural deprivation	Many poor and ethnic minority youths are socialized within homes and communities that prevent them from acquiring the cognitive skills and cultural characteristics needed to succeed in school.	To compensate for the cognitive deficits and dysfunctional cultural characteristics that many poor and ethnic minority youths bring to school.	Compensatory educational experiences that are behavioristic and intensive, e.g. Head Start and Follow Through programs in the United States.
Language	Ethnic and linguistic minority youths often achieve poorly in school because instruction is not conducted in their mother tongue.	To provide initial instruction in the child's mother tongue.	Teaching English as a Second Language programs; bilingual–bicultural education programs.
Racism	Racism is the major cause of the educational problems of non-white ethnic minority groups. The school can and should play a major role in eliminating institutional racism.	To reduce personal and institutional racism within the schools and the larger society.	Prejudice reduction; anti-racist workshops and courses for teachers; anti-racist lessons for students: an examination of the total environment to determine ways in which racism can be reduced, including curriculum materials, teacher attitudes and school norms.
Radical	A major goal of the school is to educate students so that they will willingly accept their social-class status in society. The school cannot help liberate victimized ethnic and cultural groups because	To raise the level of consciousness of students and teachers about the nature of capitalist, class-stratified societies; to help students and teachers to develop a commitment to radical reform of the social and	

	it plays a key role in keeping them oppressed. Lower-class ethnic groups cannot attain equality within a class-stratified capitalist society. Radical reform of the social structure is a prerequisite of equality for poor and minority students.	economic systems in capitalist societies.	
Genetic	Lower-class and ethnic minority youths often achieve poorly in school because of their biological characteristics. Educational intervention programs cannot eliminate the achievement gap between these students and majority-group students because of their different genetic characteristics.	To create a meritocracy based on intellectual ability as measured by standardized aptitude tests.	Ability-grouped classes; use of IQ tests to determine career goals for students; different career ladders for students who score differently on standardized tests.
Cultural pluralism	Schools should promote ethnic identifications and allegiances. Educational programs should reflect the characteristics of ethnic students.	To promote the maintenance of groups; to promote the liberation of ethnic groups; to educate ethnic students in a way that will not alienate them from their home cultures.	Ethnic studies courses that are ideologically based; ethnic schools that focus on the maintenance of ethnic cultures and traditions.
Cultural difference	Minority youths have rich and diverse cultures that have values, languages and behavioral styles that are functional for them and valuable for the nation-state.	To change the school so that it respects and legitimizes the cultures of students from diverse ethnic groups and cultures.	Educational programs that reflect the learning styles of ethnic groups, that incorporate their cultures when developing instructional principles, and that integrate ethnic content into the main-stream curriculum.
Assimilationism	Ethnic minority youths should be freed of ethnic identifications and commitments so that they can become full participants in the national culture. When schools foster ethnic commitments and identifications, this retards the academic growth of ethnic youths and contributes to the development of ethnic tension and balkanization.	To educate students in a way that will free them of their ethnic characteristics and enable them to acquire the values and behavior of the mainstream culture.	A number of educational programs are based on assimilationist assumptions and goals, such as cultural deprivation programs, most Teaching English as a Second Language programs, and the mainstream curriculum in most Western nations. Despite the challenges that they received during the 1970s, the curricula in the Western nations are still dominated by assimilationist goals and ideologies.

The Cultural Deprivation Paradigm

Cultural deprivation theories, programs and research often develop during the first phase of an ethnic revitalization movement. Cultural deprivation theorists assume that lower-class youths do not achieve well in school because of family disorganization, poverty, the lack of effective concept acquisition, and other intellectual and cultural deficits that these students experience during their first years of life. Cultural deprivation theorists assume that a major goal of school programs for 'culturally deprived' children is to provide them with cultural and other experiences that will compensate for their cognitive and intellectual deficits. Cultural deprivation theorists believe that lower-class students can learn the basic skills taught by the schools, but that these skills must often be taught using intensive, behaviorally oriented instruction (Bereiter and Engelmann, 1966).

Programs based on cultural deprivation theory, such as most of the compensatory education programs in the United States, are structured in such a way that they require students to make major changes in their behavior. Teachers and other educators are required to make few changes in their behavior or in educational institutions. Such programs also ignore the cultures that students bring to school and assume that poor minority children are 'culturally deprived' or 'disadvantaged'. Some of these programs in the United States have been able to help poor and minority youths to experience achievement gains, but these gains are often not maintained as these students progress through the grades.

The Language Paradigm

Often during the early phase of ethnic revitalization or when a large number of immigrants settle in a nation and enroll in the schools, educators view the problems of these groups as resulting primarily from their language or dialect differences. When the West Indians and Asians first enrolled in British schools in significant numbers in the 1960s, many British educators believed that if they could solve the language problems of these youths then the youths would experience academic success in British schools. The early responses by British educators to the problems of immigrant children were almost exclusively related to language (Schools Council, 1970). Special programs were set up to train teachers and to develop materials for teaching English as a second language to immigrant students. French educators also viewed the problems of the North African and Asian students in their schools in the late 1970s as primarily language related (Banks, 1978).

In the United States the educational problems of Puerto Ricans and Mexican Americans are often assumed to be rooted in language. Proponents of bilingual education in the United States argued during the 1970s that if the language problem of these students were solved, they would experience academic success in the schools. As bilingual programs were established in the United States educators began to realize that many other factors, such as social class, learning styles and motivation, were also important variables that influenced the academic achievement of Hispanic ethnic groups in the United States.

The experiences with programs based on the language paradigm in the Western nations teach us that an exclusive language approach to the educational problems of ethnic and immigrant groups is insufficient. Languages are integral parts of cultures. Consequently, any attempt effectively to educate students from diverse language and cultural groups must be comprehensive in scope, and focus on variables in the educational environment other than language. An exclusive language approach is doomed to fail.

The Racism Paradigm

At an early point in an ethnic revitalization movement, ethnic minority groups and their liberal allies usually state that institutionalized racism is the only or most important cause of the problems of ethnic groups in school and society. This claim by ethnic minorities usually evokes a counter-claim by those who defend the status quo, and an intense debate ensues. This debate usually takes place during the first phase of ethnic revitalization, when ethnic polarization and tension are high. The debate between those who claim that racism is the cause of the problems of ethnic groups and those who deny their claim is usually not productive because each side in the argument sets forth extreme and competing claims.

A major goal of the racism advocates is not so much to convince others that racism does, in fact, cause all of the problems of victimized ethnic groups as to legitimize racism as a valid explanation and to convince leaders and those who defend the status quo that racism is an important and tenacious part of Western societies. The debate between radical reformers and conservative defenders of the status quo remains stalemated and single-focused until the existence of racism is acknowledged by the dominant group and meaningful steps are taken to eliminate it. Until this acknowledgement is made in official statements, policies and actions, radical reformers will continue to state that racism is the single cause of the social, economic and educational problems of victimized ethnic groups.

Radical reformers will not search for or find more complex paradigms that explain the problems of victimized ethnic groups until mainstream leaders acknowledge the existence of institutionalized racism. In other words, institutionalized racism must become legitimized as an explanation, and serious steps must be taken to eliminate it, before an ethnic revitalization movement can reach a phase in which other paradigms will be accepted by radical reformers who articulate the interests of groups that are victims of institutionalized racism. Societies and nations are successful in making the racism paradigm less popular when official bodies and leaders validate the racism paradigm, acknowledge that racism exists in the society, and take visible and vigorous steps to eliminate it, such as enacting legislation that prevents discrimination and hiring minorities for influential jobs in the public and private sectors.

The Importance of the Racism Paradigm

In the later and final phases of an ethnic revitalization movement, when conservative forces emerge and challenge educational programs related to ethnic and cultural diversity, the racism paradigm serves an essential function. It emphasizes that racism is a tenacious part of Western societies and that racism reduction techniques must be part of any educational program designed to bring about educational equality.

The focus on racism as a major factor that causes educational inequality is especially important during the later and final phases of ethnic revitalization movements. It is during these periods that educational programs related to ethnic groups and educational equality, such as multicultural education, tend to sidestep issues and problems related to institutional racism and to focus on the cultural characteristics of ethnic minority groups and how their cultures differ from those of majority ethnic groups. As Moodley points out in Chapter 3, this focus on the cultural differences of ethnic minority groups often results in the perpetuation of cultural stereotypes and the trivialization of the historical and sociological experiences of these groups. A focus on cultural differences often encourages teachers to evade questions related to institutional racism, social-class stratification, power struggles, and other important issues and concepts related to the subjugation of ethnic groups in modernized Western societies. In the United States, which is experiencing the final phase of ethnic revitalization, many explicit programs designed to reduce institutional racism in the schools and in the larger society have been eliminated. Consequently, educational programs designed to eliminate racism are usually described using other concepts and terms. Strategies for eliminating racism in US schools must be implicit and thoroughly integrated into the total school curriculum rather than highly visible and explicit.

To implement educational programs that help all students attain educational equality, teachers must understand how culture affects the lives of their students as well as how *racism* and *culture* interact to cause educational problems for many ethnic minority students. The curriculum should also help students to view concepts, events and issues from diverse ethnic and cultural perspectives. Teachers do not have to decide whether to include a study of cultural differences *or* a study of racism in the curriculum. Both concepts should be an integral part of the multicultural curriculum. However, the complexity and dynamic nature of cultures should be studied and the intersection of racism and culture should be examined. For example, blacks in the United States maintain many ethnic institutions because, historically, racism has prevented them from participating fully in mainstream US society.

To be effective, multicultural education must have a strong, effective and systematic component designed to reduce personal and institutional racism. Strategies that are effective in reducing racism in the curriculum and the school must be comprehensive in scope and focus on all aspects of the school environment, including the hidden curriculum, institutional norms, school policy, the counseling program, assessment and testing procedures, the formalized course of study, teaching methods and materials, and the attitudes and expectations of the school staff.

Helping Teachers to Develop Positive Racial Attitudes

Whether educational programs designed to foster educational equality succeed or fail ultimately depends on the characteristics and skills of the classroom teacher. Teachers are human beings who bring their cultural perspectives, values, hopes and dreams to the classroom.[2] They also bring their prejudices, stereotypes and misconceptions. Teachers' values and perspectives mediate and interact with what they teach, and influence the way that messages are communicated and perceived by their students.

Because the teacher mediates the messages and symbols communicated to the students through the curriculum, it is important for teachers to come to grips with their own personal and cultural values and identities in order for them to help students from diverse racial, ethnic and cultural groups to develop clarified identities and relate positively to each other. I hypothesize that self-clarification is a prerequisite to dealing effectively with and relating positively to outside ethnic and cultural groups. An Anglo-American teacher who is confused about his or her identity and who has a non-reflective conception of the ways that Anglo-American culture relates to other groups in the United States will have a very difficult time relating positively to outside ethnic groups such as Afro-Americans and Mexican Americans.

Pre-service and inservice teacher training programs should help teachers to explore and clarify their own ethnic and cultural identities and to develop more positive attitudes towards other racial, ethnic and cultural groups. To do this effectively, we must design and implement training programs for teachers that are keyed to their particular attitudes, perceptions, levels of knowledge, interest and experiences. We cannot assume that all teachers, of any race or ethnic group, will benefit from identical training approaches and models. When planning multiethnic experiences for teachers, we tend to assume that ethnic groups are monolithic and have homogeneous needs and characteristics. In designing multiethnic experiences for teachers, and when teaching them to work with multiethnic populations, we need to take their cultural experiences, personality and levels of knowledge into consideration.

To reflect the myriad and complex characteristics and cultural and ethnic identities of teachers in training programs, we must make some attempt to identify them. I have developed a typology which attempts to outline the stages of cultural or ethnic identity that are exemplified by teachers and students (Banks, 1981). The typology describes six stages (see Figure 1.1).

A primary goal of staff development programs for teachers (using this typology) should be to help them to develop increasingly higher levels of cross-cultural competency. We should help teachers at Stages 1 and 2 to move to Stage 3, etc. However, I hypothesize that different techniques and training strategies are needed to help teachers to develop higher levels of cross-cultural competency, depending on where they are on the typology outlined above and briefly described in Figure 1.1. I hypothesize that Stage 1 and 2 teachers require training experiences that will help them to clarify and come to grips with their own cultural or ethnic identities. Self-understanding is a prerequisite to understanding and accepting others. I hypothesize that teachers are ready for powerful affective techniques – such as racism awareness training models that are designed to help them to develop acceptance of and empathy with other groups – only when they have reached Stage 3 (cultural or ethnic identity clarification).

I am not suggesting that we should not introduce ethnic minority cultures or racism awareness to teachers until they have attained cultural identity clarification. *Studying others is often an effective way to understand oneself better and to come to grips with one's personal values and attitudes.* However, I am suggesting that until teachers have

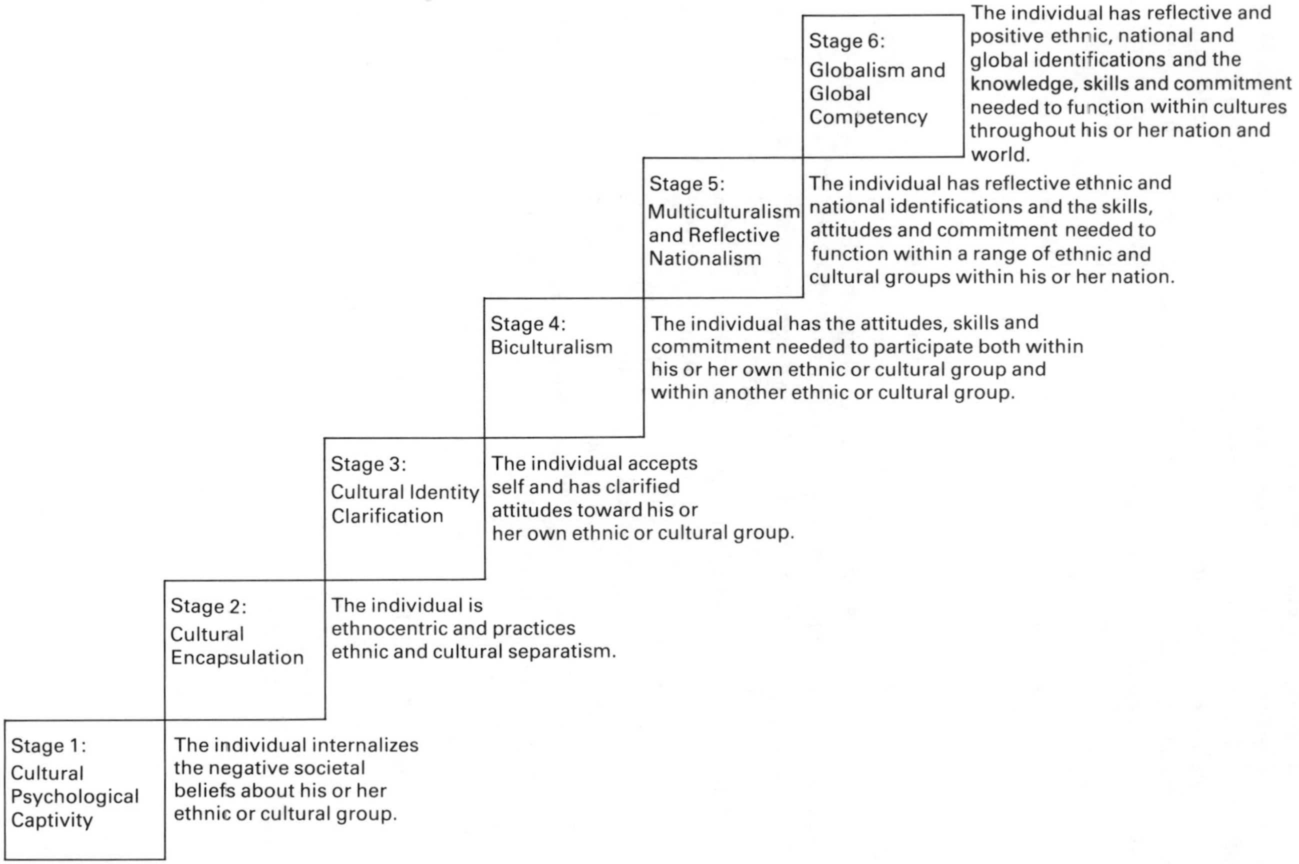

Stage 1:
Cultural
Psychological
Captivity

The individual internalizes the negative societal beliefs about his or her ethnic or cultural group.

Stage 2:
Cultural
Encapsulation

The individual is ethnocentric and practices ethnic and cultural separatism.

Stage 3:
Cultural Identity
Clarification

The individual accepts self and has clarified attitudes toward his or her own ethnic or cultural group.

Stage 4:
Biculturalism

The individual has the attitudes, skills and commitment needed to participate both within his or her own ethnic or cultural group and within another ethnic or cultural group.

Stage 5:
Multiculturalism
and Reflective
Nationalism

The individual has reflective ethnic and national identifications and the skills, attitudes and commitment needed to function within a range of ethnic and cultural groups within his or her nation.

Stage 6:
Globalism and
Global
Competency

The individual has reflective and positive ethnic, national and global identifications and the knowledge, skills and commitment needed to function within cultures throughout his or her nation and world.

Figure 1.1 *The stages of ethnic and cultural development.* From Banks, J.A. (1981) *Multiethnic Education: Theory and Practice*, p. 220. Boston: Allyn and Bacon. Reproduced with the permission of the publisher.

come to grips with their own personal and cultural identities and are comfortable with them it will be difficult for them to develop empathy with the experiences of victimized racial and cultural groups. More research and theory need to be developed about the kinds of training strategies and teaching techniques that work best with different kinds of teachers and students. Current theory, research and practice suggest that specific techniques may have different effects on teachers with different life histories, personalities, levels of knowledge and cultural identity stages (Ford, 1979).

The Radical Paradigm

A radical paradigm tends to develop during the early or later stage of ethnic revitalization. It is usually reproductionist or neo-Marxist in orientation. While the other paradigms assume that the school can successfully intervene and help ethnic minority youths to attain social and political equality, the radical paradigm assumes that the school is part of the problem and plays a key role in keeping ethnic groups oppressed. Thus, it is not possible for the school to help liberate oppressed groups because one of its central purposes is to educate students so that they will willingly accept their assigned status in society. A primary role of the school is to reproduce the social-class structure.

The radical paradigm stresses the limited role that schools can play to eliminate racism and discrimination and to promote equality for low-income students. Christopher Jencks (Jencks et al., 1972) was an influential 'ineffectiveness of school' theorist in the United States. He argues that the most effective way to bring about equality for poor people is to equalize incomes directly rather than to rely on the schools to bring about equality in the adult life of students. He suggests that the schooling route is much too indirect and will most likely result in failure. Bowles and Gintis (1976) wrote a neo-Marxist critique of schools in the United States which copiously documents the way in which schools reinforce the social-class stratification within society and make students politically passive and content with their social-class status.

The radical paradigm argues that multicultural education is a palliative to keep excluded and oppressed groups such as blacks from rebelling against a system that promotes structural inequality and institutionalized racism. It does not deal, contend the radical critics, with the real reasons for ethnic and racial groups being oppressed and victimized. It avoids any serious discussion of class, institutionalized racism, power or capitalism. Multicultural education, argue the radical critics, diverts attention from the real problems and issues. They argue that we need to focus on the institutions and structures of society rather than on the characteristics of minority students and cultural differences.

The radical critics of multicultural education tend to be cogent and explicit when they criticize the school but vague and ambiguous when they propose strategies for school reform. Bowles and Gintis (1976) are perceptively critical of the school but vague when they describe school reform strategies. While the radical critics offer a number of insights that practicing educators can incorporate into effective school programs (e.g. the need to focus on institutional racism and to raise students' levels of consciousness), they provide teachers with few teaching techniques and methods they can use in the classroom or to reform the school. Radical approaches to school reform have little chance of success in most Western societies. Most teachers in these societies perceive themselves as guardians of their nations' liberal democratic traditions. Consequently, they are likely to reject summarily radical approaches to school reform without giving them serious analysis or consideration.

The Genetic Paradigm

The ideology and research developed by radical reformers do not go unchallenged. An ideological war takes place between radical reformers and conservatives who defend the status quo. While radical and liberal reformers develop ideology and research to show how the major problems of ethnic groups are caused by institutionalized racism and capitalism, anti-egalitarian advocates and researchers develop ideology and research which state that the failure of ethnic groups in school and society is due to their own inherited or socialized characteristics.

Both radical reformers and conservative scholars tend to develop single-cause paradigms during the early phase of ethnic revitalization. While those developed by radical theorists tend to focus on racism and other problems in society, those developed by conservative researchers usually focus on the characteristics of ethnic students themselves, such as their genetic characteristics and their family socialization.

In the United States the most popular anti-egalitarian theories focus on the genetic characteristics of black and poor students and were developed by researchers such as Jensen (1969), Shockley (1972) and Herrnstein (1971). Jensen argues that the genetic characteristics of blacks are the most important reason that compensatory educational programs designed to increase the IQ of black students have not been more successful. Shockley developed a theory about the genetic inferiority of blacks that is less accepted by the academic community than Jensen's. Herrnstein published his controversial article, which argued that social class reflects genetic differences, in the *Atlantic Monthly*, a widely circulated and highly respected popular magazine. Herrnstein's views evoked more controversy than Jensen's, perhaps because he argued that social class rather than race was related to heredity. The genetic paradigm is often embraced by educators who are not committed to educational equality for lower-class and ethnic minority students. It is often used as an alibi for their educational neglect.

Competing Paradigms

Particularly during the later stage of ethnic revitalization, when aspects of ethnic diversity are being implemented within the schools, an intense clash of ideologies and paradigms is likely to occur between those committed to ethnic pluralism and those who endorse assimilationism and are committed to preserving the status quo. The language paradigm (which often includes a call for bilingual education), the racism paradigm and the radical paradigm are especially likely to evoke strong responses from assimilationists, who are committed to nationalism and to developing strong national commitments and identifications. In the United States the call for bilingual education and the federal legislation and court decisions that promoted it stimulated one of the most acid educational debates in recent history.

A cultural pluralism paradigm tends to emerge during the first phase of ethnic revitalization. It maintains that a major goal of the school should be to help students develop commitments and attachments to their ethnic group so that they can participate in its liberation. Cultural pluralists believe that ethnicity and ethnic cultures have a significant influence on the socialization of students, and thus should strongly influence the formulation of educational policies and programs. As the ethnic revitalization movement develops, more moderate paradigms emerge, such as the cultural difference and bicultural paradigms. The cultural difference paradigm maintains that ethnic minority youths often do not achieve well in school not because they have a deprived culture, but because their cultures are different from the culture of the school. The school should therefore modify the educational environment in order to make it more consistent with the cultures of ethnic minority youths. If this is done, they will experience academic gains in the school.

Assimilationists often oppose pluralist programs such as bilingual education and ethnic studies because, they argue, these programs prevent students from learning the skills needed to become effective citizens of the nation-state and from developing strong national loyalties. They also argue that pluralist educational programs promote ethnic attachments and loyalties which contribute to ethnic conflict, polarization and stratification. Assimilationists maintain that the primary goal of the school should be to socialize students so that they attain the knowledge, attitudes and skills needed to become effective citizens of their nation-states. During the final phase of ethnic revitalization, assimilationist paradigms tend to become increasingly conservative. In the United States during the late 1970s assimilationism developed into a neo-conservative ideology that was strongly nationalistic and reactionary (Steinfelds, 1979).

THE NEED FOR A MULTI-FACTOR PARADIGM AND HOLISM

The field of multicultural education is replete with single-factor paradigms that attempt to explain why lower-class and minority students often achieve poorly in school. Proponents of these paradigms often become ardent in their views and insist that one major variable explains the problems of minority students and that their educational problems can be solved if major policies, related to a specific explanation or paradigm, are implemented. Many existing reforms in multicultural education, such as compensatory education and bilingual programs, are based on single-factor paradigms. Proponents of the ethnic additive and self-concept development paradigms believe that ethnic content and heroes can help minority students to increase their academic achievement; cultural deprivation proponents view cultural enrichment as the most important variable influencing academic achievement; radical scholars often view the school as having little possibility of significantly influencing the life chances of poor and minority students.

Experiences in the major Western nations since the late 1960s teach us that the academic achievement problems of ethnic minority students are too complex to be solved with reforms based on single-factor paradigms and explanations. Education is broader than schooling, and many of the problems that ethnic minority students experience in the schools reflect the problems in the wider society. The radical critique of schooling is useful because it helps us to see the limitations of formal schooling. However, the radical paradigm is limited because it gives us few concrete guidelines about what can be done after we have acknowledged that schools are limited in their ability to bring about equality for poor and minority students.

When designing educational reform strategies, we must be keenly sensitive to the limitations of formal schooling. However, we must be tenacious in our faith that the school can play a limited but cogent role in bringing about equal educational opportunities for poor and minority students and helping all students to develop cross-cultural understandings and competencies. In order to effectively design school programs that will help ethnic minority youths to increase their academic achievement and to help all students to develop ethnic literacy and cross-cultural competency, we must conceptualize the school as a system in which all of its major variables and components are highly interrelated. *A holistic paradigm, which conceptualizes the school as an interrelated whole, is needed to guide educational reform* (see Figure 1.2). Viewing the school as a social system can help us to derive an idea of school reform that can help minority students to increase their academic achievement and help all students to develop more democratic attitudes and values. Although our theory and research about multicultural education are limited and developing, both research and theory indicate that educators can successfully intervene to help students to increase their academic achievement (Weinberg, 1977) and to develop more democratic attitudes and values (Katz, 1976).

Conceptualizing the school as a social system suggests that we must formulate and initiate a change strategy that reforms the total school environment in order to implement multicultural education successfully. Reforming any one variable, such as curriculum materials and the formal curriculum, is necessary but not sufficient. Multiethnic and sensitive teaching materials are ineffective in the hands of teachers who have negative attitudes to different ethnic and cultural groups. Such teachers are likely to use multiethnic materials rarely or to use them in a detrimental way when they do. Thus, helping teachers and other members of the school staff to develop democratic attitudes and values is essential when implementing multicultural programs and experiences.

When formulating plans for multicultural education, educators should conceptualize the school as a microculture that has norms, values, roles, status and goals like other cultural systems. The school has a dominant culture and a variety of subcultures. Almost all classrooms in Western societies are multicultural because white students, as well as black and brown students, are socialized within diverse cultures. Teachers in schools in Western societies also come from many different ethnic groups and cultures. Many teachers were socialized in cultures other than the Anglo dominant one, although these may be forgotten and repressed. The school is a microculture where the cultures of students and teachers meet. *The school should be a cultural environment where acculturation takes place: both teachers and students should*

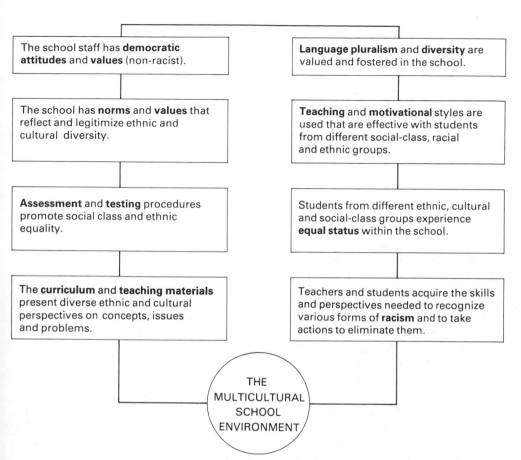

The school staff has **democratic attitudes** and **values** (non-racist).

Language pluralism and diversity are valued and fostered in the school.

The school has **norms** and **values** that reflect and legitimize ethnic and cultural diversity.

Teaching and **motivational** styles are used that are effective with students from different social-class, racial and ethnic groups.

Assessment and **testing** procedures promote social class and ethnic equality.

Students from different ethnic, cultural and social-class groups experience **equal status** within the school.

The **curriculum** and **teaching materials** present diverse ethnic and cultural perspectives on concepts, issues and problems.

Teachers and students acquire the skills and perspectives needed to recognize various forms of **racism** and to take actions to eliminate them.

THE MULTICULTURAL SCHOOL ENVIRONMENT

Figure 1.2 *A reformed school environment based on a multi-factor paradigm (holism).* This figure describes the characteristics of a multicultural school environment that has experienced reform based on a multi-factor, holistic paradigm. The total school environment is conceptualized as a system which consists of a number of identifiable factors, such as the staff attitudes and values, assessment and testing procedures, and the curriculum and teaching materials. In the reformed, idealized multicultural school, each of these variables has been changed and reflects ethnic, cultural and social-class equality. While any one of these factors may be the focus of initial school reform, changes must take place in each of them to create and sustain a school environment in which students from diverse groups experience equality.

assimilate some of the views, perceptions and ethos of each other as they interact (see Figure 1.3). Both teachers and students will be enriched by this process and the academic achievement of students from diverse cultures will be enhanced because their cosmos and ethos will be reflected and legitimized in the school.

Historically, schools in Western societies have had assimilation rather than acculturation as their major goal. The students were expected to acquire the dominant culture of the school and society, but the school neither legitimized nor assimilated parts of the students' cultures. Assimilation and acculturation are different in important ways. Assimilation involves the complete elimination of cultural differences

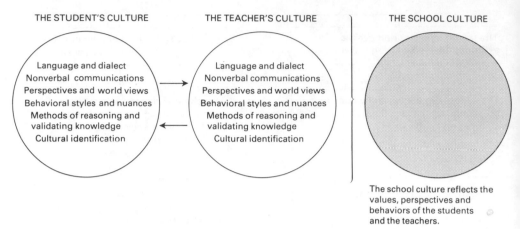

Figure 1.3 *Acculturation as a school goal.* When the student assimilates elements of the teacher's culture and the teacher assimilates elements of the student's culture, the school culture becomes a synthesized cultural system that reflects the cultures of all of its participants.

and differentiating group identification. When acculturation occurs, a culture is modified through contact with one or more other cultures but maintains its essence (Theodorson and Theodorson, 1969).

Both acculturation and accommodation should take place in today's schools in Western democratic societies. *When accommodation occurs, groups with diverse cultures maintain their separate identities but live in peaceful interaction.* It is essential that schools in Western democracies acculturate students rather than foster tight ethnic boundaries, because all students, including ethnic minority students, must develop the knowledge, attitudes and skills needed to become successful citizens of their cultural communities, their nation-states and the global community.

If they are to function successfully in their nation-states, ethnic minority students must develop competency in the national language or languages and acquire the skills needed to participate in the national civic culture. They must also develop commitment to the overarching democratic ideals of their nation-states, such as equality and justice. Acquiring the knowledge, skills and attitudes needed to participate in their nation-states and in the global community means that all students, including majority group students, will often find it necessary to assimilate cultural components that are not a part of their first culture. However, ethnic minority students can assimilate essential aspects of the mainstream culture without surrendering the most important aspects of their first culture or becoming alienated from it. The school should help students to develop the knowledge, skills and attitudes needed to function effectively in their community culture, in the mainstream national culture, and within and between other ethnic cultures and subsocieties (see Figure 1.4). The school should not require students to become alienated from their families and communities in order to acquire the knowledge, attitudes and skills needed to function effectively in the national civic culture.

While students will find it necessary to assimilate values, knowledge and skills from the mainstream culture, educators should also assimilate some of the values, ethos

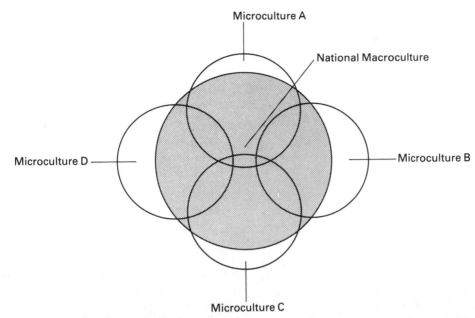

Figure 1.4 *Microcultures and the national macroculture.* In this figure the national macroculture is represented by the shaded area. This culture is shared by all ethnic and cultural groups and citizens of the nation-state. A, B, C and D represent microcultures that consist of unique institutions, values and cultural elements that are not universal and are shared primarily by members of specific ethnic and cultural groups. A major goal of the school should be to help students to acquire the knowledge, skills and attitudes needed to function effectively within the national macroculture and their own microcultures, and within and across other microcultures. Adapted from Banks, J.A. (1981) *Multiethnic Education: Theory and Practice*, p. 81. Boston: Allyn and Bacon. Used with the permission of the publisher.

and perspectives of their ethnic minority students. Only in this way will a workable and humane form of accommodation develop and will educators be able to create a school culture that validates and legitimizes the cultures of students from diverse ethnic and cultural groups. By incorporating some of the ethos, values and perspectives of ethnic groups into the curriculum and into their cosmos, teachers will be able not only to help ethnic minority youths to attain equality but to enrich their personal lives and be better able to improve the human condition.

NOTES

1. Parts of this chapter were adapted from a paper, 'Ethnic revitalization movements and education', presented at the Second National Conference on Multicultural and Intercultural Education, sponsored by the Canadian Council for Multicultural and Intercultural Education, Toronto, November 7–10, 1984, and published in *The Educational Review*, June 1985. Reprinted with permission.
2. This section of this chapter is based on 'Multicultural teacher education: knowledge, skills, and processes', a paper presented at the conference on Intercultural Training of Teachers, sponsored by the National Swedish Board of Universities and Colleges, Vildmarkshotellet, Kolmarden, Norrköping, Sweden, 10–14 June 1985.

REFERENCES

Apter, D. E. (1977) Political life and cultural pluralism. In Tumin, M. M. & Plotch, W. (ed.), *Pluralism in a Democratic Society*, pp. 58–91. New York: Praeger.

Banks, J. A. (1977) A response to Philip Freedman. *Phi Delta Kappan*, **58**, 695–7.

Banks, J. A. (1978) Multiethnic education across cultures: United States, Mexico, Puerto Rico, France, and Great Britain. *Social Education*, **42**, 177–85.

Banks, J. A. (1981) *Multiethnic Education: Theory and Practice*. Boston: Allyn and Bacon.

Banks, J. A. (1984) Values, ethnicity, social science research, and educational policy. In Ladner, B. (ed.), *The Humanities in Precollegiate Education*, Eighty-third Yearbook of the National Society for the Study of Education, Part II, pp. 91–111. Chicago: University of Chicago Press.

Baratz, S. S. & Baratz, J. C. (1970) Early childhood intervention: the social science base of institutional racism. *Harvard Educational Review*, **40**, 29–50.

Bereiter, C. & Engelmann, S. (1966) *Teaching Disadvantaged Children in the Preschool*. Englewood Cliffs, N.J.: Prentice-Hall.

Bowles, S. & Gintis, H. (1976) *Schooling in Capitalist America*. New York: Basic Books.

Clark, K. B. (1963) *Prejudice and Your Child*. Boston: Beacon Press.

Ford, M. (1979) 'The development of an instrument for assessing levels of ethnicity in public school teachers'. Doctoral dissertation, University of Houston.

Herrnstein, R. J. (1971) IQ. *Atlantic Monthly*, September, 43–64.

Jencks, C. et al. (1972) *Inequality: A Reassessment of the Effect of Family and Schooling in America*. New York: Basic Books.

Jensen, A. R. (1969) How much can we boost IQ and scholastic achievement? *Harvard Educational Review*, **39**, 1–123.

Katz, P. A. (ed.) (1976) *Towards the Elimination of Racism*. New York: Pergamon Press.

Kuhn, T. S. (1970) *The Structure of Scientific Revolutions*, second edition, enlarged. Chicago: University of Chicago Press.

Park, R. E. (1950) *Race and Culture*. Glencoe, Ill.: The Free Press.

Patterson, O. (1977) *Ethnic Chauvinism: The Reactionary Impulse*. New York: Stein and Day.

Porter, J. (1975) Ethnic pluralism in Canadian perspective. In Glazer, N. & Moynihan, D. P. (ed.), *Ethnicity: Theory and Experience*, pp. 267–304. Cambridge, Mass.: Harvard University Press.

Schools Council (1970) Schools Council Working Paper 29, *Teaching English to West Indian Children: The Research Stage of the Project*. London: Evans Brothers.

Shockley, W. (1972) Dysgenics, geneticity, raceology: a challenge to the intellectual responsibility of educators. *Phi Delta Kappan*, **53**, 297–307.

Steinfelds, P. (1979) *The Neoconservatives*. New York: Simon and Schuster.

Stone, M. (1981) *The Education of the Black Child in Britain: The Myth of Multiracial Education*. Glasgow: Fontana.

Theodorson, G. A. & Theodorson, A. G. (1969) *A Modern Dictionary of Sociology*. New York: Barnes and Noble.

Weinberg, M. (1977) *Minority Students: A Research Appraisal*. Washington, DC: United States Government Printing Office.

BIBLIOGRAPHY

Banks, J. A. (1981) *Multiethnic Education: Theory and Practice*. Boston: Allyn and Bacon. This book includes a discussion of the theoretical and conceptual issues in multiethnic education, and guidelines for formulating educational programs that reflect ethnic diversity.

Banton, M. (1983) *Racial and Ethnic Competition*. Cambridge: Cambridge University Press. This well reasoned and researched book presents thoughtful theoretical perspectives on race relations and examples from several nations, including South Africa, the United States and the UK.

Barton, L. & Walker, S. (ed.) (1983) *Race, Class and Education*. London: Croom Helm. Thoughtful radical perspectives on issues related to race, class and education are presented in this book.

Batelaan, P. (1983) *The Practice of Intercultural Education*. London: Commission for Racial Equality. This publication is the report of an educational conference held in the Netherlands which included representatives from the UK, the Federal Republic of West Germany, Sweden and the Netherlands.

Bullivant, B. M. (1981) *The Pluralist Dilemma in Education: Six Case Studies*. Sydney: George Allen and Unwin. Case studies in multicultural education in the UK, Canada, Fiji, the USA mainland, Hawaii and Australia are included in this book. The author also presents a theory on the 'pluralist dilemma'.

Cashmore, E. E. (1984) *Dictionary of Race and Ethnic Relations*. London: Routledge and Kegan Paul. Definitions of key concepts, terms and movements in race and ethnic relations are included in this informative reference book.

Cashmore, E. E. & Troyna, B. (1983) *Introduction to Race Relations*. London: Routledge and Kegan Paul. This book includes several chapters that educators will find of particular interest, including those on education, ethnicity–youth–resistance, and media–racism–reality.

Centre for Contemporary Cultural Studies (1982) *The Empire Strikes Back: Race and Racism in 70s Britain*. London: Hutchinson. Issues related to race, gender and social class are examined in this provocative collection of papers.

Craft, M. (ed.) (1981) *Teaching in a Multicultural Society*. Lewes: The Falmer Press. Various views on ways to incorporate multicultural perspectives into teacher education are discussed in the papers that comprise this book.

Craft, M. (ed.) (1984) *Educational and Cultural Pluralism*. Lewes: The Falmer Press. The essays in this book discuss a range of issues related to multicultural education in the United Kingdom, including languages, home, school and community, and ideologies.

Glazer, N. (1983) *Ethnic Dilemmas 1964–1982*. Cambridge: Harvard University Press. Some of the major essays that Glazer has written during a period of nearly twenty years are compiled in this volume. In Part IV, the author discusses race and ethnic issues from an international perspective.

Gordon, M. M. (1964) *Assimilation in American Life*. New York: Oxford University Press. The nature of assimilation and various theories of assimilation and cultural pluralism are perceptively examined by the author. This book has had a major impact on teaching, research and writing about ethnic groups in the United States.

Husen, T. & Opper, S. (ed.) (1983) *Multicultural and Multilingual Education in Immigrant Countries*. Oxford: Pergamon Press. This book is made up of the proceedings of an international symposium held at the Wenner-Gren Center, Stockholm, in 1982. It includes a discussion of the social and psychological aspects of multicultural education.

Lynch, J. (ed.) (1982) *Teaching in the MultiCultural School*. London: Ward Lock Educational. The papers that comprise this book are grouped into four sections: theoretical perspectives, curriculum, religious and ethnic background, and resources.

Lynch, J. (1983) *The Multicultural Curriculum*. London: Batsford Academic and Educational. This book includes chapters on the teacher and multicultural education, a framework for a multicultural curriculum, the community and the multicultural school, as well as sources and guidelines for implementing a multicultural curriculum.

Marjoribanks, K. (1980) *Ethnic Families and Children's Achievements*. Sydney: George Allen and Unwin. This is an important study of the relationship between ethnicity, class and academic achievement.

Martin, J. I. (1978) *The Migrant Presence*.

Sydney: George Allen and Unwin. This book is an informative and important work on immigrant groups in Australia by a perceptive sociologist.

Megarry, J., Nisbet, S. & Hoyle, E. (ed.) (1981) *World Yearbook of Education 1981: Education of Minorities*. London: Kogan Page. Contributors from several nations discuss a range of issues related to the education of ethnic and immigrant groups in this comprehensive volume.

Pinkney, A. (1984) *The Myth of Black Progress*. Cambridge: Cambridge University Press. The author's main goal is to refute the thesis, popularized by William J. Wilson, that the significance of race in the United States is declining and that class is more important than race in explaining life chances. While the author is only partially successful in refuting Wilson's thesis, this book is important because of the counter-argument it sets forth.

Samuda, R. J., Berry, J. W. & Laferriere, M. (ed.) (1984) *Multiculturalism in Canada: Social and Educational Perspectives*. Toronto: Allyn and Bacon. A comprehensive collection of papers that discuss diverse issues related to multicultural education in Canada are included in this volume.

Sowell, T. (1984) *Civil Rights: Rhetoric or Reality*? New York: William Morrow and Co. In this controversial book, Sowell argues that the civil rights vision – which has decisively shaped events and policies in the United States since 1954 – is based on assumptions and misperceptions rather than on factual evidence.

Thernstrom, S., Orlov, A. & Handlin, O. (ed.) (1980) *Harvard Encyclopedia of American Ethnic Groups*. Cambridge: Harvard University Press. This is the most ambitious and comprehensive single volume on the diverse ethnic groups in the United States. It includes a number of thematic essays related to the education of ethnic groups.

Van Den Berg-Eldering, L. & DeRijcke, F. J. M. (ed.) (1983) *Multicultural Education: A Challenge for Teachers*. Dordrecht, Holland: Foris Publications. A group of Dutch and US educators and social scientists describe a range of theoretical and political issues in this book which resulted from a conference sponsored by the Dutch government on the occasion of the US–Dutch Bicentennial in 1982.

Verma, G. K. & Bagley, C. (ed.) (1979) *Race, Education, and Identity*. London: Macmillan. This book contains an informative collection of empirical studies that educators will find useful in their work.

Watson, J. L. (ed.) (1977) *Between Two Cultures: Migrants and Minorities in Britain*. Oxford: Basil Blackwell. This book consists of well-crafted essays on the various ethnic, cultural and religious groups in Britain.

Wolfgang, A. (ed.) (1975) *Education of Immigrant Students: Issues and Answers*. Toronto: The Ontario Institute for Studies in Education. The papers that make up this book discuss a range of issues, including philosophical and historical perspectives, practical experimental programs in action, and what research shows.

Wood, D. (1978) *Multicultural Canada: A Teacher's Guide to Ethnic Studies*. Toronto: The Ontario Institute for Studies in Education. The author describes concepts, teaching methods and materials that teachers will find helpful in incorporating ethnic content into their curricula.

PART II

Policies and Practices

The chapters that constitute this part focus on the development of multicultural education in selected Western nations in which the education of ethnic groups and the education of all students about ethnic and cultural differences have become major issues and have stimulated debate and action at local, state, provincial and national levels. The ethnic revival movements that erupted in the United States in the 1960s and 1970s echoed throughout the world. They stimulated actions by legislators and educators that influenced developments in multicultural education in many different nations.

Such developments have also been rich in the other newer nations where European peoples and cultures are dominant, including Canada and Australia. Since the Second World War, immigrants from British Commonwealth nations have settled in the United Kingdom in significant numbers and have consequently given rise to both ethnic revival and protest movements and, since the 1970s, newer developments in concepts, practices and programs in multicultural education. Most of the nations in Western Europe, such as the Netherlands, France and West Germany, have also been grappling with the problems of educating ethnic and immigrant groups since the 1970s.

The chapters in this part discuss the historical development of multicultural education within specific nations or a group of nations, changing definitions of the concept, legal and political developments, competing theories and trends, current practices including exemplary programs, and a critical assessment of the present and future status of multicultural education. Each chapter also includes a bibliography of important readings related to education and cultural diversity.

Chapter 2

Race, Ethnicity and Schooling in the United States: Past, Present and Future

JAMES A. BANKS

ETHNIC DIVERSITY IN THE UNITED STATES

Since its founding, the United States has been an ethnically and culturally diverse society. The native inhabitants of what became the United States were culturally diverse before the coming of the Europeans and Africans. They were made up of several hundred different societies and spoke more than 200 languages (Fuchs and Havighurst, 1973, p. 2). While the English and the Welsh were numerically dominant by 1790, there were substantial numbers of Scots, Germans, Dutch, Irish, French and other European groups. Blacks were the largest non-European group. They made up about 20 per cent of the total population. The non-English population, counting blacks, was about 40 per cent of the population (Bailey, 1961, p. 67).

The ethnic texture of the United States continued to deepen as the nation expanded from the Atlantic to the Pacific Ocean through wars and conquest, and as immigrants flocked from distant lands to realize the American dream that existed in myth if not in reality. A substantial number of Northern and Western European immigrants settled in the United States (about 3 778 633) between 1881 and 1890 (Banks with Sebesta, 1982). The period near the turn of the century (1901–1910) was characterized by a large influx of immigrants from Southern, Central and Eastern Europe (6 225 981) and by the rise of a nativistic movement designed to stop the flow of this group of Europeans because it was alleged that they would destroy Anglo-Saxon culture and civilization (Higham, 1972).

At the end of the United States–Mexican War in 1848, the United States acquired nearly a third of Mexico's northern territory and almost 80 000 of its former citizens. When the Spanish–American War ended in 1898, Cuba was placed under United

30

States tutelage, and the United States acquired Puerto Rico, Guam and the Philippines. Puerto Ricans became US citizens in 1917 and started migrating to the United States in significant numbers in the 1920s and 1930s. A large number of Filipinos immigrated to Hawaii and the United States mainland to work as field laborers between 1923 and 1929. In the 1860s Chinese laborers started immigrating to the United States in significant numbers. They were followed by the Japanese after 1868.

THE EDUCATION OF ETHNIC GROUPS IN THE UNITED STATES

Very early in Colonial American history, the English became the dominant cultural group and gained control of most of the nation's social, economic and political institutions. A primary goal of the school was to *Americanize* (which meant to Anglicize) the immigrants and help them to attain the language, values and behavior needed to succeed in American culture and institutions. By the time that the masses of Southern, Central and Eastern European immigrants began to enter the nation near the turn of the century, most of the 'old' European immigrants (from Northern and Western Europe) viewed themselves as culturally Anglo-Saxon and joined with the groups of British descent to express alarm about the immigration of the 'new' immigrants from Southern, Central and Eastern Europe. The fact that most of the new immigrants were Catholic also alarmed the old immigrants, who were largely Protestant and by now considered themselves native Americans.

American leaders and educators believed that the schools could and should play a major role in Americanizing the new immigrants. Wrote Cubberley, the famed educational leader (1909, pp. 15–16):

> Everywhere these people [immigrants] tended to settle in groups or settlements, and to set up their manners, customs, and observances. Our task is to break up these groups or settlements, to assimilate and amalgamate these people as part of the American race, and to implant in their children, as far as can be done, the Anglo-Saxon conception of righteousness, law, and order, and popular government, and to awaken in them a reverence for our democratic institutions and for those things in our national life which we as a people hold to be of abiding worth.

Educational historians have traditionally maintained that the schools played a major role in Americanizing the Southern, Central and Eastern European immigrants and in helping them to attain upward social mobility. However, revisionist historians contend that the role of the school in assimilating the immigrants and helping them to attain social mobility has been greatly exaggerated. These historians maintain that the immigrants usually attended school irregularly, learned about American society primarily from their jobs, and experienced social mobility primarily because of an expanding economy. Writes Berrol (1982, p. 41): 'In reality, it was the expanding economy rather than formal schooling that was the generator of acculturation in New

York. The immigrants learned about the city as they labored in it'. Whether the school succeeded or not, its primary goal was to eradicate the students' ethnic cultures and to assimilate them.

The educational experiences of the native Indians epitomize the assimilationist goals of education in the United States. In the late nineteenth century, the education of Indians became the responsibility of the Bureau of Indian Affairs. The Bureau totally disregarded the rich cultural diversity among the Indians and established boarding schools designed to 'civilize the natives' (Fuchs and Havighurst, 1973, p. 6). The educational 'civilization' of the Indians was often harsh. Indian students were removed from their homes – sometimes by force – to attend boarding schools that were usually long distances from their homes. Write Fuchs and Havighurst (p. 6): 'Old abandoned army forts were converted into boarding schools . . . the use of Indian languages by children was forbidden under the threat of corporal punishment, students were boarded out to white families during vacation times, and native religions were suppressed.'

The education of non-white ethnic groups, such as American Indians, blacks and Mexican Americans, has historically been characterized by Americanization and neglect. When the Mexican–United States War ended in 1848, the Mexicans who became new citizens of the United States found themselves foreigners in their native land. The treaty that ended the war made them American citizens and guaranteed them certain rights. However, these new United States citizens soon realized that they did not enjoy many of the benefits of other Americans. Anglo-dominated institutions showed little respect or tolerance for their language, cultures and values. In schools throughout the Southwest, the 'No Spanish' rule was imposed and Mexican students were forbidden to speak Spanish in school. If they were caught speaking Spanish they often received corporal punishment. In the early years of the twentieth century, most Mexican children dropped out of school after the primary grades; school was viewed by educational authorities primarily as an agency to assimilate the Mexican; and Mexican children were frequently segregated in schools, particularly in the early grades (Carter, 1970, pp. 10–11).

EGALITARIAN IDEALS AND RACIST IDEOLOGY

When immigrant and ethnic groups were Americanized, they were taught and were inculcated with the American egalitarian ideology. At the same time as they were being taught American democratic ideals, they were victimized by structural inequality and institutionalized racism. One of the founding principles of the new American nation was that 'all men are created equal, that they are endowed by their Creator with certain unalienable Rights, that among these, are Life, Liberty, and the pursuit of Happiness' (The Declaration of Independence, 1776). This ideology was expressed and popularized by American founding fathers such as Thomas Jefferson, John Adams and Benjamin Franklin. The key constitutional and political documents in the United States, such as the Declaration of Independence, the Constitution and the Bill of Rights echo this fundamental principle.

When this principle was first articulated in the late 1700s by America's founding fathers, it applied primarily to Anglo-Saxon males with property. As other European ethnic and cultural groups immigrated to the United States in increasing numbers, the principle was expanded to include these groups if they satisfied certain conditions. They had to declare allegiance to American democratic ideals and become culturally assimilated into the dominant Anglo-American culture before they experienced the full rights of United States citizenship or were structurally included in the nation's social, economic and political life.

The European colonists justified their break from Britain on the basis of the democratic principles stated in the Declaration of Independence and the United States Constitution. These principles, as beliefs and ideologies, became institutionalized within American culture. Yet slavery, the grossly unequal education received by blacks, Indians and Mexicans, and other forms of institutionalized racism and discrimination sharply contradicted the American democratic principle that 'all men are created equal'.

The contradiction between American democratic ideals and the existence of slavery and institutionalized segregation and discrimination is an important and salient characteristic of American life that has decisively shaped its history and continues to strongly influence contemporary life in the United States (Myrdal, 1944). A key theme in American history is the attempt to reconcile an egalitarian ideology with institutionalized racist practices such as slavery, separate and unequal schools, and the more subtle forms of racism in US society today. The development of slavery, the formulation of a complex racist ideology to justify it, and the quest of blacks to attain an education in both the past and present indicate how the American egalitarian ideal is blatantly contradicted in practice. Yet it remains a powerful idea in US life.

JUDEO-CHRISTIAN PRECEPTS AND RACISM

Judeo-Christian ideas also became important early in the history of the United States. Religion played a major role in the founding of most of the American colonies. Slavery grew by leaps and bounds in the late 1600s and was established in both fact and law when the eighteenth century began (Franklin, 1980). Defenders of slavery – or the 'peculiar institution' as it came to be called – were faced with the difficult task of developing an ideology to defend the peculiar institution which was consistent with American egalitarian ideals and Judeo-Christian concepts and principles.

Racism was developed as an ideology to justify the enslavement of blacks and the colonization of other non-white peoples in the Third World (van den Berghe, 1978). The tenets of racism were developed in a way that made it consistent with both American democratic ideals and Judeo-Christian precepts. An elaborate racist ideology was formulated which defined blacks as non-human, thus making the central American tenet that 'all men are created equal' inapplicable to them. Religiously, blacks and other Third World peoples were defined as heathens who needed to be conquered, enslaved or colonized in order to be taught Christianity so that they would experience salvation. The elaborate racist ideology that was developed was used to justify laws that prevented blacks from learning to read and from attending school in the years before the Civil War.

SLAVERY AND THE GREAT BETRAYAL

The institutionalization of slavery in the Southern states and the caste-like status of 'free' blacks in the North, which had developed by the beginning of the eighteenth century, decisively shaped race relations and the education of blacks during the pre-Civil War period. The North and the South grew increasingly apart because of cultural, ideological and economic differences. The South became heavily dependent on cotton and the institution of slavery as the North experienced industrial growth.

Slavery was challenged from its beginning by black and white Northern abolitionists. As in future fights for racial justice in the United States, the abolitionists pointed out the inconsistencies between American egalitarian ideals, Judeo-Christian precepts, and the dehumanizing nature of slavery. Southern apologists for slavery countered with arguments about the innate inferiority of blacks, how slavery civilized them, and the ominous threat that racial mixing posed to the nation-state. Southerners argued that blacks were genetically inferior, while at the same time enacted laws that prohibited them from learning to read and attending school. Their belief in the genetic inferiority of blacks was apparently equivocal. The arguments about the educability of blacks that were developed during the pre-Civil War period are often echoed today, in contemporary language and symbols, by leaders who defend the status quo and those who advocate equality for the nation's victimized ethnic groups (Jensen, 1969; Green, 1981).

Slavery was one of the major causes of the United States Civil War, which raged from 1861 to 1865 and in which more than 600 000 people lost their lives. The hope that was born among blacks during the Civil War was quickly shattered by the events that took place in the South during the Reconstruction period – a period in which a defeated and broken South tried to rebuild itself. With the help and protection of the United States government and of Northerners, blacks were able to participate for the first time in their local and state governments during Reconstruction and to establish schools for black youths. However, their brief honeymoon ended when the Northern troops pulled out of the South in 1877. Some historians view this event as the Northern desertion of blacks and refers to it as the 'great betrayal' of the newly freed blacks by the North.

THE ESTABLISHMENT OF BLACK COLLEGES

In the years immediately following the Civil War, a number of black educational institutions were established with the encouragement and financial support of

Northern philanthropists. The Hampton Normal and Agricultural Institute opened in Hampton, Virginia, in 1868. The most famous graduate of the Hampton Institute, Booker T. Washington, founded the Tuskegee Institute in 1881. Both Hampton and Tuskegee were founded to give blacks a technical education. An acid debate took place about whether the newly freed blacks should be given a technical or a liberal education. Other black institutions that were founded during this period had a traditional liberal arts curriculum. These included Fish University, founded in 1866, and Morehouse College and Howard University, both founded in 1867. Various religious groups often played a key role in the founding of the first black colleges. Until recent years, most black Americans who went to college attended one of the historic black institutions of higher education that were established during the post-Civil War period. Many of these institutions, such as Fish and Morehouse, attained excellent reputations through the years. Predominantly black colleges and universities are still very important in the higher education of black students today in the United States.

THE POST-RECONSTRUCTION PERIOD AND THE 'SEPARATE BUT EQUAL DOCTRINE'

During the post-Reconstruction period blatant forms of discrimination and segregation were legally established in the South. Determined to 'put blacks back in their place', the South established a number of institutions and laws designed to re-establish slavery in form if not in substance. The poll tax was established to stop blacks from voting, the Ku Klux Klan was born, and the Supreme Court in the *Plessy* v. *Ferguson* case (1896) legitimized the concept of 'separate but equal' institutions. In this case, Homer A. Plessy, who was one-eighth black, sat in an all-white car on a train and took his case to court when he was arrested. The United States Supreme Court eventually heard the case and ruled that 'separate but equal accommodations' were constitutional. The Supreme Court judgment in the *Plessy* case sanctioned racial segregation in the South and the North for almost sixty years. Blacks also became frequent victims of lynchings and other forms of violence in the late nineteenth and early twentieth centuries.

While the *Plessy* case indicated that black and white institutions could constitutionally be separate but equal, the schools established for blacks during this period were separate but highly inferior. Textbooks, buildings and facilities, pay for teachers, and the training of teachers were highly unequal for white and black schools. Deliberately segregated schools were established in the South. Segregated black and white schools also developed in the North because of laws, customs, housing discrimination, and the gerrymandering of school district boundaries (Weinberg, 1977). Other minority groups, such as Mexicans and Indians, often attended segregated schools for many of the same reasons as blacks in the North. Education for these groups, as for blacks, was inferior, sporadic and assimilationist oriented, with little respect or regard for the cultures of ethnic minority students.

THE EDUCATION OF ETHNIC GROUPS IN THE
EARLY TWENTIETH CENTURY

The first decades of the twentieth century were a difficult time for blacks and other US ethnic minority groups. Many ethnic minority youths in the South and Southwest, who were the children of sharecroppers and farm laborers, worked long hours in the fields and attended school rarely, if at all. When ethnic minority youths did attend school, their schools were usually segregated and unequal. Black children in the South often had to walk four to eight miles to school each day as buses carrying white students passed them on the road. The walking black students were sometimes teased and taunted by the white children riding the bus.

Blacks in Northern cities and Mexicans in the Southwest often faced problems attaining an education in the first decades of this century. During the 1920s in the Harlem district of New York City, blacks often had to attend schools that were severely overcrowded, deliberately segregated, and housed in inferior buildings (Weinberg, 1977, p. 73). In 1928, at least 40 per cent of the Mexican-American school-age children in Texas were not attending school, their school year was often only half as long as that of white students, and their schools were segregated. Mexican-American children were not attending school at all in at least seventeen school districts in Texas (Manuel, 1930). Many of the individuals who were on the boards of school districts were large landowners who made educational policies consistent with their needs for cheap farm labor rather than for the academic advancement of Mexican-American youths. Writes Weinberg (1977, p. 147): 'As an instrument of exploitation, the schools often seemed to be hardly more than an extension of the cotton field or the fruit-packing shed.'

THE SECOND WORLD WAR AND THE BIRTH OF
INTERGROUP EDUCATION

Most blacks lived in the Southern states before the Second World War. However, many joined the exodus to Northern cities after the war began to seek jobs in defense-related industries. Many poverty-stricken blacks rushed to Northern cities when they heard rumors of a 'land of milk and honey' up North. Many white Southerners also migrated to the North seeking defense-related jobs during the war years. A significant number of Mexicans migrated from Mexico to the Southwestern states under the provisions of an agreement between the United States and Mexico that authorized Mexican immigrants to work temporarily in the United States.

The competition between blacks and whites for housing and jobs in Northern cities created racial tensions that culminated in some of the most serious riots in the nation's history. In 1943, race riots erupted in a number of US cities, including Detroit, the Harlem district of New York, and Los Angeles. In the Harlem riot, five people were killed, 400 were injured, and damage to property was about $5 million. Thirty-four people lost their lives in the Detroit riot and millions of dollars' worth of property was destroyed. Mexican-Americans and whites clashed in a series of 'zoot suit' riots in Los Angeles during the summer of 1943 (McWilliams, 1968).

The rash of riots deeply stunned the nation and stimulated discussions and actions designed to ease racial tensions and conflicts. Educational institutions responded with a series of reforms that became collectively known as *intergroup education* (Cook and Cook, 1954). A major goal of intergroup education was to reduce racial and ethnic prejudice and misunderstandings. Activities designed to reduce prejudice and to increase interracial understanding included the teaching of isolated instructional units on various minority groups, exhortations against prejudice, organizing assemblies and cultural get-togethers, disseminating information on racial, ethnic and religious backgrounds, and banning books considered stereotypic and demeaning to ethnic groups. A major assumption of the intergroup education movement was that factual knowledge would develop respect and acceptance of various ethnic and racial groups (Banks, 1981).

The intergroup education movement of the 1950s differed in several significant ways from the ethnic education movement of the 1960s and 1970s which it foreshadowed. The intergroup education movement was dominated by liberal educators who envisioned a more just and tolerant society. Few of the leaders of this movement were black or members of other non-white ethnic groups. Consequently, the perspectives presented within the intergroup education movement were primarily those of sympathetic liberals rather than those of racial and ethnic minorities. The ideology that dominated the intergroup education movement was primarily a liberal assimilationist one which envisioned a society made up of people who were very much alike but who were not discriminated against for having vestiges of cultural differences (Glazer, 1977). Unlike the ethnic revival movement that emerged in the late 1960s, the intergroup education movement did not assume that the school should help to maintain the cultural uniqueness of ethnic groups.

THE 1950S AND 1960S

The United States experienced a series of events related to race relations during the 1950s and 1960s that deeply influenced US society and the education of its ethnic groups. When the 1950s began, segregation of blacks and whites was deeply entrenched throughout the South and in many parts of the border and Northern states. The National Association for the Advancement of Colored People (NAACP), a major civil rights organization founded in 1910, had initially tried to bring about equal education for black students by working to get their separate schools equal. However, it was obvious to NAACP leaders by the 1930s and 1940s that black and white schools were not going to become equal. With this realization, the NAACP began a fight in the courts to get segregated schools declared unconstitutional.

The battle was long and hard. The NAACP began with colleges and universities in its fight to desegregate the nation's educational institutions. In 1950 it had a major legal victory when the Supreme Court struck down state laws that prevented blacks from attending state universities in Oklahoma and Texas (the *McLaurin* v. *Oklahoma State Regents* and the *Sweatt* v. *Painter* cases). After victories in breaking down segregation in higher education in the Southern and border states, the NAACP started working to get racial segregation in the public schools declared unconstitutional. In a landmark decision on 17 May 1954 (*Brown* v. *Board of Education of Topeka*), the Supreme Court ruled that segregated schools were 'inherently unequal' and that they denied black children 'the equal protection of the laws guaranteed by the Fourteenth Amendment' to the Constitution. The Court thus reversed its own decision that it had made nearly sixty years before in the *Plessy* case (1896), when it upheld the principle of 'separate but equal accommodations'.

THE BLACK REVOLT AND THE RISE OF ETHNIC REVITALIZATION MOVEMENTS

A number of events gave rise to the black civil rights movement that arose in the 1960s and stimulated the rise of a rash of ethnic movements among other ethnic groups. The Supreme Court cases that declared segregation unconstitutional in state universities in the Southern and border states, President Truman's Executive Order in 1948, which prohibited segregation in the armed forces, and the landmark *Brown* decision were significant events that paved the way for the black revolt that erupted in the 1960s. These events created hope and enabled blacks to see the possibility of change. The attempt by the federal government and the federal justice system to eliminate the most blatant forms of discrimination stimulated blacks to seek more rights that were guaranteed by the Constitution. The egalitarian ideology which is the cornerstone of the Constitution and the Bill of Rights was used by blacks to justify and to legitimize their quest for full citizenship rights.

The Montgomery bus boycott led by Martin Luther King in 1955 was a significant event that signaled the beginning of the civil rights movement. The movement gained increasing momentum as the sit-ins, freedom rides, and marches took place to force an end to segregation and to push for equality for all Americans. Liberal legislation, designed by the federal government to halt the growth of the civil rights movement, actually gave it more momentum. The Civil Rights Act of 1964, the most comprehensive in the nation's history, responded to many of the concerns and stimulated the growth of the civil rights movement.

The civil rights movement grew increasingly militant as younger and more strident black leaders, such as Stokely Carmichael and H. Rap Brown, emerged and challenged established leaders such as Martin Luther King and Roy Wilkins. A militant group had emerged within the civil rights movement by the mid-1960s and the legitimacy of the established leaders was becoming increasingly challenged. A series of serious race riots and rebellions occurred in the nation's cities during the mid- and late 1960s. Thirty-five people lost their lives in the riot that occurred in the Watts district of Los Angeles in August 1965. Hundreds of others were injured and $40 million worth of property was damaged or destroyed. The worst rebellion of the period broke out in Detroit on Saturday evening, 22 July 1967. At least 44 people lost their lives during the outbreak and about 2000 were injured.

A NATIONAL COMMISSION ON CIVIL DISORDERS IS ESTABLISHED

The riots in the 1960s deeply stunned the nation and stimulated actions by a range of government and private agencies and institutions, including the federal and state governments, volunteer agencies and public educational institutions such as schools and colleges. President Lyndon B. Johnson appointed a prestigious commission to identify the causes of the riots and to make recommendations that would help to lessen racial tension in the nation and improve the social and economic status of blacks. The commission, chaired by Governor Otto Kerner of Illinois, was criticized by militants because they viewed its members as too much a part of the establishment and as too conservative. The commission wrote cogently about the causes of the racial problems in the United States and warned that the nation was headed toward two societies: one black and one white, separate and unequal (Report of the National Advisory Commission on Civil Disorders, 1968). It set forth a series of comprehensive recommendations related to employment, education, the welfare system and housing regarding ways to lessen racial tension in the nation and to improve the social and economic conditions of black Americans.

The cogent message and recommendations made by the commission had more legitimacy because its members were a part of the establishment. What was initially thought to be a shortcoming of the commission by militant observers turned out to be one of its major strengths: a group of respected members of the establishment concluded that the establishment itself was the major cause of the racial problems in the nation. The Kerner Commission Report, as it came to be called, stimulated much controversy as well as productive discussions about the plight of black Americans and the responsibility of the larger society to help them attain economic and political equality.

Some non-black minority group leaders criticized the Kerner Commission for viewing racial and ethnic problems in the United States primarily as black–white rather than multiethnic. The multiethnic dimension of the civil rights movement developed later. As the civil rights movement matured, more and more ethnic groups began to echo the voices of black Americans and to indicate how they had been victimized in US society. Mexican Americans, Puerto Ricans in the United States, American Indians and Asian Americans expressed their frustrations and hopes and, like blacks, made demands on educational and other institutions. Later in the movement, white ethnic groups expressed their ethnic rage and demanded redress

THE EDUCATIONAL RESPONSE TO ETHNIC MOVEMENTS

During the late 1960s ethnic groups made a number of demands on educational and other institutions. They demanded that textbooks be integrated so that their children could see themselves reflected in the curriculum, that more minorities be hired as teachers and administrators, that their languages be legitimized and/or taught in the public schools, and that their histories become a part of the school and college curriculum. Ethnic groups also demanded that more minorities be admitted to colleges and universities.

Because of the racially tense and politically polarized atmosphere in which these demands arose, educators often responded to them without careful thought and planning and in ways designed primarily to silence ethnic protest rather than to institutionalize ethnic programs or to make significant changes in existing institutions. Ethnic history courses were quickly created, individuals were sometimes hired to teach them who did not have the required credentials, and white faces in textbooks were painted brown. Most of the early ethnic studies programs in the United States were based on the assumption that only members of a particular ethnic group needed to study its history and culture. Thus black studies courses were typically found only in predominantly black schools and Mexican-American studies courses were usually found only in schools with a significant Mexican-American population.

LEGISLATIVE AND JUDICIAL ACTIONS

Legislation at the state and federal level was enacted to respond to the ethnic revitalization movements. Most of this legislation was compensatory in nature: it was designed to help minority youths to attain the knowledge, skills and attitudes needed to be assimilated into the mainstream society rather than to encourage cultural maintenance, which was often an expressed goal of advocates of education for ethnic groups. This legislation was rarely designed to change the total school curriculum so that all students could learn about the cultures and histories of ethnic groups. Among the important legislation enacted during this period were: the Title I Amendments to the Elementary and Secondary Education Act (ESEA) of 1965, designed to provide assistance to educational agencies for the education of children from low-income families; the Title VII Amendment to the ESEA (the Bilingual Education Act 1968), which provided special funds to help students who came to school speaking a language other than English; and the Title IX Amendment to the ESEA (Ethnic Heritage Studies Act 1972), which provided funds for the development and dissemination of materials related to the history and culture of ethnic groups and for training teachers to incorporate ethnic content into the curriculum.

The federal and district courts also shaped policy related to the education of ethnic groups in the 1970s. In a case decided in 1974, *Lau* v. *Nichols*, the Supreme Court ruled that the San Francisco school district denied Chinese students who did not speak

English a meaningful opportunity to participate in the public educational program and violated the Civil Rights Act 1964 when it failed to provide them with English language instruction. Many observers and supporters of bilingual education interpreted the Court's action to mean that the district was required to establish bilingual rather than Teaching English as a Second Language (TESL) programs. However, the Court allowed the San Francisco school district to decide how it would provide English language instruction to Chinese students. A federal district court in Michigan, in *Martin Luther King Jr Elementary School Children* v. *Ann Arbor School District* (Smitherman, 1981), ruled that the Ann Arbor School District must provide training for teachers so that they could better understand black English and take it into account when teaching students who spoke black English. Both the *Lau* and the *King* decisions were highly controversial and evoked acid debates about their meanings and educational implications.

THE SCOPE OF THE ETHNIC MOVEMENTS EXPANDS

As the civil rights movement entered its later phases, more and more groups that believed they were victims of discrimination began to articulate their grievances and to make demands on educational institutions and other governmental agencies. Black Americans were at the forefront of the civil rights movement when it emerged. As the movement developed, other non-white ethnic groups, such as Mexican-Americans and American Indians, joined the movement, thus expanding its focus and scope. Later, white ethnic groups, such as Jewish-Americans, Italian-Americans and Polish-Americans, pointed out ways in which they were victims of discrimination in US society and argued that they had specific entitlements. In a strongly worded book, *The Rise of the Unmeltable Ethnics*, Michael Novak (1971) expressed the frustrations and hopes of many white ethnic groups in the United States who believed that they were victims of discrimination. Most of these ethnic groups came from Southern, Central and Eastern Europe. They were made up primarily of Greeks, Italians, Poles and other Slavic groups. In 1979, the United States Commission on Civil Rights (1979) sponsored a consultation on the *Civil Rights Issues of Euro-Ethnic Americans in the United States: Opportunities and Challenges*.

The focus of the civil rights movement expanded even more when women, handicapped people and senior citizens articulated ways in which they were victims of discrimination in US society and demanded redress. Like other groups who viewed themselves as victims of discrimination, these groups pushed for legislation and educational programs designed to give them equity in US society. Women's rights groups experienced a major victory when Title IX of the 1972 Education Amendments was enacted. This title states that 'No person shall, on the basis of sex, be excluded from participation in, be denied the benefits of, or be subjected to discrimination under any education program or activity receiving federal financial assistance.'

An important Act related to the education of handicapped students was enacted by Congress in 1975: Public Law 94–142, known as the Education for All Handicapped

Children Act. This Act requires that handicapped students must be placed in the least restrictive educational environment that is consistent with their needs, and that an individualized educational program be developed for each child. This individualized program must clearly specify the services required to meet each child's educational needs.

Title IX of the 1972 Education Amendments and Public Law 94–142 not only expanded the focus of the movement concerned with ethnic rights but, like the Acts related to the education of ethnic groups, created tremendous debate and controversy among educators. Both of these Acts have major implications for the ways in which female and handicapped students are educated in the schools. Title IX became controversial in part because many educators believed that it meant they had to make major changes in their schools, such as creating the same athletic programs for girls as those that existed for boys, or lose their federal funds. Public Law 94–142 became controversial because it requires mildly handicapped students to be educated in regular classrooms, and many teachers were very apprehensive about having handicapped students in their classrooms, since few of them had any previous experience with handicapped students.

ACTIONS BY STATES AND PROFESSIONAL ORGANIZATIONS

In addition to the federal legislation that requires educational institutions to implement programs and practices related to ethnic groups, women and handicapped people, a large number of states also enacted laws that require actions and programs related to one or more of these groups. States such as Iowa, California and Minnesota enacted legislation that requires educators to develop criteria for selecting textbooks to ensure that they depict the contributions of ethnic groups and to provide training for teachers in the history and culture of ethnic groups. The training of teachers in the history and culture of ethnic groups was extensive in several states, including Iowa, Minnesota and California.

Influential national professional organizations developed and published policy statements, often adopted by their boards of directors, that urged educational institutions to implement programs and practices related to ethnic and cultural diversity. The Board of Directors of the American Association of Colleges for Teacher Education adopted a policy statement on multicultural education, 'No One Model American', in November 1973. The statement reads in part, 'Multicultural education rejects the view that schools should seek to melt away cultural differences or the view that schools should merely tolerate cultural pluralism. Instead, multicultural education affirms that schools should be oriented toward the cultural enrichment of all children and youths through programs rooted to the preservation and extension of cultural alternatives' (American Association of Colleges for Teacher Education, 1973). The Board of Directors of the National Council for the Social Studies published an influential position statement endorsing multiethnic education and describing ways that schools could implement it (Banks et al., 1976).

By the late 1970s, educational institutions in the United States were faced with a number of mandates and pressures that required or appealed to them to implement programs and practices related to various ethnic and cultural groups. These included demands made by the ethnic and cultural groups themselves, federal, state and local laws, judicial decisions, and recommendations and requirements by professional and accreditation organizations. In May 1977 the major national organization that accredits teacher education programs, the National Council for the Accreditation of Teacher Education, adopted a standard requiring its member institutions – made up of about 80 per cent of the institutions in the United States that train teachers – to have multicultural components in their teacher education programs. The standard states that 'Provision should be made for instruction in multicultural education in teacher education programs. Multicultural education should receive attention in courses, seminars, directed readings, laboratory and clinical experiences, practicum, and other types of field experiences' (National Council for the Accreditation of Teacher Education, 1977, p. 4).

THE DEVELOPMENT OF MULTICULTURAL EDUCATION

The earliest educational responses to the ethnic revitalization movements of the 1960s were specialized ethnic studies courses and programs that focused on specific ethnic groups, such as Afro-Americans and Mexican-Americans. As more and more ethnic groups demanded specialized attention in the curriculum, ethnic studies courses and programs that focused on several ethnic groups were developed.

As the ethnic studies movement matured, educators began to realize that incorporating ethnic content into the curriculum was necessary but not sufficient to help ethnic minority youths to experience educational equality. Consequently, ethnic studies evolved into a larger educational movement that included the teaching of ethnic content as well as changes in aspects of the school environment. This movement became known as *multiethnic education*: it focuses on all the major variables of the school environment, including teacher attitudes and expectations, the languages that are respected and taught in the school, the school culture, the norms and values of the school, the curriculum, and assessment and testing procedures. The most important goal of multiethnic education is to reform the major variables in the school environment so that students from all ethnic and racial groups will experience educational equality (Banks, 1981).

As more and more groups, such as women and handicapped people, began to demand that the school reflect their cultures and promote equality for them, educational institutions began to view these diverse groups as a collectivity and to respond to their needs with single courses, programs and projects. *Multicultural education* emerged as a concept in the United States to incorporate the concerns and needs of a wide range of cultural and ethnic groups. Multicultural education is sometimes conceptualized in a way that includes a wide range of groups, including ethnic, religious, language, social-class, sex, and age groups as well as handicapped individuals (Gollnick and Chinn, 1983).

The attempt in the United States to conceptualize and implement a highly inclusive kind of multicultural education has stimulated debate and controversy. Some ethnic minorities believe that when multicultural education is conceptualized in a way that includes many different groups it directs attention away from the real victims of racism and discrimination, non-white ethnic groups. Some critics of multicultural education in the United States believe that a broad concept of multicultural education focuses too little or not at all on institutionalized racism. A few observers believe that one of the major purposes of multicultural education is to divert attention away from racism and thus away from the problems of the nation's non-white ethnic minorities.

Some people feel that multicultural education, when conceptualized in a broad and inclusive way, does not deal adequately with the unique problems of any of the various groups because their problems are too individual to be dealt with adequately in such a generalized way. Geneva Gay (1983) is concerned that multicultural education is becoming too broad. She writes (p. 563):

> Another potential threat to multiethnic education comes from within. Although any educational idea must grow and change if it is to stand the test of time, such growth must remain within reasonable boundaries and retain a certain degree of continuity. If many new dimensions are added too rapidly, the original idea may be distorted beyond recognition. This may be beginning to happen to multiethnic education.

SCHOOL DESEGREGATION: AN UNFULFILLED DREAM

Nearly every phase in the development of multicultural education in the United States has been dominated by debate and controversy. Since its beginning, school desegregation has been characterized by acid debate, controversy, and sometimes violence. After years of delay, violence and conflict, the South eventually succeeded in desegregating its public schools. The battle for school desegregation then shifted to the North and the West, where school segregation developed because of housing segregation and the gerrymandering of school district boundaries rather than because of laws.

The major battles over desegregation in the 1970s were fought in the North and West, and not in the South. The resistance to school desegregation in Northern cities was often as tenacious and violent as it had been in the South. The North could no longer point its finger at the South and call it racist. White parents in the North argued that they opposed school desegregation not because they disliked blacks but because they wanted neighborhood schools. Many Northern white parents fled to the suburbs or sent their children to private schools rather than send them to desegregated public schools in the cities. The flights to the suburbs became known as 'white flight'. While there are a few cities in the United States in which school desegregation is working, such as Austin, Texas, and Seattle, Washington (National Education Association, 1984), the hope promised by the *Brown* decision and school desegregation remains largely unfulfilled.

The South worked hard and succeeded in desegregating its public schools. However, many schools in the South are becoming resegregated as whites move out of the city or send their children to private schools. School segregation in the nation's largest cities in the North and West is also increasing. Many large urban school districts are becoming predominantly ethnic minority. In 1984, non-white ethnic minorities constituted the majority of school enrollments in 23 of 25 of the nation's largest cities (American Council on Education, 1984). A significant number of middle-class ethnic minorities are also deserting the public schools for private schools (Coleman et al., 1981). Consequently, the public schools in the nation's largest cities are becoming not only increasingly non-white but also increasingly poor.

Even within desegregated schools, classes are often segregated because white students are found disproportionately in classes for the academically gifted. Gifted education is a movement that has mushroomed in recent years in the United States. Middle-class white parents who choose to keep their children in the public schools often get them placed in special classes for gifted and talented students. Ethnic minority parents, a disproportionate number of whom are poor, are not nearly as skilled in manipulating the school system to get special benefits and classses for their children. The result is that gifted and special classes and programs are composed mostly of whites in many desegregated city school districts.

Many parents from all cultural and racial groups have lost faith in school desegregation, or 'busing', as it is euphemistically called. Many black parents believe that blacks have paid the greatest price for school desegregation and that the gains from it have been illusory. Many white parents oppose school desegregation because they have lost faith in many city school districts and are uncomfortable when their children are bused to schools that have large numbers of children from diverse ethnic and social-class groups. Some Hispanic parents oppose desegregation because they want their children to be educated in their local communities in schools that reflect their cultures, language and traditions.

Despite the fact that many groups have lost faith in school desegregation and in the dream legalized in the *Brown* decision, school desegregation is still the law of the land in the United States. Most school districts are doing what is legally required to desegregate their schools, despite the odds. A few, such as Seattle and Austin, are succeeding.

The attempt to desegregate its public schools dramatizes the persistent US dilemma: the US commitment to egalitarian ideals, the inconsistency between these ideals and the reality, and the failure to make the ideals a reality but the tenacity to keep trying. The United States has not given up the effort to desegregate its public schools because segregated schools and a segregated society are inconsistent with US egalitarian ideals. The continuing but fledgling attempt to desegregate the nation's schools will no doubt continue because of the laws of the land and the egalitarian ideals upon which the laws are based.

THE IDEOLOGICAL DEBATE OVER MULTICULTURAL EDUCATION

School desegregation is only one of the issues related to multicultural education on which Americans are deeply divided and debate vigorously. Affirmative action policies, bilingual–bicultural education, the extent to which the school should reflect and promise cultural diversity, and the best ways to bring about equality for the nation's ethnic minority groups are other issues on which both the US public and scholars are deeply divided. Americans often disagree sharply about these issues because they have divergent beliefs and ideologies about what should be the proper role of state-supported schools, about the nature of race and ethnicity in US society, and about what the posture of the common schools should be in the maintenance of the values, cultures and languages of ethnic minority youths.

It is difficult to categorize the range of opinions and ideologies related to the education of ethnic and cultural groups in the United States. However, the various opinions and ideologies range from strong assimilationists who argue that the major goal of the schools should be to socialize ethnic youths so that they will become effective participants in the nation's mainstream culture (Thernstrom, 1980) to strong pluralists who believe that the school should play a major role in helping ethnic youths to retain their first cultures and languages and acquire the values and skills needed to participate in the radical reform of US society.

The goals and concepts of education held by assimilationists and pluralists differ sharply. Assimilationists assume that the directions and nature of US society are essentially what they should be, and that the major problems of ethnic groups result from the fact that they are not full participants in society. The assimilationists assume that ethnic groups are not structurally integrated into US society primarily because they lack the knowledge, skills and attitudes needed to participate fully in the common culture. When they acquire the requisite knowledge, skills and attitudes, they will be able to become structurally integrated into the mainstream society.

Assimilationists believe that the major goal of education for ethnic and cultural minorities should be to help them attain the knowledge, attitudes and skills needed to participate in the mainstream society. Programs that foster cultural maintenance, such as bilingual education and ethnic studies, will retard the ethnic child's ability to function in the mainstream US culture. Assimilationist educators view modernity and traditional ethnic cultures as inherently contradictory. Ethnic youths must be freed of ethnic group affiliations and cultures in order to attain success in the shared culture of the nation-state.

The pluralist educator believes that ethnic individuals cannot attain equality in US society until their groups acquire structural inclusion into the society because ethnic people are treated first as members of groups and only secondarily as individuals (Dickeman, 1973). Pluralists thus reject the assimilationists' 'individual opportunity' view of US society. They believe that education should foster cultural maintenance and ethnic identity, and help youths to acquire the knowledge, attitudes and skills needed to participate in the reformation of US society and to make it more just for their own and other ethnic groups. Pluralists believe that education should foster cultural maintenance and societal reform and not merely assimilate ethnic youths into the existing society.

A group of educators has emerged in the United States whose members might be called biculturalists or multiculturalists (Ramirez & Castaneda, 1974). They believe that it is important for ethnic youths to acquire the knowledge, attitudes and skills needed to function effectively in the mainstream culture. However, they also believe that the national culture needs new ideals and that it can be enriched by the values, perspectives and points of view that are parts of ethnic minority cultures (Greenbaum, 1974). Biculturalists also believe that a curriculum that reflects the cultures, perspectives and histories of ethnic groups will help ethnic students to achieve at higher levels because students learn best in an educational environment that validates their cultures and is consistent with the ways in which they learn.

Pluralists and biculturalists influenced the nation's curriculum and educational policies significantly in the 1960s and 1970s. Many textbooks were revised so that they reflected more accurately the experiences and cultures of ethnic groups; minorities were hired for the first time in many schools, colleges and universities; multicultural programs, offices and projects were established in many school districts; and many educators became much more knowledgeable about and sensitive to the cultures and needs of ethnic minority students. However, the influence of pluralist and bicultural educators has waned tremendously in recent years. A neo-conservative movement has arisen in the United States which is characterized by a strong push for assimilation, national pride and patriotism. Many recent textbooks include less information about ethnic groups than their counterparts in the early 1970s; many school districts have abandoned their offices for multicultural education; and ethnic issues have a low priority on the agenda of many schools and colleges.

As has been the case in the past when pluralism raised its head to challenge the dominance of assimilationism in US life, the assimilationists won the battle to control the nation's schools during the 1960s and 1970s. However, their victory is neither total nor complete. Bits and pieces of the ethnic reform movement are slowly becoming institutionalized in the nation's schools, colleges and universities. The strong pluralist movement of the 1960s and 1970s left a lasting legacy. While there are fewer blacks and Hispanics in textbooks today than there were during the height of the ethnic revival movement in the early 1970s, almost every history and social science textbook includes some information on the experiences of the nation's ethnic minorities. Many school districts have developed and require the use of criteria that stipulate that the adopted textbooks should reflect accurately the cultures and experiences of ethnic groups and women.

There are other signs that the ethnic movement of the 1960s and 1970s left a mark on US society and that the nation can never take ethnic issues off its agenda. The NCATE standard that requires teacher-education institutions to have multicultural education in the curriculum is one of the most significant legacies of the ethnic movement of the last decade. Many of the nation's teachers are, in some form or fashion, learning about the cultural diversity in US society and its implications for teaching. The tremendous growth in the ethnic population in the United States between 1970 and 1980, which resulted largely from immigration from Mexico, China, Korea, Indochina and the Philippines, makes it essential that the nation not only acknowledge but deal creatively and effectively with the education of its increasing ethnic minority population.

The powerful assimilationist, patriotic and nationalistic forces rampant in the United States today are giving pluralistic ideals and developments a serious challenge. Yet ethnic and cultural pluralism is too entrenched in US life to be eradicated: it is irrepressible. The war between assimilationism and pluralism will continue to exist in US society (Apter, 1977). Neither force will ever experience a complete victory. The pendulum will continue to swing toward one force and then the other. Assimilationism and pluralism are destined to co-exist in the United States in a delicate but tense balance.

REFERENCES

American Association of Colleges for Teacher Education (1973) *No One Model American* (pamphlet). Washington, DC: The American Association of Colleges for Teacher Education.

American Council on Education (1984) Minority changes hold major implications for US. *Higher Education and National Affairs*, 9 March, p. 8.

Apter, D. E. (1977) Political life and pluralism. In Turmin, M. M. & Plotch, W. (ed.), *Pluralism in a Democratic Society*, pp. 58–91. New York: Praeger.

Bailey, T. A. (1961) *The American Pageant: A History of the Republic*, second edition. Boston: D. C. Heath and Company.

Banks, J. A. (1981) *Multiethnic Education: Theory and Practice*. Boston: Allyn and Bacon.

Banks, J. A. et al. (1976) *Curriculum Guidelines for Multiethnic Education*. Washington, DC: National Council for the Social Studies.

Banks, J. A. with Sebesta, S. (1982) *We Americans: Our History and People*, vol. 2. Boston: Allyn and Bacon.

Berrol, S. (1982) Public schools and immigrants: the New York experience. In Weiss, B. J. (ed.), *American Education and the European Immigrant*, pp. 31–43. Urbana: University of Illinois Press.

Carter, T. P. (1970) *Mexican Americans in School: A History of Educational Neglect*. New York: College Entrance Examination Board.

Coleman, J. S., Hoffer, T. & Kilgore, S. (1981) *Public and Private Schools*. Chicago: National Opinion Research Center.

Cook, L. & Cook, E. (1954) *Intergroup Education*. New York: McGraw-Hill.

Cubberley, E. P. (1909) *Changing Conceptions of Education*. Boston: Houghton Mifflin.

The Declaration of Independence (1776). Reprinted in *The Annals of America* (1968), pp. 447–9, vol. 2. Chicago: Encyclopaedia Britannica.

Dickeman, M. (1973) Teaching cultural pluralism. In Banks, J. A. (ed.), *Teaching Ethnic Studies: Concepts and Strategies*, pp. 5–25. Washington, DC: National Council for the Social Studies.

Franklin, J. H. (1980) *From Slavery to Freedom: A History of Negro Americans*, fifth edition. New York: Knopf.

Fuchs, E. & Havighurst, R. J. (1973) *To Live on this Earth: American Indian Education*. Garden City, NY: Doubleday (Anchor Books).

Gay, G. (1983) Multiethnic education: historical developments and future prospects. *Phi Delta Kappan,* **64**, 560–3.

Glazer, N. (1977) Cultural pluralism: the social aspect. In Tumin, M. & Plotch, W. (ed.), *Pluralism in a Democratic Society*, pp. 3–24. New York: Praeger.

Gollnick, D. M. & Chinn, P. C. (1983) *Multicultural Education in a Pluralistic Society*. St Louis: Mosby.

Green, P. (1981) *The Pursuit of Inequality*. New York: Pantheon Books.

Greenbaum, W. (1974) America in search of a new ideal: an essay on the rise of pluralism. *Harvard Educational Review,* **44**, 411–44.

Higham, J. (1972) *Strangers in the Land: Patterns of American Nativism 1860–1925*. New York: Atheneum.

Jensen, A. (1969) How much can we boost

IQ and scholastic achievement? *Harvard Educational Review,* **39**, 1–123.

McWilliams, C. (1968) *North from Mexico: The Spanish-Speaking People of the United States.* New York: Greenwood Press.

Manuel, H. T. (1930) *The Education of Mexican and Spanish-Speaking Children in Texas.* Austin: Fund for Research in the Social Sciences, University of Texas.

Myrdal, G., with the assistance of Sterner, R. & Rose, A. (1944) *An American Dilemma: The Negro Problem and Modern Democracy.* New York: Harper and Brothers.

National Council for the Accreditation of Teacher Education (1977) *Standards for the Accreditation of Teacher Education,* p. 9. Washington, DC: The National Council for the Accreditation of Teacher Education.

National Education Association (1984) *Three Cities that are Making Desegregation Work.* Washington, DC: The National Education Association.

Novak, M. (1971) *The Rise of the Unmeltable Ethnics.* New York: Macmillan.

Ramirez, M. & Castaneda, A. (1974) *Cultural Democracy, Bicognitive Development and Education.* New York: Academic Press.

Report of the National Advisory Commission on Civil Disorders (1968) New York: Bantam Books.

Smitherman, G. (1981) What go round come round: King in perspective. *Harvard Educational Review,* **51**, 40–56.

Thernstrom, A. M. (1980) E pluribus plura: congress and bilingual education. *The Public Interest,* **60**, 3–22.

United States Commission on Civil Rights (1979) *Civil Rights Issues of Euro-Ethnic Americans in the United States: Opportunities and Challenges.* Washington, DC: The United States Commission on Civil Rights.

van den Berghe, P. (1978) *Race and Racism: A Comparative Perspective,* second edition. New York: Wiley.

Weinberg, M. (1977) *A Chance to Learn: A History of Race and Education in the United States.* Cambridge: Cambridge University Press.

BIBLIOGRAPHY

Appleton, N. (1983) *Cultural Pluralism in Education: Theoretical Foundations.* New York: Longman. This book includes a thoughtful theoretical analysis of the concept of cultural pluralism and its implications for schooling.

Baker, G. C. (1983) *Planning and Organizing for Multicultural Instruction.* Reading, MA: Addison-Wesley. This introductory book is designed to introduce educators to multicultural education. Topics include planning for instruction, organizing for instruction, and instruction.

Banks, J. A. (1981) *Multiethnic Education: Theory and Practice.* Boston: Allyn and Bacon. This book discusses the historical, conceptual and philosophical issues in the fields of multiethnic and multicultural education. It also includes a chapter on teaching strategies for multiethnic education.

Banks, J. A. (1984) *Teaching Strategies for Ethnic Studies,* third edition. Boston: Allyn and Bacon. Teaching strategies, with grade levels designated, and bibliographies for teachers and students are key features of this book. A historical overview and a chronology of key events for all major ethnic groups in the United States are also included.

Clark, R. M. (1983) *Family Life and School Achievement: Why Poor Black Children Succeed or Fail.* Chicago: University of Chicago Press. In this case study of ten children, the author describes family characteristics that facilitate the academic achievement of black students.

Garcia, R. L. (1982) *Teaching in a Pluralistic Society: Concepts, Models, Strategies.* New York: Harper and Row. This introductory book on ethnic diversity and American education discusses a range of topics, including schools and their communities, and various models and strategies related to teaching cultural diversity.

Glazer, N. & Moynihan, D. P. (ed.) (1975) *Ethnicity: Theory and Experience.* Cambridge, Mass.: Harvard University Press. An outstanding and seminal collection of essays which focus on ethnicity in the United States and in other nations. Martin Kilson, Milton Gordon, Talcott Parsons and Andrew Greeley are among the contributors.

Gollnick, D. M. & Chinn, P. C. (1983) *Multicultural Education in a Pluralistic Society.* St. Louis: The C. V. Mosby Co. Multicultural education is conceptualized broadly in this book, which discusses ethnicity, religion, language diversity, socioeconomic status, sex and gender, age, and exceptionality.

Gordon, M. (1964) *Assimilation in American Life: The Role of Race, Religion, and National Origins.* New York: Oxford University Press. This seminal and classic work has deeply influenced ethnic studies teaching and research in the United States.

Longstreet, W. (1978) *Aspects of Ethnicity: Understanding Differences in Pluralistic Classrooms.* New York: Teachers College Press. The author presents an interesting definition of ethnicity and describes a process that teachers can use to study ethnic behavior in their own classrooms.

Obgu, J. U. (1978) *Minority Education and Caste: The American System in Cross-Cultural Perspective.* New York: Academic Press. In this book, a social anthropologist presents a theory which suggests that a major goal of education in the United States is to prepare minority groups for their caste-like status in society. Comparisons are made with the education of ethnic groups in Britain, New Zealand, India and Japan.

Philips, S. U. (1983) *The Invisible Culture: Communication in Classroom and Community on the Warm Springs Indian Reservation.* New York: Longman. In this study, the author describes patterns of verbal and nonverbal communication among Anglo and Indian children. She describes the conflicts that Indian children experience when they function in their home cultures and in the school.

Ramirez, M. & Castaneda, A. (1974) *Cultural Democracy, Bicognitive Development, and Education.* New York: Academic Press. This important book describes ways in which the learning styles of Mexican-American students often differ from the learning styles favored by the schools. The authors suggest the need to match teaching better with students' learning styles.

Samuda, R. (1975) *Psychological Testing of American Minorities: Issues and Consequences.* New York: Dodd, Mead. Important psychological and sociological issues related to the testing of ethnic minority groups are discussed in this book.

Thernstrom, S., Orlov, A. & Handlin, O. (ed.) (1980) *Harvard Encyclopedia of American Ethnic Groups.* Cambridge: Harvard University Press. This important reference book includes an essay on the education of ethnic groups as well as many other articles that will help educators to better understand and interpret the experiences of ethnic groups in the United States.

Weinberg, M. (1977) *A Chance to Learn: A History of Race and Education in the United States.* Cambridge: Cambridge University Press. This well-researched history of the education of ethnic groups in the United States focuses on school desegregation efforts and treats the education of blacks, Mexican-Americans, American Indians and Puerto Ricans on the United States mainland.

Chapter 3

Canadian Multicultural Education: Promises and Practices

KOGILA A. MOODLEY

PATTERNS OF IMMIGRATION

Canada has always been an ethnically heterogeneous society. The roots of this diversity lie in four major phases of settlement:

1. Prior to European contact, indigenous native people constituted some fifty distinct segments and spoke over a dozen languages. They ranged from nomadic hunting and gathering groups to cultivators of the soil.
2. From the sixteenth and seventeenth centuries, up until 1760, spurred by the fur trade, there was an influx of French traders and colonizers. At this time most accounts estimate the native population to have been over 200 000. By the latter half of the 1800s these numbers had dwindled to 100 000 due to conquest and genocide. French–Aboriginal contact gave rise to the distinctive Metis population.
3. Following the French came the British, in the eighteenth century, after Canada was ceded to Britain at the Treaty of Paris in 1763. Subsequent phases of migration, at first by the United Empire loyalists after the American Declaration of Independence in 1776, and then by other immigrants from Britain, marked the beginnings of a firm British presence. By the mid-nineteenth century, they were to outnumber the French.
4. The need to settle the prairie provinces led to a call for 'other' immigrants who were recruited from Europe and parts of Asia. Northern European immigrants, especially of Dutch and German origin, predominated. By 1871, German immigrants constituted the largest group, numbering some 200 000 (Hawkins, 1972). In 1896 they were joined by Eastern Europeans, in particular Ukrainians. Despite their lack of the prized Anglo-mainstream ancestry, they were nevertheless recruited because of their agricultural backgrounds, which 'fitted' them for the development of the prairies. For the same reasons, nonconformist sects such

51

as the Hutterites and Mennonites were given tracts of land to farm as communities. Asians, most of whom were brought in as contract labourers to work on the Canadian Pacific Railway, numbered 23 700 in 1901. Among these were some 4700 Japanese and 1700 East Indians. Lord Sifton's disapproval of Asian immigration led to the imposition of a 'head tax' for Chinese immigrants in 1900 and 1903, but this did not deter them from coming. By 1921, the Chinese population in Canada had increased to 40 000, the Japanese to 16 000 and the East Indians of Sikh origin to 5000. Over half the Chinese, and the majority of Japanese and Sikhs, settled in British Columbia (Palmer, 1975, pp. 7–10).

The period after the Second World War marked a resumption in immigration. In addition to the continuing influx of British settlers, there came Europeans, notably of Italian, German, Dutch and Polish origin, from different social and occupational backgrounds. In the mid-1960s, with a booming Canadian economy, the future was optimistic. Canada needed immigrants to meet the needs of a complex industrialized, urbanized society. Previous sponsored immigration requirements gave way in 1967 to a more selective policy known as the point system. It was based on level of education, occupational skills, local demand and personal adaptability. The new admission procedure replaced the racial and ethnic discriminatory practices of the past through the use of universalistic admission criteria. After 1967, Canada's ethnic mosaic began to permit, for the first time, a significant number of non-white people. By 1971, non-charter group[1] immigrants constituted 25.3 per cent of the overall population, and have been referred to as a 'third force'.

Unlike earlier waves of immigration aimed at opening up the interior of the country, with involvement in agricultural pursuits, recent immigrants, particularly Asians, preferred to settle in the major metropolitan centres. Toronto, for instance, has become home to over a third of all new immigrants (Richmond, 1969), changing its character radically from a provincial British-dominated city to a lively culturally heterogeneous metropolis. The range of ethnic origins and the differing group strengths in Canada are reflected in the 1981 census (Table 3.1). Increasingly more immigrants in the 1970s originated in Third World countries, so that in 1980 exactly 50 per cent of all new arrivals came from Asian countries. This shift led to renewed racial tensions in Canada and prompted an unprecedented activity on the part of public and private bodies to ease adjustment problems and combat racism.

The changing proportions of immigrants to Canada from different regions of the world are illustrated in Table 3.2.

This diversity is reflected in the populations of most major cities and, consequently, in the composition of schools. In Vancouver in 1982, of 55 000 students, 46 per cent were identified as children for whom English was a second language. 'Forty-three per cent of these were of Chinese origin, 16 per cent East Indian, 9 per cent Italian, 5 per cent Portuguese, 4 per cent Greek, 3 per cent German and 3 per cent Tagalog; and smaller percentages of Japanese, Serbo-Croatian, Vietnamese, Spanish, French and Korean' (Allan, 1982, p. 1). Toronto has a slightly larger ESL[2] population – 47 per cent. Added to the range of home languages other than English is the presence of dialects of English (Masemann, 1984, p. 351). This Babylonic situation clearly gave new impetus to the practical aspects of the policy of multiculturalism.

Table 3.1 *Population by selected ethnic origins,[a] Canada, 1981*

Total population[b]	24 083 500
Single origins	22 244 885
African	45 215
Armenian	21 155
Asian Arab	60 140
Austrian	40 630
Balkans	129 075
Baltic	50 300
Belgian and Luxembourg	43 000
British	9 674 245
Czech and Slovak	67 695
Chinese	289 245
Dutch	408 240
Finnish	52 315
French	6 439 100
German	1 142 365
Greek	154 365
Magyar (Hungarian)	116 390
Indochinese	43 725
Indo-Pakistani	121 445
Italian	747 970
Japanese	40 995
Jewish	264 025
Latin American	117 555
Native peoples	413 380
North African Arab	10 545
Pacific Islands	115 290
Polish	254 485
Portuguese	188 105
Romanian	22 485
Russian	49 435
Scandinavian	282 795
Spanish	53 540
Swiss	29 805
Ukrainian	529 615
West Asian	10 055
Other single origins	176 160
Multiple origins	1 838 615
British and French	430 255
British and other	859 800
French and other	124 940
British, French and other	107 080
European and other[c]	238 455
Native peoples and other[d]	78 085

Statistics Canada, Ottawa, Queen's Printer, 1983, p. 2.

[a] The 1981 Census is the first to accept more than one ethnic origin for an individual. Therefore this table includes counts of single and multiple origins.

[b] Excludes inmates.

[c] Includes multiple origins involving European, Jewish and other origins not included elsewhere.

[d] Includes multiple origins involving native peoples and British, French, European, Jewish or other origins.

Table 3.2   *Landed immigrants^a in Canada according to world regions in 1980*

Region	%
Asia	50.0
Europe	28.8
Africa	3.0
South America	3.8
Caribbean	5.2
USA	6.9
Others	2.3
	100.0

Statistics Canada, Ottawa, Queen's Printer, 1982, p. 6.
^a Landed immigrant status is granted after an individual is eligible for entry into Canada and arrives in the country. It is similar to the 'green card' in US immigration.

MULTICULTURAL POLICY

In the endless quest for the ever-elusive Canadian identity, the view that Canada values the cultural mosaic, unlike the assimilationist United States, has always held prominence. This difference was formalized in the 1971 Liberal government's policy of multiculturalism. It was initiated in response to the Report of the Royal Commission on Bilingualism and Biculturalism in the mid-1960s, and the Official Languages Act of 1961, which conferred equal status on both French and English 'as the official languages of the Parliament and Government of Canada' (Innis, 1973). The core of the government's policy presented by the then Prime Minister, Trudeau, stressed government assistance for culture maintenance:

> First, resources permitting, the government will seek to assist all Canadian cultural groups that have demonstrated a desire and effort to continue to develop a capacity to grow and contribute to Canada, and a clear need for assistance, the small and weak groups no less than the strong and highly organized.
>
> Second, the government will assist members of all cultural groups to overcome cultural barriers to full participation in Canadian society.
>
> Third, the government will promote creative encounters and interchange among all Canadian cultural groups in the interest of national unity.
>
> Fourth, the government will continue to assist immigrants to acquire at least one of Canada's official languages in order to become full participants in Canadian society.
>
> (Canada, House of Commons, Debates, 1971, p. 8546)

The policy was greeted in some quarters with great enthusiasm. On the whole, however, there has been some mixed reaction. Both the French and the native Canadians saw it as neutralizing their special claims. As founding peoples,[3] their charter rights[4] were being equalized with those of many others. Multiculturalism, native people point out, achieves nothing for the recognition of land claims and forgotten treaty rights. Although the French language is recognized as one of the two official languages, the French complained about a loss of cultural hegemony by being treated like other immigrants. Some European ethnics, especially Ukrainians, viewed cultural preservation without linguistic preservation as being certain to fail.

Ambiguities and contradictions in the policy have been argued ad nauseam (Burnet, 1975). The critique boils down to a tendency to view Canadian society and ethnic groups as though they existed independently, yet with the latter adding interest to the whole, through diverse customs and practices (Peter, 1981). Fear is expressed that ethnic groups, in sustaining their respective cultures, will undermine national unity, and this is mitigated by a meek plea to share these cultures with the rest of Canadian society, thereby enriching it. Cultural differences are at once extolled and considered a hindrance to be removed in the interests of access to equal opportunity (Moodley, 1983). Such conceptualization is said to raise legitimate concerns about the real integration of ethnic groups into the national identity. Finally, right-wing critics viewed the policy as a mere election ploy to garner the ethnic vote for the Liberal Party. It is indicative, though, that the Conservative Party, after its landslide victory in 1984, continued with the identical policy that now has virtually the unanimous support of all major political forces in the country.

PROVINCIAL RESPONSES TO CULTURAL DIVERSITY

Recognition of the potential divisiveness of the issues of culture and schooling led to the shift in control of education at Confederation from the national to the provincial arena, to allow the greatest freedom of expression of differences. Consequently, religious and linguistic diversity have been dealt with differently in each province. This educational autonomy of each province, resulting in different organizational provisions for linguistic and religious instruction, makes for a rather complex and confusing picture. A broad overview reveals great contrasts among the provinces.

A denominational system has operated in Newfoundland since the nineteenth century, providing Anglican, Pentecostal, the United Church and Roman Catholic schools with government support (Jaenen, 1977, p. 99). No such legal provisions exist for sectarian schools in New Brunswick, Nova Scotia or Prince Edward Island, but informal arrangements have been worked out in each. Special provisions exist for Acadian education in Prince Edward Island and Nova Scotia. New Brunswick has both English and French school boards. In response to the grievances of those seeking independent religious education, Ontario developed a public educational system composed of common schools[5] and separate public schools,[6] guaranteed under the BNA Act.[7] At present, financial support is provided for separate schools to the end of grade ten only.

Also guaranteed under the BNA Act was a dual confessional arrangement in Quebec. To this end, French and English instruction were made available. In Manitoba, separate language schools were available for French and English, as were bilingual schools for other ethnocultural groups. A major shift took place when English was made the sole language of instruction in 1916, effectively shattering the hopes of Franco-Manitobans for French language education, not to speak of cultural retention. Alberta, Saskatchewan and Northwest Territories offer both public and publicly funded separate school systems (Mallea, 1984, p. 78). British Columbia has never made any provision for public funding of separate schools, except for the supply of textbooks. There has been rising political pressure for government support of 'independent' schools. Where numbers warrant it, French-medium education is made available for its Francophone minority.

Although provincial autonomy in education has afforded flexibility to meet local needs, it has raised controversy. The absence of a federal guarantee of minority rights is especially notable when the language rights of different Francophone minorities are viewed (Mallea, 1984, p. 79). This state of affairs made for an initially very lukewarm reception of the policy of multiculturalism. If language education for a sizeable charter group[8] could not be guaranteed, how could linguistic and cultural preservation for a spectrum of ethnocultural groups be encouraged? Despite this contradiction, four out of ten provincial governments have officially accepted multiculturalism for implementation in educational programmes. School boards across the country have expressed various forms of commitment to multicultural education, and in some cases to race relations programmes as well. No single model of multicultural education exists. What is common is acknowledgement of a changing population, with different needs, and these concerns have been incorporated in school programmes and in inservice teacher education programmes. A few faculties of education across the country have established alternative programmes in multicultural education for pre-service teachers. It has been offered either as a separate course or as a component in sociology of education courses, where it may be discussed as part of the hidden curriculum of schools. Nowhere is it yet recognized as a mandatory requirement for all teachers.

Overt responses of schools to multiculturalism indicate a shift from the earlier benign assimilation to a greater acceptance of multiculturalism. A survey by Day and Shapson (1981) in British Columbia, involving 237 central office personnel in seventy school districts, found that most respondents favoured the inclusion of multicultural activities and programmes in the school curriculum. However, this acceptance has not been evenly integrated into practice. This is not surprising in view of the tremendous ambiguity about what multicultural education means. The survey shows that in the same sample only 20 per cent supported the inclusion of second languages as the medium of instruction for part of the curriculum. Even in provinces where the provincial government has adopted the policy, Francophones have difficulty finding education in their own language.

The main difference in multicultural policies is between an ethnocultural support-service orientation, as pursued by Ontario and Nova Scotia, and a language-based view of multicultural education, as practised in Saskatchewan, Alberta and Manitoba.

The Ontario Ministry of Education has actively initiated considerable curriculum reform. There has been a marked shift in approach from the 1950s and 1960s, when it was assumed that once immigrants acquired English language competence there would cease to be an 'immigrant problem' (Masemann, 1984). Beginning with the

Francophone minority, legislation passed in Ontario in 1968 guaranteed French-medium education. Present policy guidelines include information about the advantages of intercultural awareness in educational planning. Courses in multiculturalism are offered to inservice teachers and administrative staff. Curriculum materials are scrutinized for bias and stereotyping, and guidelines are offered to publishers and authors to promote bias-free, appropriate curriculum materials (McLeod, 1984).

Despite the controversy about offering non-official languages at public expense during regular school hours, the Heritage Language Programme established in 1977 has found increasing support. In 1980–81 44 different languages were taught after school hours, to 76 017 students (Ontario Ministry of Education 1980, p. 2). The instruction time permitted was up to two and a half hours a week. Immersion programmes in French are offered to English speakers who want greater fluency. Their success has stimulated international interest in the Canadian approach. Among other language programmes offered are the use of the minority language as a transitional language in instruction, gradually leading to mastery of the official language (Shapson and Purbhoo, 1977). Also increasingly popular are trilingual education programmes, established with community initiative. Most children in these programmes are third-generation immigrants, whose home language is English (Cummins, 1984).

Like Ontario, Nova Scotia's policy emphasizes intercultural understanding and the broader focus of equality of opportunity and access. Attempts have also been made to update inservice teacher education and to disseminate bias-free resources (McLeod, 1984), though this does not seem to have reached official curriculum guides and handbooks (Wilson, 1984).

In contrast to the intercultural awareness and after-school language programmes of Ontario and Nova Scotia, Manitoba, Alberta and Saskatchewan implement more integrated language programmes. English and French were until 1978 the official languages of instruction in Manitoba schools. In 1978, under the amended Public Schools Act, instruction in other languages was permitted, with school board authorization, for religious instruction, for allocated language-study time, before or after school hours, and for transitional purposes during school hours; and, with ministerial permission, other languages could be the language of instruction for up to 50 per cent of regular school hours (Manitoba, 1980, p. 42). This policy was very well received by the Ukrainian and German communities. Several pilot projects have been established and enrolment has increased notably (Mallea, 1984, p. 89). Furthermore, research evidence about the social and academic benefits of bilingual education has been positive (Shapson and Purbhoo, 1977; Cummins, 1979–80).

The integration of heritage languages as part of a sound multicultural programme is also clear in the Manitoba Teacher Society's background paper 'Multiculturalism and education in Manitoba'. Three essential components are highlighted: 'mainstream, multicultural education, immigrant orientation and New Canadian awareness [as well as] ancestral languages of established ethnocultural groups' (cited in McLeod, 1984, p. 41).

Saskatchewan's commitment to multiculturalism was evidenced in 1974 when the Saskatchewan Multicultural Act was passed. As a step toward implementing the goals of disseminating knowledge about and pride in all cultural heritages, the legislature amended section 209 of the School Act to permit the use of languages other than English for instruction. Financial incentives were offered for the development of such instruction. Bilingual instruction from Grades K to 12 and out-of-school programmes for some seventeen languages are offered.

Stimulated by the energetic efforts of the Ukrainian community of Alberta to include their cultural heritage as part of the educational process, the Alberta Schools Act was amended in 1971. School boards were empowered to introduce non-official language instruction where and when they deemed it appropriate. Wide-ranging curriculum reform was initiated. Pilot programmes using heritage languages for instruction for up to 50 per cent of the school day were established. In 1974 Ukrainian–English bilingual programmes were offered in both private and separate public schools. Currently, several variations of bilingual education are offered. Of the ten bilingual public schools in Alberta, five are Ukrainian, three Jewish and two German. In addition to these are the private schools which offer different language instruction. Saturday schools have also increased in scope and demand, and some twenty languages are taught. These schools are privately administered by the Alberta Cultural Heritage Branch (Wilson, 1984, p. 72).

British Columbia's Ministry of Education has not initiated any concerted attempts to formulate a multicultural policy. A few knee-jerk attempts such as the establishment of an ad-hoc committee in 1979 and the sponsorship of local multicultural conferences are about as far as it has gone. If anything, emphasis has been on English as a second language for immigrant children. Of late, however, some school boards, notably the Vancouver School Board, have made considerable progress in providing inservice teacher education, establishing a regular race relations advisory committee and institutionalizing a firm race relations policy in the school district. All schools have been requested to submit proposed plans for implementing multicultural education. Similarly, the Victoria School Board, with assistance from the Ministry, acted upon community members' suggestions to pilot an elementary school project entitled 'Alternatives to Racism'. The outcome is John Kehoe's *A Handbook of Selected Activities for Enhancing the Multicultural Climate of the School* (Kehoe, 1984). No significant developments in the area of bilingual education exist, other than those privately established by some ethnocultural communities. Under the current climate of budgetary restraint in British Columbia, multicultural and minority language education have been quickly defined as frills. They are readily targeted and shed as priorities.

Like the Heritage Language Programme of Ontario, Quebec's *Programme de l'enseignement des langues d'origine*, which was established in 1978, offers children of linguistic minorities the opportunitity of retaining the language of the family. The programme was developed in close collaboration with fluent native speakers from the various communities, who also had a sound grasp of the French language. The model used initially was half a school-day's instruction in native language and culture. The programme caters mainly for new immigrants and children whose parents define themselves as belonging to the particular ethnic group.

APPROACHES TO MULTICULTURAL EDUCATION

The education of minorities in Canada has been viewed from two basic and contrasting perspectives. The social-pathological perspective focuses on the cultural background or lifestyle of the minority as the source of 'the problem'. Often with benign intentions, well-meaning educators have interpreted the causes of the failure of some minorities as being culturally rooted. Canadian education is replete with instances of the forcible removal of Indian children from their homes and families in order to exorcise them of their 'malignant' cultures. Similarly, Glazer and Moynihan (1963), in their much cited study of US minorities, described what they saw as the deficiencies of the urban black family, its disorganization, instability and lack of a distinctive culture. The source of the problem was said to emanate from their home experiences, which failed to transmit the appropriate cultural patterns necessary for the types of learning required by schools and society. Characteristic of a victim-blame approach, such a perspective overlooked the complex interrelationship between the economic, social and political factors involved, which transcends the cultural basis. This view gave rise to numerous compensatory programmes which sought to make good the 'cultural deficits' through enrichment programmes certain to lead to integration.

In stark contrast to the deficit model of culture is the more seemingly egalitarian, anthropologically based, relativistic model. Unlike the former, it stresses that all cultures warrant equal respect and value. Neither is better or worse. Cultural content can be assessed only from the perspective of the 'insider'. It has its roots in the work of Malinowski (1944), Radcliffe-Brown (1952) and Herskovits (1948), to name just a few. Whereas the deficit model aimed at the integration of the outsider, the relativist model is analogous to the pluralist view, stressing the legitimacy of living within meaningful cultural collectivities outside the mainstream.

The two perspectives outlined are interwoven in the responses of the provinces toward the federal government's policy of multiculturalism. These include:

1. Programmes for the newcomer to acquire fluency in one of the official languages.
2. Cultural maintenance programmes. Interested ethnocultural groups are offered support to retain their cultures of origin through non-official language instruction and/or the cultivation of aspects of folk culture.
3. Multicultural education as an antidote to the conventional portrayal of ethnic groups. Canadian social studies curricula have depicted them for the most part as 'marginal' Canadians, as 'contributors to the dominant society', as 'beneficiaries' of the dominant society and as 'problems' (Werner et al., 1980, pp. 7–35). The acknowledgement of the valued diversity is sought.
4. Anti-racism education, which recognizes that prejudice and discrimination are potent forces which need to be addressed in a multicultural society.

It is worthwhile to examine each of these approaches in more detail, citing specific Canadian initiatives to concretize their practice.

Official Language Education

Official language education has aimed at enabling the minority child to function effectively both in the school and in the world outside. Three types of classes exist in different schools: (a) total integration, where the child is placed in a regular classroom; (b) withdrawal classes, where some time each day is spent in the language education class and the rest in the regular class; and (c) reception classes, where intensive training in language is provided to newcomers only (Ashworth, 1975).

In recent years, major Canadian language education journals portray a shift away from the more technical aspects of language learning alone to wider issues of language and culture. There has been a heightened awareness of the assimilationist hidden agenda of most language teaching to speakers of non-official languages.

An experiential programme of Anglo-Canadian cultural immersion was in effect at what used to be the Main Street School in Toronto's East End. With a sympathetic bilingual or multilingual staff of eight teachers it worked sensitively with 72 children of twelve years and above. Though the school no longer exists, it best characterizes the approach. The operative perspective was that the problems which immigrant children experience are best described as cultural problems rather than language problems. The route taken was to expose them to the language, namely English, through the culture. Teaching took place through informal interchanges with staff and peers and, more crucial, daily life experiences through field trips in the city. The approach was very orally based. There was no pressure to change their own ways of life; only ways of integrating their cultures with that of the mainstream were stressed. While the school was very popular with those it served, reports from subsequent schools attended by the children might be summarised as 'Your kids speak good English but they can't write'. Evaluations of the programme were not all that favourable either. As Lind comments:

> It was naive to try to prepare for the tedium of high school by having 'set pupils free to explore and discover the topography and inscapes of their community' . . .
> To flood one small school . . . with progressivism was to offer the kids no real purchase on the school system.
>
> (Lind, 1974, p. 110)

Above all, despite its benign motives, a programme such as this, by pushing culture first, ensured an assimilationist outcome.

In contrast to this 'cultural immersion' approach is the use of languages of origin for 'transitional' purposes in acquiring the new official language. The latter is used as a temporary bridge, to facilitate learning the new language. It aims at greater security without retarding academic progress in the process. While two languages may be used in the classroom, as is the case with the Italian programme in Toronto, the established language facilitates the learning of the new (Shapson and D'Oyley, 1984, p. 7).

Cultural Maintenance Programmes

Cultural maintenance programmes have taken different forms. In some Vancouver schools with a sizeable minority of native Indian children, cultural enrichment programmes are offered. One approach has been to withdraw native Indian children from regular classes to expose them to aspects of Indian cultural heritage, from stories to folk arts, for an assigned time daily. Since this was found by some teachers to set them back even further from other children in the classroom, an alternative has been arranged. The whole class is exposed to native Indian cultural materials for a given amount of time each week. Similar programmes have been established in black studies elsewhere. The aim of these programmes is to raise the self-esteem of the minority child. What is overlooked, however, is that high self-concept does not come only from knowledge of a cultural heritage. Characteristic of a victim-blame approach, the assumption here, despite benign intentions, is that if the group would feel more positively about itself, its members' life chances would be different. What is ignored is the daily relegation of the group to a caste-like lower status from which there is little chance of escape. Instead of an uncritical celebration of cultural heritage in a vacuum, what is needed is, as Banks illustrates, the development of a sense of political efficacy and the knowledge and skills to influence public policy toward greater equality (Banks with Clegg, 1977). Only if teachers' awareness of cultural backgrounds were to be harnessed toward effective teaching styles, reflecting a sensitive understanding as well as being actively demanding of standards through high expectations, could cultural content serve such groups well.

On the other hand, some immigrant parents from non-official language backgrounds have expressed a desire for the education of their children in their home languages, to prevent increasing alienation from their heritage cultures. Members of a Chinese community in Toronto, for instance, in the early 1970s appealed for greater compatibility between home and school culture for their children, by offering instruction in Chinese language and culture during the school day. Children are withdrawn for thirty minutes daily for instruction. Subsequent evaluation showed that academic achievement was unaffected, that children's information about their backgrounds increased and above all that their self-esteem had improved considerably (Bhatnagar, 1982, p. 171).

Similarly, Greeks in Eastern Canada have initiated and implemented a separate programme for trilingual education in English, French and Greek, using styles of teaching valued by the community. The schools operate within the Catholic or Protestant systems in Montreal, and more recently in Toronto as well. The president of the Greek community speaks in glowing terms of its success: 'In 1971, only 4 per cent of our high school graduates went to university. Today, our special schools send 84 per cent of graduates into post-secondary education' (House of Commons, 1984, p. 114).

There is, however, a danger of generalizing from the above successes. Clearly, sound pedagogic arguments have been advanced in favour of home language and cultural retention for effective school performance, as Verma and Bagley (1982) and others have pointed out. However, a few prerequisites for their success need to be mentioned. It goes without saying that an ongoing heritage culture with a language in use in the community is one of them. Another is a concerted, organized initiative from the community itself; this ensures cooperation through increased motivation of the children. Where enrichment programmes have been offered by the school board as a corrective for poor performance, it is clearly an imposed programme, lacking some of the components for success.

In this respect the call of the Native Indian Brotherhood for control of their own education and the increasing number of qualified native teachers have given rise to more successful outcomes in alternative programmes which have been run with native people. The true test will lie in the acceptability of their graduates in the market-place.

Multicultural Education

A broader definition of multicultural education also exists in the public awareness. It entails the celebration of difference, often the exotic. Usually 'the curriculum' is left intact and the celebration is an 'add-on' activity. In a recent survey in British Columbia by Shapson and Day there was a suggestion that 'after school programmes are probably most appropriate for some of the goals and objectives of multiculturalism' (cited in Wilson, 1984, p. 69). The inclusion of multicultural content is most prevalent at elementary levels, and mostly relegated to social studies programmes. Its non-integration in the curriculum is reflected in McLeod's comment about the status of multicultural education in secondary schools: '[They] have been slower than elementary schools in adopting multicultural education because they are more discipline and subject-oriented, and their teachers have been less innovative' (McLeod, 1984, p. 41).

A clear distinction exists between programmes focusing on culture and lifestyles and those focusing on race relations, power and life chances. There is more consensus about the former, which is viewed as non-controversial and 'positive', and it is the preferred, safer route for most teachers. The latter, being controversial and dealing with conflict, is defined as 'negative' and has been avoided for the most part. Of course, many who pursue the culture and lifestyle approach see as their goal the valuing of differences as a long-term path to better race relations. A common trend is to increase information *about* the different groups, in the hope that this will lead to greater tolerance. Sufficient historical evidence, as well as contemporary empirical studies, exists to show that this is not the only possible outcome (Katz, 1976; Moodley, 1981). Given the complexity of cultures, they are frequently trivialized in presentation in the elementary curriculum. Werner et al. refer to the common, isolated use of artifacts and other aspects of the material culture of people, without a holistic interpretation, as the 'museum approach'. It reinforces the 'us'–'them' difference and highlights a 'hierarchy of cultures' based on the way the outsider perceives the minority (Werner et al., 1980, p. 31).

A popular programme which addresses the issue of differences in lifestyles is 'Exploring Likeness and Differences with Film' (Hood, 1980), which is a twelve-week social studies unit for the intermediate grades. Through the use of selected films portraying the ordinary lives of children from different cultures, as well as the physically handicapped, children are taught to draw out the similarities and differences. The individuals portrayed talk about their own lives, thereby providing the 'insider's' perspective. A carefully worked out set of questions encourages observers to participate by drawing out their own, similar experiences. Evaluation of the programme was done by the developer herself, as well as in two separate evaluations. While the developer experienced very positive results, and the first evaluation (Kehoe, 1978) showed positive change in most schools, the second evaluation, using pre- and post-tests (Echols, 1981) 'showed inconsistencies and mixed results' (Kehoe, 1984, pp. 145–7). Despite limitations in implementation, the project has been very popular. This is not surprising, given its uncontroversial nature, its use of film, the clarity of accompanying guidelines and activities and, above all, the 'positive' focus on similarities.

Accentuating similarities is also the guiding thread of work done by Kehoe in *A Handbook of Selected Activities for Enhancing the Multicultural Climate of the School* (Kehoe, 1984). It integrates a concern with the broader issues of equality of opportunity and the hidden curriculum and links these with the way in which cultural diversity has been treated. The similarities between the attributes of minority groups and others are emphasized. Like the programme discussed above, this is a popular approach. It advises against the use of 'historical bad news', such as dwelling on Canadian treatment of minorities, and the tendency to connect 'poverty' with immigrants. Based on sound short-term evaluations, the concern with victimization is seen as not necessarily ensuring empathy of the learner with the victim. This approach is not without argument about the value of in-depth education for long-term immunization against discriminatory behaviour.

Also emphasizing children's better understanding of themselves and a respect for the differences of others is a programme from Alberta, known as the Society for the Prevention and Elimination of Discrimination and Stereotyping (SPEDS). Through a variety of themes, it highlights the uniqueness of individuals, in terms of their needs, abilities, values, ideas, beliefs, emotions, feelings and the forms of expression they choose. Students are taught an appreciation of the complementary nature of differences. Dislike and prejudice are distinguished, as well as the costs of the latter to all human beings. These themes are raised in 36 suggested lessons, using an activity-oriented, experiential approach. The SPEDS course was offered as one of two approaches. The other was an ethnic studies course. Careful evaluation using pre- and post-tests showed the SPEDS approach to have more positive effects on attitudes than the ethnic studies course.

Most programmes in multicultural education focus on accepting and respecting differences and recognizing similarities. Diverging from this is the concern of the Association for Values Education and Research at the University of British Columbia, which looks at issues of moral education. It sees multiculturalism as a moral concern, since it is concerned with how cultural minorities are treated and conflicts resolved. The distinction between cultural and ethical relativism is considered necessary in order to understand the moral principles basic to multiculturalism. Knowledge of the concepts of person, society, culture, prejudice and stereotyping, and the ability to distinguish factual and value claims, are considered essential in the formulation of valid arguments and the testing of moral principles. From this perspective, what multicultural education lacks is a clearly defined moral stance.

Multicultural education must develop the modes of reasoning for arriving at rational judgement concerning how people of different backgrounds should be treated . . . The aim has to be one of developing beliefs and modes of reasoning by which we can make intelligent decisions concerning how the needs, interests, and feelings of people should be construed, and how conflicts of interest should be resolved.

(Wright and La Bar, 1984, p. 118)

This can be accomplished, it is maintained, through educational efforts which promote sound reasoning and develop a concept of person, a sense of self-worth, a sense of society and the understanding of such concepts as prejudice and stereotyping. This approach has the advantage of being applicable to all children. It makes neither saints nor villains of either majority or minority group.

While values-education programmes would seem basic to any sound educational initiatives, they lack the flair and visibility demanded of other overtly multicultural programmes. They resemble the way in which true multicultural programmes ought to be inconspicuously incorporated as part of the normal human experience in a culturally diverse society.

Anti-racism Education

A growing number of programmes have been concerned with prejudice and racism in Canadian society, and this has more recently been known as anti-racism education. It differs from multicultural education in several ways. The shift is from a preoccupation with cultural difference to an emphasis on the way in which such differences are used to entrench inequality. It draws attention to the rhetoric of multiculturalism compared with its practice. The prime concern is with systemic discrimination in all its manifestations, ranging from the treatment of minorities in history to the hidden curriculum of schools. A dynamic rather than a static view of culture is taken. Instead of a preoccupation with the 'customs of the past' approach, it looks at the ways in which people transform their lives and respond to injustice, especially through various forms of collective action. In the school curriculum, this has been accomplished through seeking out appropriate literature, oral histories, biographies, music, poetry and art. In so doing, the lived experiences of all children are maximized and made part of 'school knowledge' (Thomas, 1984). The shared interests of people along class lines are emphasized in contrast to their 'primordial' ethnic ties. In light of its political, controversial nature, however, teachers have been somewhat reluctant to venture in this direction. It has also been viewed as a 'negative' approach. On the other hand, more astute programmes of multicultural education have incorporated racism as a concern.

A few school boards have included anti-racism as part of their goal of multicultural education. Toronto and North York led the way in the late 1970s and Vancouver has followed suit more recently. Both addressed manifestations of racism within the school system through the establishment of race relations sub-committees, consulting school personnel, students and the community.

A 'total community approach' has been advocated. The 1982 Vancouver School Board Race Relations Policy brochure states:

1. That the Board opposes and condemns any expression of racial/ethnic prejudice by its personnel, students and trustees.
2. That the Board [will] direct the Superintendent, in cooperation with all employee, parent and student organizations and trustees, to devise guidelines for the implementation of the race relations policy.
3. That the Superintendent [will] communicate . . . the Board's race relations policy and guidelines to all personnel and students . . . [and] the entire school community . . . methods will be devised at the school level whereby school personnel make employee, parent and student organizations aware of the policy . . . and . . . steps taken to implement it . . . and
13. That the Board [will] direct the Superintendent to encourage Vancouver schools to develop programs within and among schools to increase multicultural understanding. Such programs should involve all school personnel as well as students and parents.

(Vancouver School Board, 1984)

Schools were requested again in 1983 to submit detailed action plans for their proposed implementation of the district's policy of multicultural education and race relations. Along with this request was included a reminder that 'each school's action plan be a cooperative endeavour of the school staff, school consultative committee, racial/ethnic groups represented in the student population, and the student councils of secondary schools' (Vancouver School Board, 1984, p. 2). The responses of 83 schools indicate for the most part verbal commitment to an integrated, community-inclusive approach. What the content of the actual practice will be is of course difficult to gauge at this stage. It may be speculated that some of the plans are quick responses to the request for a submission, and therefore not really organically developed. However, the whole district policy is an interesting example of how behavioural change, based on policy directives and legal pressure, can be effective even if it precedes attitudinal change.

The preoccupation, albeit at the ideological level, with multiculturalism has given short shrift to the concerns of native people, as the original inhabitants of the country. They constitute 2 per cent of the population, including Inuit and those of mixed ancestry, the Metis. No longer definable in physical and cultural terms alone, two legal categories ('status' and 'non-status') serve to distinguish their claims to various rights. Natives of both categories number 300 000 and an estimated half a million respectively (Frideres, 1983). Subject to educational colonization, they have come to occupy a caste-like position in Canadian society. In an attempt to modernize native people and rid them of 'undesirable cultural practices', most were converted to Christianity, their children were forcibly removed to residential or day schools away from the community, and they were forbidden the use of their home languages. Indian education, unlike that of other minorities, has been under federal control, reflecting the paternalistic notions of natives as wards of the state. Under these circumstances the lack of identification of native people with mainstream education, and the extraordinarily high drop-out rate of Indian children, seem a logical consequence of educational colonization. Suffice it to say that the history of native education runs counter to all that multiculturalism purports to value.

In the literature on multicultural education, however, native Indian education has largely been ignored. This may have happened for several reasons. Indians are construed as an integrated part of what constitutes indigenous Canadian culture. Like the flora and fauna, natives are portrayed as natural fixtures, frequent objects in biased social studies curricula (Werner et al., 1980). For most immigrants, a country of origin still exists as a manifestation of a viable culture. For natives, on the other hand, the material basis of a cultural tradition has been drastically altered, so that Indian culture is seen as putative rather than real, relegated to the museum rather than being an everyday-life world. While early Indian folklore and mythology have been glorified, contemporary Indian life is widely stereotyped in pathological terms. Loss of fluency in their languages of origin, which mainstream educational institutions have both directly and implicitly aided, is then cited as evidence for the absence of an enduring culture worthy of preservation, like those of the other groups. The fact that Indian education is federally controlled and financed has served to act as a legitimate reason to ignore to some extent the need for concern about the group at the crucial regional level.

POLICY TRENDS IN RACE RELATIONS

The debate about race relations has climaxed in the 1984 report on visible minorities entitled *Equality Now* (House of Commons, 1984). The report will shape the implementation of multiculturalism for years to come, particularly as regards affirmative action programmes. It is a landmark in the ongoing controversy about immigration policy and race relations in Canada. The extensive cross-country hearings by an all-party committee of the House of Commons under the Chairmanship of Liberal MP, Bob Daudlin, resulted in eighty recommendations on new policies from social integration to employment, changes in the legal and justice system to media representations and educational issues. Regardless of how the government bureaucracy will respond to the proposals for affirmative action in many realms, the report has already received the almost unanimous endorsement of ethnic organizations that would be difficult to ignore.

Despite the widespread support for this imaginative and well intentioned blueprint, it is necessary to subject the document to a critical review. Many reservations have been forthcoming from voices that dislike a multiracial immigration policy in the first place, not to speak of special considerations for disadvantaged visible minorities. However, it raises fundamental questions to be asked even by those who will benefit from this progressive state intervention.

From a sociological perspective the most startling shortcoming of the report lies in its treatment of visible minorities as more or less monolithic. Aboriginal people, blacks in Nova Scotia, and Chinese and Indo-Canadians in British Columbia are subsumed under the concept 'visible minority communities'. While a common bond may lie in their exclusion, the histories of these four major visible groups in Canada are so different, their expectations and claims so varied, and their experience of and reaction to discrimination so distinct, that the common denominator of being 'non-white' makes the formulation of a common policy problematic. In addition to these intergroup distinctions, there are significant intra-group differences that make the racial label meaningless, except to those who have invented it. The crucial distinction between ethnic and racial groups is not adequately dealt with by the report. Ethnic characteristics based on cultural heritage or common territory are usually considered worthy of preservation by group members as long as their individual identity is bound to this origin. In this sense, aboriginal people form an ethnic group or a 'first nation' whose visibility merely overlaps with ethnicity. The same applies to religious or language groups.

Unlike ethnicity, however, racial characteristics have no intrinsic social significance of their own. Racial characteristics acquire salience because of discrimination. Exclusion serves as a bond only as long as discrimination lasts. In and of themselves, racial classifications have no more meaning than eye or hair colour. The conceptual confusion in advocating multiracialism as a component of multiculturalism (House of Commons, 1984, p. 143) is evident. Non-racialism, but not multiracialism, can be a worthy ideal. Colour blindness, however, remains the logical outcome of 'eradicating racism'. To aim at both – multiracialism and the eradication of racism – is surely an unrecognized contradiction. If one wishes to combat racism and achieve colour blindness as much as possible, one cannot simultaneously 'activate positive racial attitudes' (House of Commons, 1984, p. 124). All racial attitudes, whether positive or negative, represent stereotypes. Positive multiracialism is a dangerous supplement to a praiseworthy multiculturalism because it heightens invidious racial perceptions where multiculturalism is rightly silent on the question of race.

The report fails to distinguish between immigrants and conquered or colonized groups. Visible minorities in Canada belong to both categories. The far greater portion of the estimated 1.9 million 'visibles' (7 per cent of the population) can be found in the immigrant group, while the aboriginal people or blacks in Nova Scotia (who migrated as slaves or escapees from US slavery) would be examples of colonized or conquered segments.

There are two important differences between the two categories:

1. Conquered people can lay legitimate claims to restitution for past injustices. The native people in particular can evoke ownership rights to land and other symbolic resources. Visible immigrants do not possess such entitlement. The state does not owe immigrants anything more than equal rights.
2. Colonized people often form what the Nigerian anthropologist, John Ogbu (1978), refers to as 'caste-like minorities'. They have, until recently, internalized their stigmatization. A self-fulfilling prophecy reinforces low expectations which lock many members of these groups into a vicious circle of poverty, under-achievement, low status and general anomie. No such destiny normally befalls voluntary immigrants in search of economic improvement. With the backing of an extended family and a culturally transmitted work ethic of high motivation, many Asian immigrants to Canada soon outperform the average member of the dominant group.

On both grounds (entitlement to restitution and need) a good argument can therefore be made that colonized minorities in Canada and, above all, native people, both deserve and need affirmative action programmes, while this is not so for visible immigrants. It is simply not true that the statistics about 'missed opportunities to education and job skills' characterizing aboriginal people are 'applicable to other visible minorities as well' (House of Commons, 1984, p. 133). The report recommends, for example, that 'post-secondary institutions need to identify recruitment procedures which encourage more visible minorities to take advantage of their programs' (House of Commons, 1984, p. 133). If this advice were to apply to Canadian students of South and East Asian origin, and if the US situation where detailed racial statistics are kept is any guide, Canadian universities would most likely find that students from the two largest visible groups (Chinese and Indo-Canadians) would be proportionally overrepresented, at least in certain disciplines. If an ill-advised racial quota system were to apply, it could in fact be used to restrict such upward mobility, since the racist backlash would want to claim its proper quota. In short, visible immigrants do not need affirmative action.

Affirmative action for Asian-Canadians and other visible immigrants can hardly solve continuous racism. On the contrary, a good case can be made against affirmative racial action, in that it perpetuates invidious distinctions by attaching advantage to them. Affirmative action institutionalizes race. Visible minority groups will perceive a strategic value in classifying themselves as racially distinct as long as a quota favours them in the market over competitors. The proposed changes require a racial categorization of the population. This is stated in a matter-of-fact manner in the report, as some items to be included in the census. Nowhere is the morality of requesting information about racial descent questioned. Once census data on invidious distinctions are collected both the racists and their victims find more justifications for fortifying the barriers. How liberal philosophy, which traditionally espouses universalism and the unity of humankind, can lend itself to unofficial pigmentation of Canadian society remains to be explained by the well-meaning authors of *Equality Now*. Where are the lines to be drawn for children of 'mixed' marriages? Will the immigrants from the Middle East qualify for visibility or will they have to undergo a test for skin fairness? When the entire civilized world abhors the compulsory race classification laws of South Africa, regardless of its benign intentions Canada is about to institutionalize voluntary apartheid.

The shortsightedness of such a policy is evident in the counterproductive implications for those members of visible minorities who succeed in the absence of affirmative action. They will have to cope with the suspicion that they owe their position more to the colour of their skin than to their merit, whereas now those who have made it at least are accepted as having reached their position on their own, despite racial obstacles. Once this certainty is removed, all members of visible minorities will labour under the suspicion of incompetence and psychological insecurity. They will be restigmatized through the very efforts meant to destigmatize visibility.

CONCLUSIONS

Much of the ambiguity surrounding the policy of multiculturalism also applies to multicultural education. It incorporates notions of cultural pluralism, special needs and, more recently, anti-racism as a change of attitudes. Underlying these, a sense of cultural harmony is pervasive, but overlooks the prime goals of equality of opportunity and equality of condition.

A somewhat static conception of 'culture' is implicit in most views of multicultural education. Culture is seen as a set of more or less immutable characteristics attributable to different groups of people. These are used to identify people and often produce stereotypes, contrary to intention (Rosen, 1977). The notion of culture which the Royal Commission's Book IV (1969, p. 11) espouses as an afterthought under the heading 'The cultural contributions of other ethnic groups' reveals a lyrical fiction that bears little resemblance to minority reality. 'Culture', the Commission waxes, 'is a way of being, thinking and feeling. It is a driving force animating a significant group of individuals united by common tongue and sharing the same customs, habits and experiences.' If one takes the public definition of the two most stigmatized ethnic minorities in Canada, native people and 'East Indians', neither of the cultural attributes fits their experience. Native people are united neither by indigenous language nor by customs and habits. So-called Indo-Canadians, who arrived in Canada from four continents and as members of three world religions (Hinduism, Christianity and Islam) and various subsects (e.g. Ismailis, Sikhs, Protestants), are even more divided in the ideological lenses they use to interpret different experiences. What unites all groups, regardless of origin, is not an alleged common culture but common exposure to manifold discrimination and being an 'outsider'. It is this experience of conflict with and uneasy accommodation to mainstream culture that unites the minorities.

Past ideological formulas for making sense of a different social environment in precolonial America or post-colonial India do not always offer a useful guide to coping with Canadian challenges, apart from giving a sense of dignity to contrast with the low status in the country of adoption. Uncritical heritage maintenance per se can be a hindrance rather than an aid to meaningful survival. The cultural baggage of immigrants is continually examined for what is useful and meaningful in the new society and some aspects are discarded as being culture-specific to another place and time. The outcome of this process amounts to a new ethnicity that has little in common with the reified notion that official multiculturalism intends to preserve; nor is it identical with melting into a dominant mainstream.

The extension of welfare state provisions, together with the much more diverse ethnic and occupational composition of immigrants since the late 1960s, has created a new ethnicity in Canada. This is reflected in a much greater variety of responses on the part of newcomers and hosts alike that in turn amounts to a new Canadian cultural configuration for educational policy.

It is this dynamic aspect of culture which is everywhere visible and yet ignored. Seemingly homogeneous groups are in fact disparate, are at different stages of acculturation, are geographically dispersed, hail from different parts of the world, and represent a tremendous array of regional, linguistic and religious difference. Above all they seem unified only by their goal of success in mainstream society. There are few societies which better illustrate Malinowski's view that culture contact produces a third cultural reality for immigrants, which is neither the original nor the new host culture (Malinowski, 1945, pp. 20–26).

The complex problem of perpetuating different cultural traditions within the school in a pluralistic configuration is evident. Foremost is the challenge to teachers as unauthentic agents of cultural transmission. Expecting teachers to communicate cultural content from highly complex cultures, without reifying, fragmenting and trivializing them to the ridiculous, is not unproblematic. In many instances the value incongruence between mainstream teachers and those of other groups is a real barrier. This is not to deny the need for teachers to come to terms with their own ethnocentrism, and to have knowledge of the cultural backgrounds of their students. However, as David Kirp (1979, p. 132) points out, the paths to be avoided are a descent into mindless multiculturalism and a determined effort to preserve the past for the sake of preservation.

Education about different cultures in schools need not imply a challenge to the hegemony of mainstream education. In South Africa, for example, ethnically based education has been used to limit the aspirations of subordinated groups. As Farrukh Dhondy and others have argued in Britain, about the history of the Raj in India, 'Two hundred years of rule may have bred a complete understanding of Indian civilization, culture and habits, but this understanding did not alter the structure of Empire' (Stenhouse et al., 1982, p. 18). Similarly, Jones and Kimberley suggest that uncritical use of multiculturalism has been seen as a way of defusing conflict and pacifying vocal members of affected minorities (Tierney, 1982, pp. 143–4).

While knowledge of other cultures is important for teachers, on balance it is clearly less important than the concern about race issues, and how racism permeates society and the school through teacher attitudes, negative racial images, and racial bias in schools and society (Affor, 1983, p. 9). Teacher attitudes stand out as a crucial concern. Indeed an unbiased teacher working with biased materials within an ethnocentric curriculum may well be preferable to a biased teacher working with multiethnic learning materials and teaching ethnic history (Affor, 1983, p. 10). Insensitive, naive use of aspects of non-Western cultures that are non-functional in Canada can just as easily undervalue and ridicule heritages out of context, thereby entrenching their second-class status. As Kirp (1982, p. 132) maintains, it is in fusing what deserves to endure with the contribution of the present that the educational system will most effectively respond to the issues of race.

On the whole, competence, not culture, is the major concern of minority-group parents. While the two are not mutually exclusive, it is foremost the mastery of modern knowledge, as well as the retention of functional aspects of their own traditional knowledge, to which the parents most aspire. The former serves their instrumental, survival needs, which are the priority in the country of adoption, and the latter their expressive needs, for which they themselves assume responsibility. Whereas diverse cultural inclusion in the school curriculum is an important device for raising the self-concept of minority children, most minority parents see their children as educationally deprived rather than culturally deprived. In this respect there has been a tendency to overstate low self-concept as a cause of minority children's failure (Stone, 1981; Musgrove, 1982). On the other hand, we overlook the fact that self-concept emerges not only from cultural recognition but also from being able to have greater mastery over one's life.

What most minority parents want for their children is not condescending teaching of fragmented, diluted versions of their culture, taught second-hand by a non-authentic group member. They expect committed, demanding teaching aimed at the mastery of basic skills, the success in English, math and science required to survive in the new home country. In many instances this was the prime reason for leaving the country of origin. Musgrove articulates a similar view for minorities in Britain. 'What "other cultures" want from us many would see as most worthy, distinguished, and indeed central in our educational tradition (though perhaps a little old-fashioned) – high moral teaching and good learning: a sense of values and a strenuous disciplined pursuit of knowledge . . . The arguments are educational, the imperialism pedagogic' (Musgrove, 1982, p. 180).

Along the same lines, Maureen Stone (1981) points to progressive multicultural teaching as contributing to West Indian children's failure in adapting to child-centred teaching and learning approaches. Quoting Gramsci, she stresses the need for minority children to acquire dominant forms of knowledge in order better to challenge it.

In these instances, despite the cultural differences of the minorities studied, the conflict with dominant society and the system of education is about pedagogies. This overrides cultural differences. It is clear, then, that cultural content in the school curriculum takes second place to other forces which stand in the way of academic achievement. The most successful communities are those which have taken cultural and religious education into their own hands while entrusting public schools with the training for the market-place.

What does this leave for schools to do with the multicultural curriculum? It does not preclude having information and awareness of the cultural backgrounds of pupils, in order better to diagnose strengths and weaknesses, as well as differences in cognitive styles. It assumes provision for learning of heritage languages for all students who so choose. It still calls for an active anti-racism awareness, examining teacher expectations, stereotyping and bias in school materials. It calls for appreciation of diversity in the curricula material, but integrated thematically in a global perspective and not as an end in itself.

These basic achievement aspirations are the substance that all minority groups share, transcending the specific differences of country of origin, language, religious affiliation or race.

The promises of multiculturalism in Canada will depend on the ways in which an informed multiethnic education is located in the broader economic, political and social structures. Only then can ethnic inequalities be effectively addressed.

NOTES

1. 'Non-charter group' refers to groups other than those of French or Anglo-Canadian origin.
2. Speakers of English as a Second Language.
3. Indians now claim 'first nation status' based on indigenous occupancy.
4. Charter rights refer to the special position of the two legal founding groups, the French and the English, and the indigenous native people. The former have special rights to language and legal codes, while the latter have special aboriginal rights.
5. Common schools refer to provincially funded, non-sectarian public schools open to all children.
6. Unlike the US policy to deny state aid to separate schools, in Canada constitutional provisions were made to guarantee state aid to both private denominational and non-denominational schools. Since education is a provincial matter its implementation has varied. For an analysis of this issue, see Wilson, J. D. & Lazerson, M. (1982) Historical and constitutional perspectives on family choice in schooling: the Canadian case. In Manley-Casimir, M. (ed.), *Family Choice in Schooling*, pp. 1–22. Lexington: D. C. Heath.
7. The British North America (BNA) Act was the British parliamentary statute passed in 1867 which granted independence to Canada. It provided for the federal union of three British North American provinces, Canada (Ontario and Quebec), Nova Scotia and New Brunswick, into one dominion under the name Canada. Subsequently, Newfoundland, Prince Edward Island, Manitoba, Saskatchewan, Alberta, British Columbia and the Northwest Territory were included. There was little specifically relating to education in the Act, with the exception of Section 93, which confirmed provincial jurisdiction in education.
8. The reference here is to the French minority who, though entitled to language rights, have not found implementation easy.

REFERENCES

Affor (All Faiths for One Race) (1983) *Issues and Resources: Handbook for Teachers in a Multicultural Society*. Birmingham: Russell.

Allan, J. (1982) *Race Relations: Studies in Success*. CEA convention presentation, 29 September.

Ashworth, M. (1975) *Immigrant Children and Canadian Schools*. Toronto: McClelland and Stewart.

Banks, J. A. (1984) *Teaching Strategies for Ethnic Studies*, third edition. Boston: Allyn and Bacon.

Banks, J. A., with Clegg Jr, A. (1977) *Teaching Strategies for the Social Studies: Inquiry, Valuing and Decision-Making*, second edition, Reading, Mass: Addison-Wesley.

Bhatnagar, J. (1982) Language and cultural maintenance programmes in Canada. In Bagley, C. & Verma, G. (ed.) *Self Concept and Multicultural Education*. London: Macmillan.

Burnet, J. (1975) *The Definition of Multi-*

culturalism in a Bilingual Framework, paper presented at Conference on Multi-culturalism and Third World Immigrants, Edmonton, September.

Cummins, J. (1984) Heritage languages and Canadian school programs. In Mallea, J. R. & Young, J. C., *Cultural Diversity and Canadian Education*, pp. 477–500. Ottawa: Carleton University Press.

Day, E. & Shapson, S. (1981) *Multiculturalism: A Survey of School Districts in British Columbia*. Burnaby, BC: Simon Fraser University.

Echols, F. (1981) An evaluation of exploring likenesses and differences, unpublished manuscript. Vancouver: University of British Columbia.

Frideres, J. S. (1983) *Native Peoples in Canada*, second edition. Scarborough, Ontario: Prentice-Hall, Canada.

Glazer, N. & Moynihan, D. P. (1963) *Beyond the Melting Pot*, Cambridge, Mass. MIT Press.

Hawkins, F. (1972) *Canada and Immigration:*

Public Policy and Public Concern. Montreal: McGill-Queens University Press.

Herskovits, M. J. (1948) *Man and His Works*. New York: Knopf.

Hood, B. (1980) 'Exploring Likenesses and Differences with Film'. Vancouver: National Film Board of Canada.

House of Commons (1984) *Equality Now*. Ottawa: Queen's Printer.

Innis, H. R. (1973) *Bilingualism and Biculturalism*. Toronto: McLelland and Stewart and Information Canada.

Jaenen, C. (1977) Multiculturalism and public education. In Wilson, J. D. (ed.), *Policy and Process: Perspectives on Contemporary Canadian Education*. London: Alexander Blake.

Katz, P. (ed.) (1976) *Toward the Elimination of Racism*. New York: Pergamon Press.

Kehoe, J. (1978) An evaluation of exploring likenesses and differences, unpublished manuscript. Vancouver: University of British Columbia.

Kehoe, J. (1984) *A Handbook of Selected Activities for Enhancing the Multicultural Climate of the School*. Vancouver: WEDGE, University of British Columbia.

Kirp, D. (1979) *Doing Good by Doing Little: Race and Schooling in Britain*. Berkeley: University of California Press.

McLeod, K. A. (1984) Multiculturalism and multicultural education: policy and practice. In Samuda, R. J., Berry, J. W. & Laferriere, M. (ed.), *Multiculturalism in Canada: Social and Educational Perspectives*. Toronto: Allyn and Bacon.

Malinowski, B. (1944) *A Scientific Theory of Culture and Other Essays*. Chapel Hill, NC: University of North Carolina Press.

Malinowski, B. (1945) *The Dynamics of Culture Change*. New Haven: Yale University Press.

Mallea, J. R. (1984) Cultural diversity in Canadian education. In Samuda, R. et al. (ed.) *Multiculturalism in Canada*. Toronto: Allyn & Bacon.

Mallea, J. R. & Young, J. (ed.) (1984) *Cultural Diversity and Canadian Education*. Don Mills. Ottawa: Carleton University Press

Manitoba, *Public Schools Act* (1980) Winnipeg: Government of Manitoba, 1980.

Masemann, V. (1984) Multicultural programs in Toronto schools. In Mallea, J. R. & Young, J. (ed.), *Cultural Diversity and Canadian Education*, pp. 349–69. Don Mills.

Moodley, K. (1981) Canadian ethnicity in comparative perspective. In Dahlie, J. & Fernando, T. (ed.), *Ethnicity, Power and Politics in Canada*. Toronto: Methuen.

Moodley, K. (1983) Canadian multiculturalism as ideology. *Ethnic and Racial Studies,* **6**(3), 320–31.

Moodley, K. (ed.) (1985) *Multicultural Education and Race Relations*, Vancouver: University of British Columbia.

Musgrove, F. (1982) *Education and Anthropology, Other Cultures and the Teacher*. Toronto: John Wiley.

Ogbu, J. (1978) *Minority Education and Caste*. New York: Academic Press.

Palmer, H. (1975) *Immigration and the Rise of Multiculturalism*. Toronto: Copp Clark Publ.

Peter, K. (1981) The myth of multiculturalism and other political fables. In Dahlie, J. & Fernando, T. (ed.), *Ethnicity, Power and Politics in Canada*. Toronto: Methuen.

Radcliffe-Brown, A. R. (1952) *Structure and Function in Primitive Society*. London: Routledge and Kegan Paul.

Richmond, A. H. (1969) Immigration and pluralism in Canada. *International Migrations Review,* **4**, 5–24.

Rosen, D. (1977) Multicultural education: an anthropological perspective. *Anthropology and Education Quarterly,* **8**.

Royal Commission on *Bilingualism and Biculturalism, Book IV* (1969) Ottawa: Queen's Printer.

Samuda, R. J., Berry, J. W. & Laferrière, M. (ed.) (1984) *Multiculturalism in Canada*. Toronto: Allyn and Bacon.

Shapson, S. & Purbhoo, M. (1977) A transition program for Italian children. *The Canadian Modern Language Review,* **33**, 486–96.

Shapson, S. & D'Oyley, V. (ed.), (1984) *Bilingual and Multicultural Education: Canadian Perspectives*. Clevedon: Multilingual Matters.

Statistics Canada (1982) *1980 Immigration Statistics,* p. 6. Ottawa: Queen's Printer.

Stenhouse, L., Verma, G., Wild, R. & Nixon, J. (1982) *Teaching about Race Relations: Problems and Effects*. London: Routledge and Kegan Paul.

Stone, M. (1981) *The Education of the Black Child in Britain: The Myth of Multiracial Education*. Glasgow: Fontana.

Tierney, J. (ed.) (1982) *Race, Migration and Schooling*. Eastbourne: Holt, Rinehart and Winston.

Thomas, B. (1984) *Principles of Anti-Racist Education*, Currents, **2**(3), 20–24.

Vancouver School Board (1984) *Report on School Multicultural Action Plans 1983–84*. Vancouver: Program Services.

Werner, W., Connors, B., Aoki, T. & Dahlie, J. (1980) *Whose Culture? Whose Heritage? Ethnicity within Canadian Social Studies Curricula*. Vancouver: University of British Columbia.

Wilson, J. D. (1984) Multicultural programmes in Canadian education. In Samuda, R. et al. (ed.) *Multiculturalism in Canada*, Toronto: Allyn & Bacon.

Wood, D. W. (1978) Multicultural Canada: *A Teacher's Guide to Ethnic Studies*, Toronto: Ontario Institute for Studies in Education.

Wright, I. & La Bar, C. (1984) Multiculturalism and morality. In Shapson, S. & D'Oyley, V. (ed.), *Bilingual and Multicultural Education: Canadian Perspectives*, pp. 112–29. Clevedon: Multilingual Matters.

BIBLIOGRAPHY

Aaron, W. (ed.) (1975) *Education of Immigrant Students. Issues and Answers*. Toronto: Ontario Institute for Studies in Education. A variety of issues confronting teachers, relating to the education of immigrant students, are examined in depth. Authors reflect a range of disciplinary backgrounds. The common focus is on the promotion of positive self-concept or identity among immigrants, ways of optimizing the learning environment and ways of facilitating communication between educators and immigrant students. In addition, practical experimental programmes in action are presented.

Dorotich, D. (ed.) (1981) *Education and Canadian Multiculturalism: Some Problems and Some Solutions*. Saskatoon: Canadian Society for the Study of Education (CSSE). Papers address: (a) the outcome of a decade of multicultural policy in Canada; (b) critical perspectives on the consequences of multicultural education; (c) comparative perspectives on multicultural education, including a chapter on multiculturalism in the USSR; and (d) language and literature in a multicultural curriculum.

Kehoe, J. (1984) *A Handbook for Enhancing the Multicultural Climate of the School*. Vancouver, University of British Columbia, Faculty of Education, Western Education Development Group. One of the few attempts to combine informed theoretical tenets with practical approaches for implementation. Multicultural needs in school and community are assessed; the hidden curriculum and equality of opportunity with special reference to particular cultural groups and the formal curriculum and curriculum development, is discussed.

Moodley, K. (ed.) (1985) *Multicultural Education and Race Relations*. Vancouver, University of British Columbia, Centre for Curriculum Studies. A critical review of multicultural policy and race relations issues, as well as detailed review of research on prejudice reduction and the role of cultural diversity, migration and cognitive style.

Samuda, R., Berry, J. W. and Laferrière, M. (ed.) (1984) *Multiculturalism in Canada*. Toronto: Allyn and Bacon. A comprehensive volume incorporating a wide range of contributions. Major foci are: (1) the policy of multiculturalism and the historical and philosophical bases of cultural diversity in Canada; (2) research on the origins of ethnic attitudes and prejudice, and attitude change through innovative approaches; (3) issues and programmes from the perspective of language, adaptation, assessment and counselling.

Shapson, S. and D'Oyley, V. (ed.) (1984) *Bilingual and Multicultural Education: Canadian Perspectives*. Clevedon: Multilingual Matters. The volume views: (1) the school's response to bilingualism

through second language teaching programmes and French immersion programmes; (2) the school's response to
multiculturalism; (3) future directions for
educational policy.

Wood, D. W. (1978) *Multicultural Canada:
A Teacher's Guide to Ethnic Studies*.
Toronto: Ontario Institute for Studies in
Education. This was one of the earlier
attempts to help teachers bridge the gap
between awareness and meaningful
change in Social Studies education and
Canadian Studies. It blends the practical
and theoretical in what, how, and why to
teach Ethnic Studies in Social Studies
curriculum. Some resources are suggested.
An introductory statement has raised
some concern about the writer's view on
ethnocultural retention, namely, 'in
English Canada, ethnic diversity is no
longer seen as a barrier to assimilating all
Canadians into English-Canadian culture.'

Chapter 4

Multicultural Education in the United Kingdom

MAURICE CRAFT

A PLURAL SOCIETY

Migration has been a permanent feature of international history. Whether individuals are naturally inert until pushed or pulled by economic or political necessity, or naturally wanderers who may decide to settle for a period, is unanswerable. What is clear is that population movements, while varying in intensity, have been a continuing feature in all societies. In Europe, the last thirty years have seen a massive northward migration from Mediterranean countries into the industrial centres of Germany, France, Switzerland, Belgium and Holland. In turn, the Mediterranean has received immigrants from still less developed countries:

> . . . as Sicilian men leave the land to work in German factories, North African migrants have come to Sicily to do agricultural work; similarly, there are Pakistanis doing low-paid work in Greece which has been abandoned by Greeks who have gone to work in German factories.
>
> (Braham, 1982, p. 14)

Nor is this process confined to manual work, for while British doctors have emigrated to the United States and Canada, so Indian doctors have come to Britain (Braham, 1982). It was estimated in 1974 that fifteen million immigrant workers and their families were living in Western Europe, and that immigrant workers made up 25 per cent of the Swiss labour force, 11 per cent of the French and 10 per cent of the German (O'Donnell, 1981), these immigrants coming to fill the less attractive, less well-paid occupations unable to recruit workers during the post-war period of full employment.

In Britain, post-war immigration had several sources. Under the British Nationality Act 1948, immigrants from the Commonwealth were allowed free entry, and during

76

the 1950s and 1960s flowed in freely – mainly from the Caribbean, the Indian sub-continent and the Far East – to fill jobs often advertised overseas. Immigrants also came from elsewhere in Europe, although subject to some restriction, and significantly from Poland, Yugoslavia and the Baltic. But the United Kingdom was far from being an ethnically homogeneous society before 1945; cultural mixing has a much longer history. The Roman occupation brought legionaries from throughout the empire. Viking raiders and the Norman conquest left indelible cultural imprints, the Jews were a significant minority until their expulsion in 1290, and there were Hanseatic, Flemish, Italian and other merchants, as well as a continuous flow of settlers into England from Ireland, Scotland and Wales. At the close of the seventeenth century came many thousands of French Huguenots.

The Jews returned to Britain in the seventeenth century, and eventually came to be one of the largest of its ethnic minorities. By 1800 they numbered some 25 000, mostly in London, reaching perhaps 65 000 by 1880 (Kosmin, 1982a), but Russian repression brought much greater numbers to Britain in the 1880s and 1890s. The Aliens Act 1905 reduced this immigration, but it is estimated that by 1914 the total Jewish population was around 300 000, more than half of them in London (Kosmin, 1982b). During the 1930s, Nazi persecution again increased Jewish immigration, and today this minority group is estimated at around 400 000 (Kosmin, 1982a).

Another of Britain's most significant minorities, the Irish, began to arrive in larger numbers during the eighteenth century as early industrialisation created opportunities in the growing English cities, and with the great famine this became a flood from the 1840s. By 1851, approaching three-quarters of a million Irish immigrants had settled in England and Wales, almost 3 per cent of the total population (Rees, 1982). As Walvin (1984) puts it, 'It was quite simply the most massive influx of people English society had ever experienced.' More than a century later, by 1971, the Irish still formed one of the largest minority groups, with 709 000 people resident in Britain.

But it is perhaps the post-war immigration from the New Commonwealth and Pakistan which has attracted most attention in terms of British social and educational policy, because of colour. As indicated earlier, this influx reached a peak in the 1950s and early 1960s, before the restrictions which came with the Commonwealth Immigrants Acts of 1962 and 1968, the Immigration White Paper 1965, the Immigration Act 1971 and the Nationality Act 1981. But black immigrants had been known since at least the sixteenth century and their numbers grew as the slave trade flourished. As Walvin reports,

> By the mid-18th century, there was a sizeable black population in London, its members engaged in various occupations, though mainly used as domestics. By 1764, *The Gentleman's Magazine* thought there were 20 000 in London alone.
>
> (Walvin, 1984, p. 33)

The developing network of world trade, and the acquisition of new territories in the last quarter of the nineteenth century, brought an increase in black settlement in Britain, and the establishment of small communities in the ports of Cardiff, Liverpool and South Shields. It was not until the late 1940s that New Commonwealth immigration on a large scale began to develop, and particularly after the McCarran-Walter Act 1952 which curbed Jamaican immigration to the United States. West

Indians seeking employment opportunities in Britain were sometimes aided by the colonial government, as in Barbados, or were recruited by the British Transport Commission, London Transport and the National Health Service. Walvin notes that 'By late 1958, London Transport employed almost 4000 black workers, about one-quarter of whom had been recruited directly from the Caribbean' (Walvin, 1984). A mere 15 300 West Indians at the 1951 Census had become 171 800 ten years later.

Asians were not unknown in the UK before the 1940s, but it was in the mid-1950s that immigration from India and Pakistan grew very rapidly, rising from 35 800 in 1951 to 106 300 in 1961. By 1980, the total number of Asian and Afro-Caribbean residents in Britain was altogether assessed at about 2.2 million, of whom almost half had been born in Britain, and constituting 4.1 per cent of the population (Holmes, 1982; Peach, 1982). While these two are the largest of the UK minorities, each is of course extremely varied in composition, and together they encompass numerous cultures, languages and religions. The West Indians came from mainland Guyana, and from Jamaica and most of the smaller islands in the Caribbean. The Asians are very largely from several specific regions: the Punjab and the Gujerat in western and northern India, from northern Pakistan, from Bangladesh, and from East Africa (as a result of the expulsion in 1972).

The UK is thus a plural society. Taking account of the statistical ambiguities – transient immigrants on their way elsewhere, for example, and the increasing difficulty of identifying ethnic minority members who were *born* in Britain – there is no doubt about the nation's cultural diversity. In addition to the Irish, the Jews and those originating in the New Commonwealth and Pakistan, there are well over half a million from Germany, Poland, Italy, Spain and elsewhere in Europe, and about one-third of a million from New Commonwealth territories in Africa, the Mediterranean (e.g. Cyprus) and the Far East. The overall figure of around 5–6 per cent of Britain's total population is very small compared, say, with Australia, where some 25 per cent of the population were born elsewhere. On the other hand, this 5–6 per cent is not evenly spread and is located mainly in the conurbations. There are also much smaller ethnic minority communities all over Britain. The Maltese, for example, live mainly in London, but communities of 200 or more exist in half a dozen cities; the Chinese are mainly in London and Liverpool, but small communities may be found in more than twenty other urban centres from Plymouth to Edinburgh; while the Cypriots can be found from Brighton to Glasgow. Outside London there are communities of 1000 or more Italians in six British cities, and communities of Poles in nine or ten (Craft, 1984).

POLICIES FOR MULTICULTURAL EDUCATION

Educational policies in the UK have adapted to ethnic diversity in several ways. The traditional approach has been simply to seek to absorb any newcomers without fuss or special provision. A small number of Jewish schools had been agreed to in areas of more concentrated Jewish settlement by the early twentieth century, parallel to the special provision for Roman Catholics and Anglicans. But this was exceptional, and all such special provision was generally made privately by minority communities. When the numbers of New Commonwealth immigrants increased substantially in the 1950s and 1960s, absorption remained the aim, although combined with often quite strenuous efforts to meet the particular needs of ethnic minority children. A more recent response, however, has been to recognise, accept and celebrate cultural differences, combined with a growing awareness that *all* children should be more fully prepared for membership of a plural society. The transition from one policy to another has generally been viewed as a move from *assimilation* to *integration*, and to *cultural pluralism*.

Assimilation

The assimilationist position placed emphasis on minimising cultural differences and on preserving the presumed cultural homogeneity of the host society. The Second Report of the Commonwealth Immigrants Advisory Council in 1964, for example, was quite explicit:

> . . . a national system of education must aim at producing citizens who can take their place in a society properly equipped to exercise rights and perform duties which are the same as other citizens' . . . [it] cannot be expected to perpetuate the different values of immigrant groups.
>
> (CIAC, 1964, para. 10)

Considerable emphasis in the 1950s and 1960s was accordingly placed upon English language teaching. In 1963, the then Ministry of Education published *English for Immigrants* (Ministry of Education, 1963), followed in 1965 by a Government Circular which defined the role of education as, 'the successful assimilation of immigrant children', and similarly stressed the need for immigrant children to learn English as quickly and effectively as possible in order to be able to participate fully in normal school work (DES, 1965). Special language centres drawing in non-English-speaking children from the neighbouring schools were established by a number of local education authorities, and many schools with large numbers of immigrant pupils set up special reception classes and withdrawal groups. In-service courses for teachers in the teaching of English as a second language appeared, and several major urban areas built up teams of peripatetic teachers for language teaching in schools where the number of non-English-speaking children was insufficient to justify a special reception or withdrawal class. Birmingham, for example, had a peripatetic team of 52 such teachers by 1968.

A second major feature of assimilationist thinking in the early 1960s was the policy of *dispersal*, first enunciated in the Second Report of the Commonwealth Immigrants Advisory Council in 1964. The Report declared:

> The presence of a high proportion of immigrant children in one class slows down the general routine of working and hampers the progress of the whole class, especially where the immigrants do not speak or write English fluently. This is clearly in itself undesirable and unfair to all the children in the class . . .

> The evidence we have received strongly suggests that if a school has more than a certain percentage of immigrant children among its pupils the whole character and ethos of the school is altered. Immigrant pupils in such a school will not get as good an introduction to British life as they would get in a normal school, and we think that their education in the widest sense must suffer as a result
>
>   (CIAC, 1964, paras. 24 and 25).

To counter a de facto segregation, the Report advised dispersal. In November 1963 the Minister of Education, Sir Edward Boyle, had told the House of Commons: 'If possible, it is desirable on education grounds that no one school should have more than about 30 per cent of immigrants', and he went on, 'I must regretfully tell the House that one school must be regarded now as irretrievably an immigrant school. The important thing is to prevent this happening elsewhere' (27 November, 1963). In 1965, the Government's Circular 7/65 declared, 'as the proportion of immigrant children in a school or class increases, the problems will become more difficult to solve and the chances of assimilation more remote' (DES, 1965). Later that year, a Government White Paper underlined the one-third limit and stated, 'Local Education Authorities are advised to arrange for the dispersal of immigrant children over a greater number of schools in order to avoid undue concentration in any particular school' (Home Office, 1965).

   A third feature of the assimilationist thinking of the 1950s and early 1960s was reflected in the tendency to disregard cultural differences in the ability testing of immigrant pupils. Many children had left more traditional, rural settings in the Caribbean and the Asian sub-continent for the industrial centres of the UK, and were in many schools required to respond to verbal reasoning and other 'objective' tests standardised on indigenous school populations, which were much more familiar with such devices. They were also, of course, tested in standard English, which was a different language or dialect for most. As crude tests of levels of mental functioning in a new environment they might have been of some limited value, but as indicators of potential or predictive guides to placement they were seriously deficient, and probably contributed to the substantial over-representation of minority children in schools for the mentally handicapped which subsequently came to light.

Integration

By the end of the 1960s, crude assimilationist thinking was coming under review. In 1966 the Home Secretary, Roy Jenkins, had given what came to be regarded as a classic definition of integration: 'Not a flattening process of assimilation but . . . equal opportunity, accompanied by cultural diversity, in an atmosphere of mutual tolerance' (23 May 1966, at a meeting in London). This was an early recognition of some of the shortcomings of the assimilationist position, and as Troyna (1982) has observed, in the late 1960s and early 1970s, 'integrationist views came to be adopted as the working paradigm for educational policy and decision-makers'. But it was, perhaps, a difference in degree rather than of kind. Cultural differences were now given some recognition, but the absorption of ethnic minorities remained the aim. Teachers began to acquire some knowledge of the social and cultural background of ethnic minority children so that they might better understand their pupils' origins and needs, and numerous books, pamphlets and articles appeared with this in view. Inservice courses and conferences were mounted in many regions, and more specialist inservice advisers and inspectors were appointed. 'Black studies' appeared on the curricula of urban schools with many immigrant children on the roll.

At the same time, the dispersal policy began to wane. It had only ever been partially implemented in fact, and not at all in two-thirds of the areas involved. Some local education authorities (London and Birmingham, for example) had felt that it violated the principle of the neighbourhood school, and all the advantages of home–school contact which this involves, particularly where young children are concerned. Others rejected it because it seemed to be discriminatory – it used ethnic origin rather than educational need as the criterion – and further, there were practical difficulties in finding empty school places to which pupils could be moved if only minority children were to be 'bussed'. The dispersal policy was thus officially abandoned in 1971 (DES, 1971), and it was left to local education authorities to decide upon the most appropriate policy according to local need. It was this same Government Report in 1971 which gave a further clear indication of the ideological shift towards integration. There was now a recognition that '. . . the arrival of immigrant pupils in the schools has greatly enriched the lives of other children . . . the new musical, dramatic, dance and visual art forms which they have introduced . . . have given fresh colour and vigour to the life and work of many schools.' The Report continued: the education service could

> . . . help promote the acceptance of immigrants as equal members of our society . . . [while also] permitting the expression of differences of attitudes, beliefs and customs, language and culture . . . which may eventually enrich the main stream of our cultural and social tradition.
>
> (DES, 1971, p. 120)

So minority experience was not to be totally devalued. But acculturation and assimilation were still main agenda items.

Cultural Pluralism

The movement towards a greater understanding and recognition of, and respect for, ethnic minority cultures continued during the 1970s. This deeper and more widespread sensitivity to diversity was progressively reflected in educational practice, and came to be termed 'cultural pluralism'. As a societal phenomenon, it might be thought to reflect the greater recognition of individual autonomy, and an aspect of the deference to be paid to gender, religious, regional or social class membership characteristic of our times. The 'ethnic revival' charted by Te Selle (1973), Smith (1981) and others is widely regarded as an emerging human right in many societies.

The national collection of ethnic minority statistics by the Department of Education and Science, begun in 1966, had probably reflected a growing regard for the distinctive needs of minority pupils. Its discontinuation in 1972 perhaps indicated a growing anxiety about the preservation of human rights.

The systematic underachievement of minority pupils, at first encompassing all but latterly focused more on West Indian, Muslim and Turkish children, began to generate widespread concern, and led to a national committee of inquiry and the publication of the Rampton Report (DES, 1981b). The committee continued its wide-ranging study into the education of ethnic minority children under the chairmanship of Lord Michael Swann, and produced its final report in 1985. At the same time, minority community groups were establishing a network of voluntary supplementary schools, both for culture maintenance activities, and also – especially among West Indians – to improve children's basic skills. Pressure has increased for the provision of culturally acceptable school meals, and for the rights of Sikh boys to wear the turban and of Muslim girls to wear traditional dress rather than skirts. Dissatisfaction of some Asian parents with secular and coeducational schooling has produced demands for single-sex schools, and also for separate schools.

Many of these developments have been accompanied by the publication of formal policy statements on multicultural education by local education authorities and by individual schools. The policy statements of the cities of London and Bradford and the county of Berkshire were among the most widely publicised, and each involved close collaboration with ethnic minority community groups. Similarly, the democratisation of school governing bodies has enabled more ethnic minority parents to articulate a view, as has the growing number of ethnic minority councillors elected to local government: by 1982, 72 councillors of West Indian or Asian origin had been elected in London (cited in Tomlinson, 1984). Schools in areas where many immigrants have settled (and where the majority of minority *children* may have been born) frequently have home-visiting programmes and Asian mothers' groups, to take account of the role, status and literacy in English of many Asian women. School notices are often translated into minority languages, and interpreters are employed by the larger education authorities.

Developments in language seem to offer a particularly dramatic illustration both of the nature of ethnic diversity in the UK and of pluralist responses in education. The Inner London Education Authority's language census in 1983, for example, identified 147 spoken languages in London schools, with 16 per cent of the school population (i.e. 50 353 children) using a language other than or in addition to English at home (ILEA, 1983a), and studies of a number of smaller British provincial towns and cities have illustrated similar findings (Linguistic Minorities Project, 1983). Indeed, at least half of all local education authorities in England and Wales have a *minimum* of one primary school with over 10 per cent of pupils who are bilingual (Tansley & Craft, 1984). A strong movement for the provision of ethnic minority community languages as part of the modern languages curriculum in secondary schools, and as transitional bilingualism for younger children, has met with some success. There is also growing support for bidialectalism in the case of West Indian children whose native creole had hitherto been regarded as 'defective English', and an increasing number of schools now offer opportunities for the use of West Indian creole in their language and literature work. The tendency is for all such home languages to be accorded far greater respect than was the case in the 1960s and 1970s. As Bolton observed in 1979, 'the early ideas of assimilation and integration were patronising or . . . offensively dismissive of other cultures and life-styles', and he advocated a pluralism more accepting of other cultures, so as 'to allow equal opportunity for all to play a full part in society' (Bolton, 1979, p. 6).

As to the education of *all* children growing up in a plural society, the late 1970s and 1980s have seen far more effort being devoted to the multicultural 'permeation' of the primary and secondary school curriculum. The natural ethnocentrism of any educational system has to be balanced by a sensitivity to the diverse origins of the majority culture and to the range and contributions of any minority cultures, and by an awareness of the tensions and hostilities between cultures. Teachers and textbook writers are beginning to consider a wider range of exemplification in literature, language, history and the arts – and particularly in religious education and home economics; and they are also giving attention to the worldwide origins of 'Western' science and mathematics (Lynch, 1981, 1983; Craft & Bardell, 1984). They are also examining ways in which specific subjects or topics can help to identify and reduce intercultural prejudice and racist attitudes and practices. In 1977, a Government consultative document, *Education in Schools* (DES, 1977) declared, 'Our society is a multicultural, multiracial one, and the curriculum should reflect a sympathetic understanding of the different cultures and races that now make up our society'. The major Government document, *The School Curriculum*, published in 1981, was equally explicit:

> What is taught in schools, and the way it is taught, must appropriately reflect fundamental values in our society . . . the work of schools has to reflect many issues with which pupils will have to come to terms as they mature, and schools and teachers are familiar with them. First, our society has become multicultural and there is now among pupils and parents a greater diversity of personal values . . .
>
> (DES, 1981a, para. 21)

The most recent national survey reports that the great majority of local education authorities in England and Wales are, in principle, 'committed to changing teaching and curricula to reflect the pluralistic nature of society', although this may be less true of independent schools, which are traditionally associated with the social élite (Cashmore & Bagley, 1984).

CONTROVERSIES

Inevitably, the post-war arrival in many urban UK classrooms of large numbers of children from overseas families, many of them non-English-speaking, created much controversy, and this will have been apparent in the foregoing pages. But the controversies have been of various kinds. While some have led to frustration and even disillusionment on the part of both minority and majority culture activists in multicultural education, others have stimulated a fuller debate, new lines of enquiry or modes of practice, and ultimately, more sensitive educational policies.

Particular Needs

An early debate, touched on above, was whether multicultural education is essentially concerned with the particular needs of ethnic minority children, or whether its main long-term purpose is the achievement of a more liberal and less ethnocentric education for *all* children. Provision for minority needs continues, although English as a second language now takes a lower priority than English language support across the curriculum and the identity problems of children growing up in two worlds. But the balance of concern has shifted increasingly towards the education of all children (*including* those of overseas origin), as the 'particular needs' problem declines in scale.

One aspect of the particular needs problem which is proving resistant, however, is the under-achievement of children of West Indian origin, and a recent controversy has consequently centred on teaching methods for these children. Stone (1981) has argued that to stress their cultural background and to place emphasis on pupil self-esteem is to encourage teachers to be social workers, and to 'neglect their primary role of instruction'. Stone's 'back to basics' argument recommends the use of more formal teaching methods with West Indian children throughout primary and secondary education: 'These methods are understood and approved of by West Indian (and other working class) parents and in the light of the dismal failure of the present approach . . . can only offer an improvement on the present situation'. There are echoes here of the North American compensatory education movement of the 1960s, and in fact current British Government policy is not unsympathetic to this general line of thinking.

A somewhat unexpected offshoot of the West Indian under-achievement issue, however, is whether or not it *is* in fact an issue. Has under-achievement been demonstrated beyond doubt? Is the analysis flawed? To begin with, numerous commentators have observed that these studies rarely apply experimental controls for social class or sex, both of which are known to be significant variables in educational performance. It is known, for example, that the West Indian population suffers a higher level of unemployment than other minorities or whites and includes far fewer self-employed than either, and that West Indian men in particular hold far fewer higher education qualifications (*Employment Gazette*, 1983). Children of West Indian origin are therefore more likely to have parents who are skilled and unskilled manual workers and the continuing pre-eminence of socioeconomic background as a correlate of educational performance has once again been demonstrated in a recent major Government analysis (DES, 1984a). Nor is it known whether under-achievement is more or less prevalent according to island of origin: can one generalise about 'West Indian' school performance? Figueroa (1984) has cited a number of studies illustrating *above-average* levels of achievement among West Indian and other minority pupils, and he goes on to point out that many studies reporting under-achievement have serious methodological limitations. For example, West Indian children born in the UK are probably under-represented in many research samples, which would have the effect of depressing average achievement levels; there has been extensive use of teacher assessment of both performance and ethnic origin, which may have introduced a degree of error; and 'objective tests' are culturally biased. Furthermore, he notes, most of these studies have been carried out in the most disadvantaged, inner urban areas, although almost half the West Indian population in Britain is located outside London. How representative, then, can the findings be? How valid? Troyna (1984) has similarly questioned the validity and reliability of much research into West Indian under-achievement, noting additionally that the possibility of race-of-tester effects cannot be disregarded; many of the studies date back to the late 1960s and early 1970s, and may no longer be relevant; and further, the majority of inquiries have used small samples.

Anti-racism

This is a second major area of controversy in UK multicultural education. *West Indian Children in Our Schools* was the title of the 1981 Rampton Report which was referred to earlier, and which was the first outcome of the Government committee of inquiry into the education of children from ethnic minority groups (DES, 1981b). Rampton identified '. . . no single cause for the underachievement of West Indian children, but rather a network of widely differing attitudes and expectations on the part of teachers and the education system as a whole, and on the part of West Indian parents . . .'. But the report did identify *racism* in school and society as a major factor:

> Whilst we cannot accept that racism, intentional or unintentional, *alone* accounts for the underachievement of West Indian children in our schools, we believe that when taken together with, for example, negative teacher attitudes and an inappropriate curriculum, racism does play a major part in their underachievement.
>
> (DES, 1981b, p. 70)

This was one of a number of such assertions which surfaced during the 1980s. The broader social context had included the first race riots since 1958, which erupted during 1980 and 1981 in London, Manchester, Liverpool, Bristol and elsewhere. In 1981 the Home Office published an analysis of racially motivated attacks which were believed to be on the increase, and which showed that, compared with white people, both West Indians and Asians suffered disproportionately (Home Office, 1981). Reports on employment, income and housing continued to document the dispro-portionate disadvantage of black Britons (Runnymede Trust, 1980; Braham et al., 1981; Brown, 1984).

None of this was new. 'Race' had featured on the agenda of social policy since the 1960s, and had led to the Race Relations Acts of 1965, 1968 and 1976 designed to eliminate discrimination in employment and housing, and the incitement of racial hatred. A Commission for Racial Equality was established to monitor, investigate and, if need be, prosecute. In *education*, race and racism did not become a central issue until the 1980s, and teaching strategies aimed at improving intercultural relations emerged as an aspect of cultural pluralism; these strategies sought to reduce racial prejudice and discrimination in pursuit of the fullest development of a plural society (Craft & Craft, 1982). Exponents of 'anti-racist' teaching argue that the celebration of diversity is, in itself, inadequate and cannot ensure equality of opportunity without a more direct confrontation of racist attitudes and practices, i.e. demeaning imagery in school textbooks, racist graffiti, physical assaults on minority pupils, name-calling in the playground and racial slurs in the staffroom (NUT, 1982; ALTARF; NAME). The Inner London Education Authority and several others contend that '. . . "cultural pluralism" alone seriously neglects the pervasive nature of racism. More stress is needed on the economic position of black people in relation to white people, differences in access to resources and in power to affect events' (Cashmore & Bagley, 1984).

'Institutional racism', defined as the more oblique, unintended consequences of unthinking classroom or managerial practices in education which may lead to the differential labelling and tracking of both minority pupils and employees, is cited as being more widespread and equally unacceptable. The anti-racist approach advocates that each school not only should develop a policy statement which unequivocally condemns all racist behaviour, but also should conduct open discussions among teaching and ancillary staff, perhaps including 'race awareness' workshops, should consult parents, governors and minority community groups on the subject, should review the representativeness of its staff appointments, and should ensure that curriculum content and process help pupils to comprehend past and present racism, both in the UK and elsewhere. As the Berkshire education authority has argued, 'The principal emphasis in the 1980s . . . should be on *equality*. This will certainly involve attention to racism, and to measures to unlearn and dismantle racism' (Berkshire LEA, 1982, my italics). Likewise, the Inner London Education Authority has declared:

> . . . a perspective emphasising diversity and pluralism must be included in a context which addresses issues of racism, and its effects on both white and black people. The latter perspective is not indifferent to cultural differences and diversity, nor to bilingualism. Indeed, it recognises the ways in which they can be distorted unless they are seen in the wider context of promoting equality and justice.
>
> (ILEA, 1983b)

For some activists, 'anti-racism' has even become an *alternative* to multicultural education.

Advocates of multicultural rather than 'anti-racist' education, however, remain far more numerous in the UK (Cashmore & Bagley, 1984), and have offered a variety of responses. Most maintain that combating racial prejudice and discrimination has always formed a central and indispensable part of any thoroughgoing policy for cultural pluralism in education; multicultural education would otherwise be seriously deficient. Some also argue that 'anti-racist' education appears to have a quite limited concern, for if the term 'race' is to be taken literally as referring to physical differences, then anti-racist education would be concerned only with black children. But 'racial' differences are known to have wider ingroup than intergroup variation, and in any case, black Asians are 'racially' part of the white (Caucasian) grouping. The term 'race' is therefore unclear, and is far less helpful than *ethnicity*, with its emphasis on cultural heritage, and which incorporates all minorities (and majorities too, for that matter), whether black or white, and including some of the most disadvantaged (e.g. some Turks, Irish and travellers).

Some critics of 'anti-racism' argue that by 'racism' most commentators appear to mean *ethnocentrism*, cultural exclusiveness, which is a more embracing and technically meaningful term. Others cite the inconclusiveness of the evidence. Jeffcoate (1984a), for example, writes:

> If racism is the decisive factor, why do South Asian pupils, also presumably its objects, perform so well? And how is the relative success of West Indian girls, indicated by some research, to be explained; or the fact that the differences in attainment among individual West Indians are far greater than the mean differences between them as a group and other groups?
>
> (Jeffcoate, 1984a, pp. 173–4)

Recent research studies in which school racism has been found to be of limited relevance would seem to support this view (Ghuman & Gallop, 1981; Short, 1983; Murray & Dawson, 1983; Smith & Tomlinson, in press).

Finally, a number of advocates of 'anti-racism' have been felt to adopt a strident and confrontational approach which has been less than helpful in changing the attitudes of teachers and administrators – a significant disadvantage in a field where progress is still slow and the potential social costs so high.

To anti-racists, the central issue is therefore one of 'power, of dominance, and subordination', as Carby (1982) puts it, and any educational policy which claims to cater for ethnic minority children and which fails to attend to *equality* as the central issue is seriously flawed. In one dimension, this concern with the distribution of power in a diverse society reflects the continuing tension between assimilation and cultural pluralism as societal objectives: should the majority impose acculturation upon the minority? In another dimension, it takes us into an equally fundamental debate about consensus and conflict models of society: is multicultural education part of a dominant class ideology (Mullard, 1984)? Each of these controversies is reflected in the contemporary literature on multicultural education in the UK, and will now be briefly sketched in turn.

Cohesion and Diversity

The trend from assimilation to cultural pluralism in the UK since the 1950s was described earlier, and was illustrated by the introduction in different regions of more varied educational practices. Not everyone agrees, however, that change of any substance has actually occurred. Troyna (1982), for example, believes that the Department of Education and Science retains a '. . . commitment to assimilation and a conception of the society as indivisible . . . it insists that the cultural values and assumptions which underpin the society are non-negotiable'. Troyna's claim may be arguable, since most recent Government statements on education have made reference to the changing social context. The policy paper, *The School Curriculum*, for example, as quoted earlier, clearly stated:

> What is taught in schools, and the way it is taught, must appropriately, reflect

fundamental values in our society . . . society has become multicultural, and there is now among pupils and parents a greater diversity of personal values.

(DES, 1981a, para. 21)

Moreover, in its stated criteria for the approval of all courses of initial teacher training, the Department of Education and Science (1984b) states:

Students should be prepared . . . to teach the full range of pupils whom they are likely to encounter in an ordinary school, with their diversity of ability, behaviour, social background and ethnic and cultural origins. They will need to learn how to respond flexibly to such diversity and to guard against preconceptions based on the race or sex of pupils . . . They will also need to have a basic understanding of the type of society in which their pupils are growing up, with its cultural and racial mix . . .

(DES, 1984b, paras. 11–12)

But Mullard (1982) is even more critical. He considers that the policies of 'integration' and 'pluralism' are merely more sophisticated and liberal variants of the earlier assimilationist model:

Although disguised and dressed up with platitudes and good intentions, the three multiracial education models are in fact power models . . . constructed by dominant white groups for the protection of the power of white groups, for the continuation of our society as it is basically perceived by those groups.

(Mullard, 1982, p. 130)

On the other hand, is it not possible that there would be a tension between assimilation and pluralism in most societies? Bullivant (1981, 1984), who has examined this problem in some detail, argues that the dilemma is a very real one:

. . . allowing democracy full rein may cater for the educational wants of individuals and groups that are part of a society's pluralist composition, but doing so weakens the cohesion of the nation-state by interfering with the enculturation imperative – the need to have enough of a common culture passed on to each generation of children.

(Bullivant, 1981, p. 14)

Economic socialisation, the role of schooling in providing occupational credentials, as McLean (1980) points out, must involve enculturation at least to that extent. Educationalists are caught between ensuring this equality of opportunity on the one hand and facilitating the human right of minorities to retain cultural autonomy on the other. In the same vein, Craft (1984) has argued that all educational systems are essentially concerned with providing for social continuity. There is, therefore, a concern to promote *similarity* as well as *difference* through schooling. In democratic industrial societies, and particularly in those which are culturally plural, 'reproducing the type' will of course include socialisation for change, adaptability and autonomy. But there will always be a tension between the need to educate for consensus and the need to educate for diversity. How far can diversity be pursued before social cohesion is put at risk? Diversity may be preferred to conformity, but without a good measure of agreement there is likely to be social breakdown. Clearly, educational planning has to take account of both the individual *and* the societal aspects of education, and the most difficult issues arise in societies which are culturally plural: 'For educationalists have [then] to decide at what point the acculturation necessary for full participation in society becomes a repressive assimilation; and at what point the celebration of diversity ceases to enrich and becomes potentially divisive' (Craft, 1984, p. 23).

Others have put this dilemma in terms of 'the limits of pluralism'. Jeffcoate (1984b) maintains that each society develops an agreed core of values which are generally embodied in a constitution and will be reflected in its major institutions. But while '. . . a degree of value tension and value conflict may be tolerated and accommodated (a liberal democracy will regard that as one of its strengths), direct contradictions of, or threats to, those core values often cannot'. Hence, UK teachers may now be faced with acute value conflicts in relation, say, to the education of Asian girls, some of whom may be promised in marriage according to tradition despite any personal plans for higher education or a career. Other value conflicts may arise in respect of intergenerational roles and status, or other incompatibilities of traditional and secular social systems. To what extent must the host society reappraise its core values in view of demographic changes and the natural evolution of culture in all societies? To what extent must minorities modify their basic beliefs?

The upshot would seem to be that acculturation to the dominant values is likely to be a salient process in any plural society. Nonetheless, all social processes are expressed through the action of *individuals*, and the options for ethnic minority individuals may offer much greater flexibility than at first appears likely. As Gordon (1978) and others have suggested, minority group members will have social-class and regional as well as ethnic affiliations, and acculturation will not necessarily proceed – or proceed equally – in respect of all three. Ethnic identity for some may embrace all aspects of life, including religion, language, and marrying within the group, as well as dress and diet; for others it may be reduced to religion, diet or endogamy – or to complete assimilation. Minority group individuals also operate in many roles and statuses, within and outside the home, and acculturation will proceed differentially. Much, of course, will depend on the attitudes of the host society, and in particular on its attitudes to colour. Furthermore, some modification of both minority and majority cultures may occur in immigrant areas, allowing individuals the choice of acculturating to the new minority or majority cultures, or to a new merged culture. A bicultural identity, in some degree, will always remain open to the individual (Newman, 1973; Tumin & Plotch, 1977; Smolicz, 1979). Nor should the uniformities of *all* cultures – caring for the young and the old, socialisation and social control, religious beliefs and rituals, and so on – be understated in assessing the degree of individual adjustment involved.

Consensus, Conflict and Interaction

The controversies which currently preoccupy theorists, lecturers, policymakers and to some extent teachers in the UK thus cover a broad spectrum. Some may seem very focused – the teaching style best suited to children of West Indian origin, say – while others may range more broadly into the 'anti-racist' or assimilation debates. Most, however, can be incorporated within more overarching, theoretical paradigms and for some observers this is the crux of the matter. Such an approach has its risks. Grand theorists may lose touch with classroom realities, reify the mundane and allege the operation of broad 'social processes' as though they could ever be independent of their constituents, the average pupil or teacher. There may even be a 'cavalier treatment of empirical data . . . [and the use of] theoretical ingenuity to squirm out of tight corners when the facts do not fit', as Jeffcoate's (1984a) critique of the Marxist approach puts it. At the same time, to consider only individual behaviours, particular events, specific studies or local policies without speculating upon the possible existence of systematic trends, underlying pressures or more embracing 'social processes' is to lose the opportunity of discovering an explanatory theory which may generate both more effective social policies and more fruitful lines of further enquiry.

Several theoretical perspectives have already been explored – multicultural education versus 'anti-racism', and the assimilation–integration–pluralism debate with its corollary, cohesion versus diversity. Social class has been touched upon, and when put together with ethnicity and race begins to form the basis of a deeper analysis. Mercer and Prescott (1982), for example, examined ethnic minority experience from the point of view of all three. Ethnicity, a sense of peoplehood, based on a distinctive culture, history, religion or language, might explain the social cohesiveness of a minority group as well as social exclusion by the majority. It is often a reason for residential segregation. But as an explanation it is incomplete without consideration of prejudice and discrimination based upon racial differences, significantly pigmentation, and the popular stereotypes derived from a former colonial empire. Nor can either ethnicity or race disregard the 'structural' disadvantages associated with working-class status, and competition for employment and housing.

Sociologists might argue that the theoretical paradigms of consensus, conflict or interaction are even more useful. For example, functionalism, derived from the work of Durkheim or Parsons, has offered a biological model of society where each part has a definable function and all fit together as a system. Broad agreement on core values (hence 'consensus' theory) ensures that the system operates more or less in equilibrium. From this point of view, immigrants are to be assimilated if their presence is not to be dysfunctional, and this will be achieved through the main agency of socialisation – the schools. Education will convey the basic skills and core values to ensure the continuing overall integration of the social system, and also the continuing flow of talent – via meritocratic procedures – to each interrelated part. The analysis is neat, tidy and a vast over-simplification of reality. Individuals are more than actors who have predetermined roles and statuses. The assumption of value consensus is particularly contentious in view of the known variations by region, social class and religion, and it appears to deny the possibility that ethnic minority diversity in values might in fact be functional in what may sometimes be the harsh and alienating conditions of an urban, industrial civilisation. On the other hand, socialisation, social cohesion and meritocracy are useful concepts, as we have seen.

Conflict theory, based on the work of Karl Marx, also offers a 'social system' approach, but a quite different interpretation of reality. Marxists place greater emphasis on the economic foundations of society, and argue that all other social relationships, including the political, legal and educational institutions, are shaped by them. Conflict rather than consensus is thus the central feature of capitalist, industrial society, as owners and managers seek to exploit workers for maximum gain. Immigrants are significant not racially or ethnically, but because of their position in the social structure. They form part of an 'industrial reserve army', brought in to fill jobs unacceptable to indigenous workers because of low wages or poor conditions. According to Cox (1948), racism is an ideology originating in early capitalism, enabling traders to use human labour as a mere commodity, and in our own times being used as a means of depressing wage levels and dividing the working class against itself. Education is an 'ideological state apparatus' – a tool of capitalism – and socialises minority children for a lowly role in society (Sarup, 1982).

Conflict theorising has attracted increasing attention since the 1970s, and has certainly contributed to the 'anti-racist' viewpoint. It makes assertions, some of which can be substantiated empirically, such as the overseas recruitment of West Indians to work on London buses and Punjabis to work in Yorkshire mills, or the employment of Pakistanis on all-night shifts in Bradford, or the below-average position of black Britons occupationally. This is certainly the operation of a free labour market, but is claimed to be the coordinated activity of a dominant class. The Marxist view offers an important corrective in underlining the differential life chances of immigrants deriving from their position in the class structure, and their consequent deprivations in terms of employment, income, housing and so on. Minority group children certainly share all the disadvantages of other indigenous working-class children (Tomlinson, 1983) and, as we have seen, class undoubtedly remains a foremost factor in educational achievement (DES, 1984a). On the other hand, to dismiss ethnicity is to make the same error as functionalists, who may similarly perceive immigrants to be a uniform mass to be processed by the social system; in fact, the lifestyles and aspirations of South Asians, West Indians, Greeks or Turks are all quite distinctive, as were those of the Irish and Jews in an earlier generation. Both functionalists and conflict theorists would probably support an assimilationist position, but for different reasons: meritocratic absorption for the former, working-class solidarity for the latter. As for schooling, it clearly has, among other things, a sorting and sifting role for the occupational structure. But it has yet to be established that it is merely a tool of capitalism, mediating docility, conditioning children for their future roles in an exploitative system, and deliberately tracking minority pupils into an underclass.

Now, while the consensus and conflict perspectives offer large-scale, 'social systems' theories, interactionism places greater emphasis upon individuals in their relationships with each other. Nor does it so readily agree that individuals are moulded by the macro pressures of societal norms and values, or by the economic infrastructure, respectively. Social reality is thought to derive from the meanings perceived in any social situation by the actors involved. An individual's definition of the situation (which may, of course, change and develop) determines his or her behaviour. Indeed, an individual's beliefs about the way he or she is perceived by others – the 'looking glass self', as Cooley termed it arc felt to contribute very substantially to human interaction. The Rampton Report of 1981 illustrates the contribution of this third sociological perspective to multicultural education in the UK. The report placed some emphasis on the unfavourable labelling by teachers of ethnic minority children, and the consequent self-fulfilling prophecy of underachievement. West Indian children, like other working-class children and with the comparable disadvantage of lacking a command of standard English, may be regarded from the outset by teachers as less promising; they may be spoken to in all daily classroom encounters accordingly, and possibly even grouped or streamed on the basis of these teachers' perceptions. The children may accept this low valuation of their abilities and consequently underperform.

There is no doubt that this micro perspective enriches our understanding of educability in general, and of the education of ethnic minority children in particular. It adds a valuable additional dimension. On the other hand, the research evidence on the teacher expectation effect is equivocal; sometimes a self-fulfilling prophecy occurs, and sometimes it does not (Nash, 1976). Stone's celebrated study (1981) concluded that 'The West Indian children's unfavourable view of their teachers' feelings towards them did not correlate with an unfavourable view of themselves', and furthermore, that '. . . self-concept research and theory and teaching styles based on those ideas have little to contribute towards an understanding of how West Indian children in Britain should be educated'. Nor do interactionists adequately explain how teachers acquire their preconceptions in the first place, if all meanings derive from classroom encounters. Some conflict theorising has, in fact, incorporated aspects of this micro perspective, and claims that the self-fulfilling prophecy is the way in which many minority children are fed into the capitalist underclass. But we lack the empirical evidence to demonstrate this.

Certainly, the controversial 'stop and search' procedures used by the police in ghetto areas in the UK seem to illustrate the 'construction of meaning' which interactionists claim always takes place in social situations. Police patrolling such an area are probably more likely to apprehend groups of minority youngsters than they would in more affluent settings, on the unsupported assumption that they are up to no good.

CONCLUSIONS

This chapter has sought to offer a review of multicultural education in the UK, beginning with the pattern of immigration. We have noted the ethnic diversity of the country, particularly in London, but the overall figure of around 5–6 per cent of the total population is small, even though minority concentrations are very much higher in the conurbations. Secondly, the post-war policies of assimilation, integration and cultural pluralism have been briefly reviewed. The UK now espouses a pluralist view, although some local education authorities and many schools in more rural areas may not in practice have moved much beyond assimilation. Cultural pluralism is now felt to represent a more appropriate position in a social democracy which claims to respect basic human rights, and the right to a heritage has been progressively argued pragmatically and through legislation.

A third section has considered major controversies, for in as highly politicised a field as multicultural education, disagreements at all levels of theory and practice were inevitable. Even the most specific issues, the opportunities for children of West Indian origin, for example, have elicited sharply conflicting opinions. But with the emergence of 'anti-racism', controversy has raged widely, dividing the committed and endangering the reform as a whole. 'Anti-racists' have seemed to be dismissive of ethnicity, a concept far more inclusive than the dated notion of 'race', which is significant more for its power to mobilise hatred than for its power to enlighten. 'Multiculturalists', on the other hand, have too frequently understated the nature and extent of minority disadvantage and, in particular, of prejudice and discrimination – both overt and unintentional. 'Anti-racism' has alerted the movement to the harsher realities of cultural pluralism, and has played a valuable role in that.

A further controversy continues in respect of the cohesion–diversity continuum. As the UK moves further into policies motivated by a commitment to cultural pluralism, closer attention is being attracted to core values, what they comprise and how they are to be ensured through the secondary socialisation of schooling. It is these larger controversies which will be of greatest significance in the long run, for they offer the possibility of generating theories of greater explanatory power. Sociological theory in its several branches may be helpful in this. The conflict perspective, represented by contemporary Marxists, continues to articulate a challenging analysis in which class, status and power are seen as the central determinants of multicultural education. Some of this work is insightful, some purely polemical; little is documented in detail. Consensus and interactionist approaches each contribute useful concepts, but each has limitations. An *eclectic* position drawing upon several perspectives may therefore prove most helpful.

Parekh's essay (1983) on under-achievement comes to a similar conclusion:

> . . . the debate is vitiated by what I might call the fallacy of the single factor. The participants tend to look for one specific factor, be it class, racism, the West Indian family, West Indian culture, the school, or educational system, to explain the fact of under-achievement. This is obviously an inherently impossible enterprise . . . Such highly complex phenomena . . . obviously require highly complex and multi-factoral explanations . . . with few notable exceptions, the participants are deeply committed to specific theories and either ignore others or dismiss them with a bundle of sweeping generalisations. They make little attempt to arbitrate between conflicting explanations on the basis of a critical evaluation of the available experiential and research evidence . . .
>
> (Parekh, 1983, pp. 113–14)

Multicultural education in the UK has proved as difficult a field of theoretical exploration as it has in terms of practical policies. Advances have been made; and a great deal remains to be done; but progress probably now depends as much upon the style of future enquiry and debate as upon anything else. If we can avoid dogmatism and hold to Parekh's model of systematic, rational appraisal, the outlook is hopeful.

REFERENCES

ALTARF (All London Teachers Against Racism and Fascism) Newsletter and occasional publications. Lambeth Teachers' Centre, Santley Street, London SW4.

Berkshire LEA (1982) *Education for Equality*. Reading: Department of Education.

Bolton, E. (1979) Education in a multicultural society. *Trends in Education*, **4**, 3–7.

Braham, P. (1982) Migration and settlement in Britain. *Ethnic Minorities and Community Relations*, Unit 2. Milton Keynes: The Open University.

Braham, P., Rhodes, E. & Pearn, M. (ed.) (1981) *Discrimination and Disadvantage in Employment*. London: Harper & Row.

Brown, C. (1984) *Black and White Britain*. London: Heinemann.

Bullivant (1981) *The Pluralist Dilemma in Education*. London: George Allen & Unwin.

Bullivant (1984) *Pluralism: Cultural Maintenance and Evolution*. Sydney: Multilingual Matters.

Carby, H. V. (1982) Schooling in Babylon. In Centre for Contemporary Cultural Studies (ed.), *The Empire Strikes Back*. London: Hutchinson.

Cashmore, E. & Bagley, C. (1984) Colour blind. *The Times Educational Supplement*, 20 December, p. 13.

Commonwealth Immigrants Advisory Council (1964) *Second Report* Cmnd. 2266. London: HMSO.

Cox, O. C. (1948) *Caste, Class and Race*. New York: Monthly Review Press.

Craft, M. (1984) Education and diversity. In Craft, M. (ed.), *Education and Cultural Pluralism*. Lewes: Falmer Press.

Craft, M. & Craft, A. (1982) Multicultural education. In Cohen, L., Manion, L. & Thomas, J. B. (ed.), *Educational Research and Development in Britain 1970–80*, pp. 445–58. Walton-on-Thames: NFER-Nelson.

Craft, A. & Bardell, G. (ed.) (1984) *Curriculum Opportunities in a Multicultural Society*. London: Harper & Row.

Department of Education and Science (1965) *The Education of Immigrants* (Circular 7/65). London: DES.

Department of Education and Science (1971) *The Education of Immigrants*. London: HMSO.

Department of Education and Science (1977) *Education in Schools* (Cmnd. 6869). London: HMSO.

Department of Education and Science (1981a) *The School Curriculum*. London: HMSO.

Department of Education and Science (1981b) *West Indian Children in Our Schools* (Rampton Report). London: HMSO.

Department of Education and Science (1984a) *Statistical Bulletin* No. 13/84. London: HMSO.

Department of Education and Science (1984b) *Initial Teacher Training: Approval of Courses* (Circular 3/84). London: DES.

Employment Gazette (1983) Ethnic origin and economic status, pp. 424–30. London: HMSO.

Figueroa, P. (1984) Minority pupil progress. In Craft, M. (ed.), *Education and Cultural Pluralism*. Lewes: Falmer Press.

Ghuman, P. A. S. & Gallop, R. (1981) Educational attitudes of Bengali families in Cardiff. *Journal of Multilingual and Multicultural Development*, **2**(2), 127–44.

Gordon, M. M. (1978) *Human Nature, Class and Ethnicity*. Oxford: Oxford University Press.

Holmes, C. (1982) The promised land? Immigration into Britain 1870–1980. In Coleman, D. A. (ed.), *Demography of Immigrant and Minority Groups in the UK*. London: Academic Press.

Home Office (1965) *Immigration from the Commonwealth* (Cmnd. 2739). London: HMSO.

Home Office (1981) *Racial Attacks*. London: Home Office.

Inner London Education Authority (1983a) *1983 Language Census*. London: ILEA.

Inner London Education Authority (1983b) *Race, Sex and Class*, No. 2. London: ILEA.

Jeffcoate, R. (1984a) Ideologies and multicultural education. In Craft, M. (ed.), *Education and Cultural Pluralism*. Lewes: Falmer Press.

Jeffcoate, R. (1984b) *Ethnic Minorities and Education*. London: Harper & Row.

Kosmin, B. (1982a) The Jewish experience. *Ethnic Minorities and Community Relations*, Units 8–9. Milton Keynes: The Open University.

Kosmin, B. (1982b) Nuptuality and fertility patterns of British Jewry 1850–1980. In Coleman, D. A. (ed.), *Demography of Immigrant and Minority Groups in the UK*. London: Academic Press.

Linguistic Minorities Project (1983) *Linguistic Minorities in England*. London: University of London Institute of Education.

Lynch, J. (ed.) (1981) *Teaching in the Multicultural School*. London: Ward Lock.

Lynch, J. (1983) *The Multicultural Curriculum*. London: Batsford.

McLean, M. (1980) Cultural autonomy and the education of ethnic minority groups. *British Journal of Educational Studies*, **28**(1).

Mercer, N. & Prescott, W. (1982) Perspectives on minority experience. In *Ethnic Minorities and Community Relations*, Units 8–9. Milton Keynes: The Open University.

Ministry of Education (1963) *English for Immigrants*. London: HMSO.

Mullard, C. (1982) Multiracial education in Britain. In Tierney, J. et al. (ed.), *Race, Migration and Schooling*. London: Holt, Rinehart and Winston.

Mullard, C. (1984) *Anti-Racist Education: the Three O's*. National Association for Multiracial Education.

Murray, C. & Dawson, A. (1983) *Five Thousand Adolescents*. Manchester: University of Manchester.

NAME (National Association for Multiracial Education). *Multiracial Education*.

Nash, R. (1976) *Teacher Expectations and Pupil Learning*. London: Routledge & Kegan Paul.

National Union of Teachers (1982) *Combating Racialism in Schools*. London: NUT.

Newman, W. M. (1973) *American Pluralism*. London: Harper & Row.

O'Donnell, M. (1981) *A New Introduction to Sociology*. London: Harrap.

Parekh, B. (1983) Educational opportunity in multiethnic Britain. In Glazer, N. & Young, K. (ed.), *Ethnic Pluralism and Public Policy*. London: Lexington Books/ Heinemann.

Peach, C. (1982) The growth and distribution of the black population in Britain 1945–1980. In Coleman, D. A. (ed.), *Demography of Immigrant and Minority Groups in the UK*. London: Academic Press.

Rees, T. (1982) Immigration policies in the UK. In Husband, C. (ed.), *Race in Britain*. London: Hutchinson.

Runnymede Trust (1980) *Britain's Black Population*. London: Heinemann.

Sarup, M. (1982) *Education, State and Crisis*. London: Routledge & Kegan Paul.

Short, G. (1983) Rampton revisited: a study of racial stereotypes in the primary school. *Durham and Newcastle Research Review*, **10**(51), 82–6.

Smith, A. D. (1981) *The Ethnic Revival*. Cambridge: Cambridge University Press.

Smith, D. J. & Tomlinson, S. (in press) *Factors Associated with Success in Multiethnic Schools*. London: Policy Studies Institute.

Smolicz, J. J. (1979) *Culture and Education in a Plural Society*. Canberra: Curriculum Development Centre.

Stone, M. (1981) *The Education of the Black Child in Britain*. London: Fontana.

Tansley, P. & Craft, A. (1984) Mother tongue teaching and support: a Schools Council enquiry. *Journal of Multilingual and Multicultural Development*, **5**(5), 367–84.

Te Selle, S. (1973) *The Rediscovery of Ethnicity*. London: Harper & Row.

Tomlinson, S. (1983) *Ethnic Minorities in British Schools*. London: Heinemann.

Tomlinson, S. (1984) *Home and School in Multicultural Britain*. London: Batsford.

Troyna, B. (1982) The ideological and policy response to black pupils in British schools. In Hartnett, A. (ed.), *The Social Sciences in Educational Studies*. London: Heinemann.

Troyna, B. (1984) Fact or artefact? The 'educational underachievement' of black pupils. *British Journal of Sociology of Education*, **5**(2), 153–66.

Tumin, M. M. & Plotch, W. (ed.) (1977) *Pluralism in a Democratic Society*. New York: Praeger.

Walvin, J. (1984) *Passage to Britain*. Harmondsworth: Penguin.

BIBLIOGRAPHY

Brown, C. (1984) *Black and White Britain*. London: Heinemann. The third of a series of national surveys carried out by the Policy Studies Institute, and providing an up-to-date review of the demography, housing, employment, etc. of the Asian and West Indian minorities in Great Britain.

Coleman, D. A. (ed.) (1982) *Demography of Immigrant and Minority Groups in the UK*. London: Academic Press. A report of the Proceedings of the 18th Eugenics Society Symposium, which includes papers on the historical and geographical patterns of both old and new immigrant communities, and offers analyses of present and future patterns of mortality, fertility and migration.

Craft, M. (ed.) (1984) *Education and Cultural Pluralism*. Lewes: Falmer Press. A symposium by leading British specialists in multicultural education on several of its most significant dimensions: policy and ideology, curriculum and assessment, intercultural relations, language, achievement, and school–community relationships.

Craft, A. & Bardell, G. (ed.) (1984) *Curriculum Opportunities in a Multicultural Society*. London: Harper & Row. A collection of papers by teachers and teacher educators which illustrate how a multicultural perspective may be interpreted in all the main areas of the secondary school curriculum, and including advice on course content, teaching strategies and resources.

Davey, A. (1983) *Learning to be Prejudiced*. London: Edward Arnold. The report of a survey of 512 white, West Indian and Asian children aged seven to ten from schools in London and industrial Yorkshire, and of some 523 of their parents, which describes the acquisition of ethnic awareness and ethnocentrism.

Edwards, V. (1983) *Language in Multicultural Classrooms*. London: Batsford. An analysis of the development of language policies and practices in British schools (including bilingualism, TESL, mother tongue teaching, and non-standard dialect issues), and a practical examination of talk, reading and writing in the curriculum.

James, A. & Jeffcoate, R. (ed.) (1981) *The School in the Multicultural Society*. London: Harper & Row. Readings by leading specialists on critical issues in multicultural education, including curriculum construction and organisation, language, attainment, and pupil–teacher interaction.

Jeffcoate, R. (1984) *Ethnic Minorities and Education*. London: Harper & Row. A critical examination of the position of ethnic minority pupils in British schools which considers positive discrimination, integration, segregation and pluralism, in the context of equality of educational opportunity for all children.

Linguistic Minorities Project (1983) *Linguistic Minorities in England*. London: University of London Institute of Education. The report of the first such national inquiry into the extent of bilingualism among schoolchildren and adults, and of mother tongue teaching by schools and community agencies.

Lynch, J. (1983) *The Multicultural Curriculum*. London: Batsford. A review of multicultural curriculum development in Britain (and also Australia and North America) which offers an analysis of its aims, objectives and techniques, and a consideration of the practical problems and opportunities which it presents.

Runnymede Trust (1980) *Britain's Black Population*. London: Heinemann. An examination of black immigration and of official policy responses to it, and a review of this minority's experience in employment, housing, education, health and the social services.

Smith, A. D. (1981) *The Ethnic Revival*. Cambridge: Cambridge University Press.

A study of the post-1945 rise of ethnic feeling and nationalist aspirations, and of their deeper historical roots, in the growth of the modern technological state.

Tomlinson, S. (1983) *Ethnic Minorities in British Schools*. London: Heinemann. A comprehensive review of the literature on the education of British ethnic minorities (1960–82), which includes policies and practices in multicultural education, educational performance, teacher expectations and other curriculum issues.

Tomlinson, S. (1984) *Home and School in Multicultural Britain*. London: Batsford. The first systematic study of the interaction of ethnic minority homes and majority culture schools in the context of a broader literature on home–school relations, and including an examination of 'supplementary' and other forms of community-based schooling.

Walvin, J. (1984) *Passage to Britain*. Harmondsworth: Penguin. An account of British immigration since the middle ages which also reviews post-1962 legislation and political developments, and considers life in Britain's contemporary minority communities.

Watson, J. L. (1977) *Between Two Cultures*. Oxford: Oxford University Press. A summary of the research of twelve anthropologists who have examined migration and ethnicity in British society, and who have each considered a particular minority at both ends of the migration chain.

Chapter 5

Multicultural Education in Australia: An Unresolved Debate

BRIAN M. BULLIVANT

With the formal adoption of multiculturalism in November 1978 as its official ideology of pluralism, after years of assimilationist and integrationist policies towards immigrants, the Australian Liberal Party Government launched Australia into a path already followed by several other Western societies. It also endorsed multicultural education backed by an allocation of Commonwealth funding on a scale that was very generous by Australian educational standards. If nothing else, this showed that in multicultural matters, at least the Government meant business.

The following Labor Party Government, elected in March 1983 on a more socialist platform, has continued to support multiculturalism and multicultural education. This has not been without some changes in an attempt to give education a more egalitarian emphasis, and very recently to cope with a resurgence of racial discrimination against indigenous Aborigines and newly arrived immigrants from Indochina and other parts of Asia.[1] Thus the nature of Australian society is now occasionally redefined by some officials as multiracial, and multiracial education is suggested as one way of combating prejudice and discrimination. Warning signs of this latest development were apparent in the late 1970s and early 1980s, with discrimination by some trade unions against Vietnamese in such industries as fruit canning and car assembly (Lunn, 1979; Wynhausen, 1981). The situation in 1984 has been exacerbated by the Aboriginal land rights issue, by the downturn in the economy, with a high unemployment rate, and by the increasing numbers of Indochinese immigrants allowed into Australia on family reunion grounds.

As in other Western societies where multiculturalism has been introduced, the historical influences of waves of immigration have been ever-present. Also present have been periodic shifts in the official ideologies of pluralism, the influence of changes in the demographic, cultural and economic composition of the society, competing theories about the nature of Australian pluralism and pluralist education, and considerable public and at times polemical debate about such issues, fuelled by periodic public opinion polls. In principle Australia is no different from other Western countries in the way multiculturalism and multicultural education have evolved historically. However, there are variations on this original theme that are typically antipodean, but even they may give educationists in other societies a strong sense of déjà vu when seen in comparative perspective.

AUSTRALIA SINCE THE SECOND WORLD WAR

Demography

The Second World War marks the logical starting point for considering developments towards multiculturalism in Australia, as the thirty years since that time have seen periodic waves of immigrants that have completely altered the composition of the society and compelled officials to recognise its pluralist nature. Prior to the war, and even for a few years after it, this was unnecessary, as only some 203 000 people, or approximately 3 per cent of the population, were born outside Australia and the British Isles. Australia was Anglo-centric and 'white' (Jupp, 1966, p. 5). By the most recent 1981 Census the proportion of non-Australian-born people had increased, but the composition of the total population of approximately 14.6 million was still heavily weighted in favour of those born in Australia (78.2 per cent) and the British Isles (7.8 per cent) (Australian Bureau of Statistics, 1984, p. 79).

The figure of 78.2 per cent born in Australia should be treated with caution, as it does not necessarily mean that all of this number are of Anglo-Australian background. A proportion are Australians born in Australia of immigrant parents, and their ethnocultural affiliation is not known. Of the 78.2 per cent born in Australia, 88.4 per cent had parents who were also born in Australia and a further 3.7 per cent had parents born in the United Kingdom and Ireland. Only 6 per cent had parents born in other European countries, Asia and the remaining parts of the world. Thus at least 72.8 per cent of the population are Anglo-Australian by descent from Anglo-Australians, by immigration from English-speaking countries, or by birth in Australia of parents who were also Australian-born. This figure would be higher (approximately 75 per cent) if immigrants from other English-speaking countries such as New Zealand, Canada, the United States and parts of Africa were included. It is a necessary corrective to frequently reiterated official claims to bolster the ideology of multiculturalism that 30 per cent or more of the Australian population are from backgrounds that are culturally different from the majority of the society.

The Growth of Pluralist Diversity

The increase in the numbers of immigrants in Australia has been accompanied by a growth in the degree of cultural pluralism, and also by a change in the ethnocultural composition of the population. In 1945 during the period immediately after the Second World War the Labor Government launched a programme directed by the Immigration Minister, Arthur Calwell.

At first the waves of immigrants were rigorously selected to maintain a ratio of nine-tenths British and one-tenth northern European – as like British, Baltic or other 'nordic types' as possible in order not to offend Australian sensibilities (Calwell, 1972, p. 103). On arrival they still encountered a strongly nationalistic and xenophobic society harbouring pre-war suspicions, fear of Asians, and entrenched chauvinistic attitudes. Asians were thus totally rejected, even to the extent of expelling Asian wives of Anglo-Australians, and those Asians who had been wartime refugees from the Japanese. The measure was also a carry-over of the White Australia policy that dominated the inter-war period.

From the beginning of the 1950s to the present there have been continuing changes in both the kinds of immigrants allowed into Australia and the official policies governing their entry. They have also been influenced by economic conditions such as the recessions of the early 1950s and 1970–1971, international incidents such as the Hungarian uprising in 1956 and periodic refugee movements from Czechoslovakia in 1968, Chile in the early 1970s and Vietnam commencing in 1975, together with a host of factors embedded in the fluctuating and not always favourable perceptions of potential immigrants that Australia was a suitable country in which to settle. Indeed, the whole 35-year period has experienced times when settlers returned home disillusioned with conditions and life in Australia, thus reducing the net immigration gain (Martin, 1978, pp. 30–33).

Changes in the ruling Federal Government also led to new immigration policies. The conservative Liberal Party Government, which succeeded Labor in 1949, remained in power until 1972, and gradually relaxed a number of conditions governing the immigrant intake. The assisted passage programme was extended to southern European countries, in particular Italy, Greece and Spain.

In 1949 some restrictive barriers against wartime refugees were relaxed, and even Chinese living in Australia under temporary permits were allowed to stay if they could demonstrate that they could not return to Communist-controlled China. By the period 1969–1971 the intake of non-European settlers had risen to nearly 10 000 a year. Even though the Liberal Government did not relax many discriminatory practices against other non-Europeans such as New Zealand Maoris and Ugandan Asians, it was clear that the White Australia policy was virtually a thing of the past.

The groundwork for non-European 'Asian' diversification had been laid by accepting settlers from an increasing number of countries peripheral to mainland Asia. Thus in the mid-1960s the Department of Immigration began to seek immigrants in the Middle East. Lebanese began to arrive in 1964, followed by Turks in 1967, as a result of an agreement with Turkey to set up an assisted passage scheme. As Martin (1978, p. 30) comments, citing Price (1971, p. A14), to allay Australian suspicions, this was achieved 'by a subtle but decisive act of re-definition, Turkey was now "for all intents and purposes . . . an entirely European country"'.

A Labor Federal Government was swept back into power in 1972, and its reformist zeal accelerated this diversification. In August 1965 the Labor National Conference had agreed to abandon the longstanding eighty-year-old Labor policy of restrictive immigration and the concept of White Australia, and further easing of restrictions was supported at subsequent conferences in 1971 and 1975 (Australian Labor Party, 1975, p. 43). In the autumn session of Federal Parliament in 1975, the *Racial Discrimination*

Act was passed and its principles subscribed to by all political parties. An era of official discrimination against non-European immigrants had ended, in a new international context of rapprochement with Asian countries and easing of the 'populate or perish' paranoia which had been a feature of the 1940s.

Labor was ousted from government in November 1975, but the impetus to diversification in the immigration intake was not abated by developments during the next ten years. These took place initially under a newly formed Ministry of Immigration and Ethnic Affairs in the Liberal Government during 1976–1983 and then under a Labor Government elected in March 1983. They clearly demonstrate that the old policy of giving preference to British immigrants has ended and that economic realities in times of periodic recession have curbed the high numbers of settlers accepted into Australia that were a feature of the immigration boom times of the 1960s and early 1970s. Increasingly Australia has come to place reliance on the Middle East, Latin America and Asian countries as sources of migrants, while old sources such as Britain, Greece, Italy and Europe have declined in importance. Australia now has a highly diversified population culturally, ethnically, linguistically and, increasingly since 1975, racially – the last in the strictly phenotypical sense of race (see for a discussion of the most recent statistics Price, 1983, pp. 6–25).

A picture of this diversity can be gained from estimates for 1981 from the Department of Immigration and Ethnic Affairs (Menadue, 1981, cited in Kerr, 1983). Then there were 1 326 833 first-generation residents from non-English-speaking countries, who spoke 36 languages with 1000 speakers or more, 106 000 first-generation residents speaking over ninety other languages with fewer than 1000 speakers, and an additional 27 000 Aborigines speaking a variety of indigenous languages, including creoles. In Menadue's estimate some 3.75 million people, or one-quarter of the Australian population, have 'an immediate personal and family interest in a language other than English and in a culture outside the British tradition'. Such is one cultural and demographic basis for the current official policies of multicultural education.

A more contentious basis is the racial diversity that is becoming an increasing feature of Australian society. Price's (1983, pp. 9, 16) estimates for 1983 show that 96.2 per cent of the Australian population of 15 282 800 are European, 1.22 per cent Aborigines and Torres Strait Islanders, 0.17 per cent Pacific Islanders, 0.46 per cent Chinese and 2.0 per cent other races. Countries of origin of non-Europeans counted as being in Asia give some further indication of the racial diversity of the Australian population. They include, among others, Bangladesh, India, Fiji, Pakistan, Sri Lanka, Indonesia, Lebanon, Turkey, Malaysia and Singapore, Philippines, Thailand, Kampuchea, Vietnam and Laos. Other racial groups include Maoris from New Zealand and Polynesian Islanders of various origins from Oceania. As the affiliations of such groups are based as much on racial similarity as on cultural allegiance, it is doubtful whether the current policy of multiculturalism provides an adequate model for fully considering all the complexities of Australian pluralism.

Evolution of Pluralist Ideologies

The growth and diversification of Australia's immigrant and ethnic population have generated changing ideologies held by governments and officials concerning the nature of the society's pluralism. The ideologies in turn have influenced the types of and developments in policies towards immigrants and the programmes and organisations needed to implement them. No complete understanding of the current stress on multiculturalism is possible without some appreciation of the ideological basis of much official thinking about post-war demographic and cultural changes.

For our purposes, the definition of an ideology proposed by Gould (1964, pp. 315–16) is quite adequate. It is 'a pattern of beliefs and concepts both factual and normative which purport to explain complex social phenomena with a view to directing and simplifying sociopolitical choices, facing individuals and groups'. The distinction between the factual and the normative nature of an ideology highlights how it can be used. Factually, an ideology makes a substantive or descriptive statement of belief and value, i.e., truth-claims about whatever it refers to. In the present discussion, official ideologies since the Second World War have been used to describe Australian society and define its characteristics.

Normatively, an ideology makes prescriptive assertions of belief and value about what should or ought to be the case, e.g., that Australia should become a multicultural society. Because such prescriptions are couched in ideal-future terms they cannot be tested as truth-claims can, by applying empirical reality tests and examining the facts. Instead, prescriptive ideologies can be tested on grounds of their theoretical or logical consistency, and comprehensiveness, or compatibility with known trends to see whether they have some possible substance or are mainly rhetoric. Much of the debate about multicultural Australia discussed below hinges on this distinction, and is concerned with the way descriptive and prescriptive uses of 'multicultural' have been confused.

The way an ideology is used and operates depends partly on the intentions of its users. People use ideologies more or less benignly to define reality, make sense of their world, and legitimate their social relations and involvement with their sociopolitical, natural and 'metaphysical' environments (see discussion in Bullivant, 1981a; 1984). A religious ideology, for instance, can set down a whole code or charter of beliefs and values which act in these ways (Thompson & Hostetler, 1970; Bullivant, 1978). However, the ideology of Islam is not only a religious ideology, but is also used politically by rulers of Iran (among other Islamic states) to legitimate a system of political rule and the conduct of internal and external relations.

Ideology can also be used as a system of beliefs and values that bolster the power-maintaining interests of a particular social or political group. Within a stratified class society such a group can be a social class which wishes to protect its vested interests, and it is this (Marxist or neo-Marxist) sense that is most commonly, if erroneously and simplistically, associated with the term ideology. There is no denying that, in this usage, it can be a very powerful weapon of class domination and struggle, often to 'mystify social relations' and create a 'system of illusory beliefs' (Lepervanche, 1980, p. 25) about the nature of the power and control exerted by the dominant class or group over subordinate classes and groups. However, to restrict the meaning of the term only to this sense and use it, as in classical Marxist analysis, to denigrate the activities of one class in the capitalist system is to be guilty of both theoretical and ideological tunnel vision.

In an analysis of ethnoculturally pluralist societies the term 'ideology' can be used to refer to the system of beliefs and values employed by a dominant ethnocultural group to legitimate its control over the life chances of subordinate ethnocultural groups. This form of *ethnic hegemony* is discussed more fully below and elsewhere (see Bullivant, 1981b; 1981c; 1984). In essence, following Weber (1968, p. 342), it involves strategies of social closure – exclusion and inclusion – to 'maximize rewards by restricting access to rewards and opportunities to a limited circle of eligibles . . . its purpose is always the closure of social and economic opportunities to outsiders' (Parkin, 1974, p. 3). Ideologies of pluralism, as I term them, are not exempt from being considered in this way. As Lepervanche (1980, p. 25) has shown, their historical evolution in Australia can be interpreted as 'a series of ideological transformations in the recreation of hegemony'. One method by which a dominant group reproduces its hegemony over the life chances of those from minority groups is through control of the education system (Bourdieu, 1973; Apple, 1979; Bullivant, 1981b; 1983; 1984). The way ideologies of pluralism have evolved historically in Australia and influenced education provides an excellent illustration of these theoretical models.

Assimilation and Anglo-conformism

Between 1945 and the mid-1960s the predominantly Anglo-Australian monocultural and ethnically homogeneous composition of the population was matched by an ideology of assimilation. This dominated official policies which were blatantly assimilationist and Anglo-conformist towards immigrants. They were expected to fit into the society, shed their cultures and languages, and symbolically announce their new status by becoming naturalised after the statutory period of five years had elapsed. The White Australia policy formed part of the ideology, and the Government's belief in a monocultural Australia, expressed even as late as 1969 by the then Minister for Immigration, W. Snedden (1969), was accompanied by a firm belief in favour of its monoracial composition.

At the outset many Australians used pejorative names in common parlance, such as 'Pommies' (British), 'Wogs' (Italians), 'Reffos' (refugees) and 'Balts' (Lithuanians, Latvians) (Yarwood, 1964, p. 43), as symbolic boundary markers to discriminate against migrants and indicate their inferior status and exclusion from 'dinkum' (genuine, real) Australians. They held strong and well-articulated stereotyped views of themselves that served as inclusive boundary markers (Berry, 1969). Even at the quasi-official level of the Australian Citizenship Conventions instituted by the Federal Government, terms used for immigrants were less offensive but still served as markers of exclusion. In 1950, all immigrants were termed New Australians. In 1953 this term was replaced by 'migrants' as a title for immigrants from Britain, but New Australians came to refer exclusively to immigrants of non-British origin (Kovacs & Cropley, 1975, p. 72), and continued in use well into the 1960s.

As a table of events related to migrant settlement between 1950 and 1977 prepared by Martin (1978, pp. 38–45) demonstrates, the period of assimilationist thinking was marked by an almost complete absence of official or semi-official standing committees and councils, special committees of inquiry, publications of government inquiries, and even programmes and services related to immigrants. In the immediate post-war period Good Neighbour Councils were established, but initially these concentrated on British immigrants, with a 'handshake' and 'cup of tea' assimilationist approach (Jupp, 1966, p. 9), and did not accept non-British members until the 1960s. The Adult Migrant Education Service was set up in 1947 as a responsibility of the Commonwealth Office of Education. A series of Australian citizenship conventions was inaugurated in the same period, sponsored by the Department of Immigration, to bring together those involved in the work of the Good Neighbour Movement. Martin (1978, p. 28) comments that 'consensus was ensured both by what was excluded from the deliberations . . . and by the bland, self-congratulatory treatment of the subjects that were covered'. In Jupp's (1966, p. 54) view the conventions were 'carefully organised to avoid controversy'.

In the field of education, very little was done for the children of immigrants. They were seen as a 'problem', disrupting classes by their presence and irregular arrival in schools. An Anglo-Australian perspective completely dominated the curriculum. What little attention to migrant children's needs there was, in Martin's view (1978, p. 84), consisted of:

> . . . giving migrant children the minimum language skills needed for them to communicate in a monolingual society. This was accomplished with the minimum of structural change in education departments or schools; the commonly used term 'withdrawal classes' for migrant English classes signifies that the system has been kept intact by the device of taking teaching staff and migrant children out of it.

Even this is probably too rosy a picture of the general situation in the period until the mid-1960s. In very many schools, migrant children were more or less left to sink or swim, and to 'pick up' English as best they could. The Australian ideology of assimilation maintained 'that it would be contrary to the prevailing egalitarian values and detrimental to assimilation for migrants, as migrants, to be given unique privileges or consideration of any kinds' (Martin, 1972, p. 14).

With some few notable exceptions, the almost total lack of theoretical writings about immigrants in this period indicated that academics were not interested in them either. Those few who did take an interest were also locked into the prevailing ideology and at that time took it for granted. Titles of journal articles and books either used the term 'assimilation' or implied it, as in Taft's (1965) *From Stranger to Citizen*, which is basically a review of his own and West Australian associates' psychological studies of the assimilation process. Martin's (1965) *Refugee Settlers* and Zubrzycki's (1964) *Settlers of the Latrobe valley: A sociological study of immigrants in the brown coal industry in Australia* are both sociological in emphasis but do not challenge the basic assumptions underlying the ideology of assimilation. This had to wait for the more enlightened 1970s and also the change of academic fashion to a more critical school of sociology in some universities following similar developments in British and European seats of learning.

Integration and interactionism

Harbingers of a change began to be evident in the period from the late 1950s to mid-1960s, with increasing pressure of immigrant numbers, especially in the metropolitan cities of Melbourne, Sydney and the latter's industrial satellites of Wollongong and Newcastle. It was also becoming evident empirically that immigrants were not assimilating, and that they were also becoming increasingly diverse in cultural backgrounds. In many metropolitan state schools it was not uncommon for thirty or forty different nationalities to be represented, occasionally even in one classroom. Despite official efforts to maintain the 'bland, self-congratulatory treatment of the subjects that they covered', Australian citizenship conventions in the 1960s contained agenda items aimed at changing the assimilationist ideology to one that would recognise the ethnocultural diversity that was becoming so obvious in Australia (Harris, 1979).

The ideology of integration and interactionism was officially adopted by the Federal Government, which set up an Office of Integration within the Department of Immigration in 1964, headed by an Officer in Charge of Integration, J. Rooth. The normative and tentative nature of the ideology seems evident in one of his statements (Rooth, 1968, p. 61): 'We *should* not merely tolerate but also respect, and, *on occasions*, encourage cultural differences . . . As members of minority groups they can make invaluable contributions to *our Australian way of life* while retaining their ethnic identity' (my emphasis).

Other official utterances were not only normative but thoroughly rhetorical – a style ideally suited to debate in Australian citizenship conventions. In 1965 Sir John Allison spoke glowingly of the new policy which aimed to 'create in the Southern Hemisphere a united nation of nations with all that is best in European culture and traditions – a Europe of the sun, without national barriers and with a common citizenship' (Harris, 1979, p. 31). It should not need emphasising that no mention was made of Asians. Although the White Australia policy was under attack from church leaders, academics and other concerned pressure groups by the mid-1960s, it was not yet officially dead. Barriers of exclusion remained in place for Asians, but were being gradually removed de jure for European immigrants. However, considerable de facto prejudice and discrimination still existed among the general public.

The ideology of integration and interactionism that was characteristic of the late 1960s did not generate many educational changes in curriculum or schooling practice, although numerous pressures were building up. 'By the beginning of the decade [1970s], a variety of influences, separately and in combination, were working to focus public, political and bureaucratic attention on the education of migrant children as a social problem' (Martin, 1976, p. 45). Full details of these influences cannot be given here (see Bullivant, 1981b; 1984; Martin, 1976; 1978) but among others they emanated from the large numbers of immigrants settling in Australia, official state committees of inquiry and surveys, concerned academics, immigrant and political pressure groups, and the sheer weight of evidence accumulating in many metropolitan schools faced with a crisis situation that immigrant children were grossly handicapped in comparison with their Anglo-Australian peers. 'The main thrust of all these efforts was to highlight the need for a vigorous program of English teaching and the main strategy was to demonstrate the extent and nature of problems associated with lack of knowledge of English' (Martin, 1976, p. 45).

Predictably, other deficiencies were played down or ignored and the situation was defined by teachers in terms that, at least implicitly, laid the blame on immigrant children for their own failure. They were a 'social problem' for which the obvious remedy was to teach them English. Thus it was still clearly assimilationist in intent. Other structural and institutional barriers, both in education and in the wider society, that might be acting as exclusion mechanisms discriminating against immigrants were conveniently overlooked. Sociology of education as taught in most universities had yet to reach the level of theoretical sophistication needed to analyse such mechanisms. Thus 'teach them English' received the seal of approval from all but a few academic educationists, and other issues failed to get on the agenda of concern.

Some States, notably Victoria (in 1967) and New South Wales (in 1968), had implemented some measures and structures to improve the teaching of English to immigrant children, but something more was obviously required. It came through Federal Government intervention in education – until that time almost exclusively a State concern. This was the introduction of the Commonwealth Child Migrant Education Program (CMEP) by the Immigration (Education) Act of Parliament in March 1971 after extensive consultations with State Ministers of Education.

As an interim measure, in April 1970 the Minister for Immigration, P. R. Lynch (1970), made a 'Ministerial Statement' in the House of Representatives pledging Commonwealth support for a five-year programme of child migrant education in government (State) and independent (denominational or 'public') schools. The expected annual expenditure of $1.5 million was to cover:

> The salary costs of teachers employed to teach migrant children in special classes and the necessary supervisory staff; special training courses for teachers in the method of teaching English as a foreign language; the provision of approved capital equipment of the language laboratory type for special classes; and the provision of suitable teaching and learning materials.

It should be pointed out that CMEP was the responsibility of the Ministry of Immigration, as the Federal Government's Department of Education and Science was constitutionally debarred from taking a *direct* role in State-level education.

Events on the wider political scene were to prove the major catalyst for the next developments in immigrant education in the 1970s. One event was the defeat of the Liberal Government in 1972 and the election of a socialist and reformist Labor Government under Prime Minister Gough Whitlam. Even then, it took several years before sufficient reformist momentum had got under way for significant improvements in immigrant education to become apparent. As Martin (1976, p. 46) has commented of the early 1970s, 'It is much more difficult to pin down the way in which changing perspectives on the nature of Australian society and the place of migrant and other ethnic groups within it have influenced approaches to the education of migrant children in recent years'.

Numerous structural changes such as committees of inquiry, rapid expansion in tertiary education, and semi-government and government organisations were generated in the first years of Labor Government rule. One that might have been expected to take a major role in immigrant education, but at first did not, was the Schools Commission, established in 1973. The report, *Schools in Australia*, published by the Interim Committee for the Schools Commission (1973) contained only eleven lines on migrant education, with the admission (p. 107) that 'the Committee has not been able to undertake a detailed investigation into the educational problems of migrant children' (see more detailed discussion in Bullivant, 1975).

This omission could well have been due to the Commission's preoccupation with trendy compensatory education philosophies and 'political arithmetic' sociology of education then sweeping through the British and United States educational and academic worlds. In the Interim Committee's case the philosophy it adopted reflected the twin principles of discovering the needs of disadvantaged schools and their pupils in general (the 'needs principle'), in order to inject into them differential financial inputs to bring about the second principle of 'equality of outcomes'. The Schools Commission took the view that the problems of migrant children were part of the wider problems of social and economic deprivation and disadvantage also experienced by many Anglo-Australian children. Its corollary was that the state could and should effect social change and eradicate such disadvantages by improving the quality of schooling.

By the time of the Schools Commission's (1975) *Report for the Triennium 1976–78* this view had undergone dramatic change. An entire chapter (Chapter 8) is devoted to 'The Education of Migrant Children' and opens with the question-begging assertion 'Australia is a multicultural society'. It concentrates mainly on TESL provisions, but condemns the then prevalent 'withdrawal system' in schools.[2] Other aspects of education are also advocated with a degree of confidence in describing Australian society which is surprising considering that the ideology of multiculturalism had been a very recent and scarcely understood innovation only two years previously, with the publication of A. J. Grassby's (1973) *A Multicultural Society for the Future*. This is a thoroughly normative, visionary piece of writing lacking both empirical and theoretical rigour, which makes the Schools Commission's somewhat dogmatic assertions all the more surprising (p. 125):

> . . . the *multicultural reality* of Australian society needs to be reflected in the school curricula – *languages, social studies, history, literature, the arts and crafts* – in staffing and in school organisation. While these changes are particularly important to undergird the *self-esteem* of migrant children they also have application for all Australian children growing up in a society which could be greatly enriched through a wider sharing in the variety of *cultural heritages* now present in it (my emphasis).

Integration and interactionism were officially dead; multiculturalism and multicultural education were moving to centre stage.

The Origins of the Multicultural Ideology

Multiculturalism and multicultural education had been hovering in the wings for some years, foreshadowed in the writings of academics such as Zubrzycki (1968, p. 27), in a paper given to the Australian Citizenship Convention of 1968, and by this writer in the same year in a series of articles for the Melbourne *Age* newspaper. These were later edited into a book (Bullivant, 1974) which followed other publications using intercultural and pluralist models for curriculum development, teacher training and classroom practice in schools with high immigrant populations (Bullivant, 1970; 1972; 1973). Canadian and United States thinking on multiculturalism was also becoming known in Australia.

However, it was the visionary (1973) official publication of Grassby that caught the imagination of educationists. As Minister for Immigration in the Labor Government he was well placed to ensure that his views received maximum publicity through a steady stream of publications from that office and his subsequent position as Commissioner for Community Relations. In any case Grassby was then, and still is, an indefatigable publicist (e.g. Grassby, 1984) with a flamboyant personal style and astute capacity to use the mass media and any other platform to expound his views (see more detailed discussion in Bullivant, 1981b).

The educational world was ripe to receive them. It was fired up by the heady, reformist policies of the socialist Labor Government, by visions of generous grants and support for research, by rapid expansion in the tertiary sector, and by the stimulus of 'busy work' created by the explosion of educational conferences, committees of inquiry, research, and new structures that occurred in the Whitlam years of the early 1970s. These all created a bandwaggonning effect which attracted many educationists. Its momentum was fuelled in some universities by fresh ideas in the sociology of education emanating from the Open University in Britain (e.g. School and Society Course Team, 1971; Young, 1971) and from the United States (e.g. Passow, Goldberg & Tannenbaum, 1967). Progressivism and reconstructionism were in vogue, and multicultural education absorbed some of these ideas.

Not all was plain sailing, however. At the National Seminar for Teacher Educators (1974) on 'The Multi-Cultural Society', held at Macquarie University, Sydney, the concepts of pluralism and multiculturalism clearly baffled the 75 or so participants, including some half a dozen 'token ethnics'. Heated arguments were a feature of group discussions, with supporters of ESL approaches to migrant education adopting dogmatic positions in which one could detect a fear that their grip on migrant education in schools, such as it was, might be weakened if the new pluralist ideas became official policy. More positive recommendations generated by the seminar included support for an integrated approach to teacher training, incorporating concepts about multiculturalism into the training curriculum, and the desirability of employing more immigrant teacher aides in schools. The former has not happened, but the latter has become a major development of the late 1970s and 1980s.

On the educational, research and academic fronts in the 1970s, the Macquarie Seminar was the forerunner of numerous seminars, surveys and research reports, and other conferences in what quickly became a multicultural growth industry. In Hill's opinion (1977, p. 150), cited by Martin (1978, p. 119), the field of immigrant education became a 'microcosm of "intellectual cross currents" . . . with its "concatenation of critics" advocating a variety of reforms'. Martin (1978) adds a more picturesque simile: 'migrant education looks more like a harbour full of sailing boats on a sunny day . . . some are competing in a regular race, others are engaged in private little *ad hoc* battles, a few verge on collision though apparently unaware of each other's existence, some go their own independent way'.

The 1970s were also notable for the proliferation of governmental and semi-governmental organisations involved either directly or indirectly with immigrant and multicultural education. Responsibility for Adult Migrant Education Services and CMEP was transferred to the Department of Education in 1975. Task force surveys were carried out in each State during 1973 (see Bullivant, 1975). The Curriculum Development Centre (CDC) was set up in Canberra as an independent statutory body in the period following the establishment of the Schools Commission. In 1977–1978 it instituted a small grants scheme for school or community groups involved in education for the multicultural society. The Education Research and Development Committee, which originated in 1970 in Canberra, set up four priority area advisory groups (PAAGs) in 1975–1976 and gave one of these responsibility for looking at multicultural education. The series of reports generated by this committee became very influential in the late 1970s but may have contributed to its demise in 1981 along with the CDC, as a number of them were critical of government practices in education. Of the three 'knowledge-generating' organisations above, only the Schools Commission escaped the so-called 'Razor Gang' spending cuts that occurred in 1981. It has been the accomplished 'survivor', partly by adjusting its ideological sails to the prevailing political and economic winds of change in the 1970s and 1980s, and partly by absorbing other empires (Johnston, 1983).

An example of this occurred in 1975. The Child Migrant Education Program had expanded far beyond what was envisaged when it was set up, and was discontinued in 1975. The provision of funds for child migrant education, which would be administered by the States, was made the responsibility of the Schools Commission (1975, p. 130), through its General Recurrent Grants Program, with effect from January 1976. This change 'meant that henceforth the States received a block grant for "Migrant and Multi-cultural Education" and that these funds could be used at the discretion of the States for teaching English to migrant children or for a variety of programmes directed at ethnic or Australian children or both' (Martin, 1978, p. 123).

Among other Royal Commissions and Committees of Inquiry (see Martin, 1978, pp. 38–45), a Committee on the Teaching of Migrant Languages in Schools was established by the Labor Government in November 1974. Its terms of reference were 'to bring together up-to-date information about the extent of the teaching of languages of migrant groups in government and non-government schools . . . to seek and collate views about desirable courses; . . . to make suggestions about possible lines of action' (Committee on the Teaching of Migrant Languages in Schools, 1976, p. 11). The committee conducted an extensive survey and gave its report in March 1976, but its passage through the Federal Parliament was unduly protracted, and it did not receive wide dissemination until a year later. In the interim, the Labor Government had been dismissed in November 1975 and its Liberal successor was firmly in power. It had its own organisations and inquiries to promote.

One of the most influential of these was the Australian Ethnic Affairs Council (AEAC), which was established in January 1977 to advise the Ministry for Immigration and Ethnic Affairs (in itself re-established from the Department of Immigration in 1976) on a variety of issues relating to immigrants. The Council operates through three committees: Settlement Programs, Multi-Cultural Education, and Community Consultation and Ethnic Media.[3]

One of the Council's most influential publications was *Australia as a Multicultural Society* (AEAC, 1977), which was a submission on the Australian Population and Immigration Council's (1977) Green Paper, *Immigration Policies and Australia's Population*. The AEAC's publication is basically ideological in setting out a normative and prescriptive blueprint for the direction Australia should take in becoming a 'multicultural society' – a question-begging and taken-for-granted assumption that is nowhere challenged in the submission. The blueprint is posited on three key social issues – social cohesion, equality and cultural identity (AEAC, 1977, p. 5):

> The crux of our argument is that Australia is already a society of multiple cultural identities, or a multicultural society, and that equality can best be promoted (perhaps can *only* be promoted) through policies that harness it to cultural identity. Both are means and both are ends: equality depends on and strengthens multiculturalism; multiculturalism depends on and strengthens equality. They are 'ends', however, only in the sense that they are the touchstones that guide our thinking and proposals, not in the sense that we see 'an equal society' or 'a multicultural society' as a tangible final social solution . . . We shall treat equality *as equal access to social resources*.

Multicultural Australia and multiculturalism are interpreted in confusing ways even in the same document. One of its architects, Professor Jerzy Zubrzycki, then at the Australian National University,[4] appeared at the outset to be somewhat ambivalent about the nature of the society, to judge from his inaugural speech as the Council's Chairman (Zubrzycki, 1977, p. 62). In this he cautioned that its task would be stupendous 'for we must make up our minds, whether we are to look backwards on what used to be rightly called British civilization in Australia or, whether we are to have a future as a multi-lingual, multi-racial, multi-cultural society'. Similar descriptions were used in an AEAC news release in March 1980.

The confusion in theoretical views about Australian pluralism has not greatly cleared up since these early statements of the Council. In education it followed trends already endorsed by the Schools Commission, by proposing policies that in its view (AEAC, 1977, p. 13) would promote equality on the one hand and cultural identity on the other. These were concerned with English language teaching (TESL), bilingual education, community language education, and the support of ethnic (Saturday or afternoon) schools. All schools were also to be 'given incentives to develop ethnic studies programs and to infuse the curriculum in general with the reality of the pluralist nature of Australian society, with the object both of enhancing the self-esteem of students of ethnic origin and giving *all* children a more authentic view of the nature of the society than the present mono-cultural education provides'.

However, the Australian Ethnic Affairs Council was in many ways the prelude to a far more influential body. This was the Committee of Review of Post Arrival Programs and Services for Migrants under the chairmanship of Frank Galbally, a noted Melbourne criminal defence lawyer, and rumoured to be under the patronage of the then Liberal Prime Minister, Malcolm Fraser. The Review was commissioned on 1 September 1977 and the Galbally Committee, as it became known, made its report on 30 May 1978 (Galbally, 1978). It was formally presented to the Federal House of Representatives by the Prime Minister in November 1978, in a manner analogous to Prime Minister Trudeau's presentation of the Canadian equivalent to the House of Commons seven years previously (Minister of State Multiculturalism, 1978, p. 45).

Even by Australian standards of political expediency and cynical pragmatism the speed of carrying out the review was remarkable. The section on education (Galbally, 1978, Chapter 9) has many shortcomings and oversimplifications about the concepts of culture and race that indicate hasty preparation and lack of theoretical competence in the social sciences on the part of the committee members (see fuller discussion in Bullivant, 1981b, p. 187 et passim). More general recommendations were, inter alia: to phase out the Good Neighbour Movement; the establishment of multicultural resource centres, to support self-help activities by ethnic groups; special provisions for workers to be appointed by ethnic communities to work in childcare centres and pre-schools 'to foster a multicultural approach and to help bridge the gap between school and home' (Galbally, 1978, p. 14).

The review also recommended the establishment of an Australian Institute of Multicultural Affairs (AIMA) to conduct research into multiculturalism, prepare material on the cultural and racial background of immigrants, and advise the Government through the Minister on preparing programmes and policies appropriate to a multicultural society (Galbally, 1978, pp. 108–9). The Institute was set up in 1979 with Mr Galbally himself as Chairman of Council, and a former member of the Prime Minister's press corps as Director. Both appointments were criticised at the time as being political patronage.

The subsequent work of the Institute did little to counter the strong feelings among academics and ethnic communities that it was an ideological arm of the Government designed to promote multiculturalism uncritically. Its *Review of Multicultural and Migrant Education* (AIMA, 1980), published in mid-1980, was similarly criticised for ideological bias, and also for highly selective research surveys, slanted reporting of findings and even outright distortion of results (Council of the Australian Institute of Multicultural Affairs, 1984). These and other criticisms of AIMA led to its operation being reviewed during 1983 and 1984 by an independent committee. The Chairman, Frank Galbally, was asked to resign and the director's position was made vacant and advertised for open competition in November 1984. The charter and name of the Institute are to be modified. Whether all these measures will result in a significantly less biased mode of operation is unknown at the date of writing.

The educational recommendations of the Galbally Committee broadly followed those of the Australian Ethnic Affairs Council before it (Galbally, 1978, 106):

> . . . our schools and school systems should be encouraged to develop more rapidly various initiatives aimed at improving the understanding of the different histories, cultures, languages and attitudes of those who make up our society . . . for example through greater allocation of resources to the teaching of histories, cultures and languages (both English and other languages), through development of bilingual teaching . . .

Ethnic schools were strongly encouraged to teach community languages and cultures. All these measures were backed by large allocations of federal funding.

A further recommendation of the Galbally Committee was to form an Australia-wide Committee on Multicultural Education consisting of acknowledged experts in the field (Galbally, 1978, p. 108). The Committee was approved on 30 June 1978, one month after the Galbally Report was presented, and before it had been formally accepted in Parliament. The Schools Commission was authorised to establish the Committee and did so with pre-emptive alacrity. It was small, and did not contain any recognised Australian experts on ethnic pluralism or migrant education. Even before it presented its final report to the Schools Commission on 5 January 1979 (Committee on Multicultural Education, 1979), it had already made recommendations to the Schools Commission on the allocation of $0.5 million provided under the Multicultural Education Program so that the Commission could include them in its 1978 report to the Government (Schools Commission, 1978).

Again, expediency won out and educational decisions about teaching community languages were supported for what appear to have been political reasons. The Report of the Committee on Multicultural Education itself, *Education for a Multicultural Society* (the McNamara Report) was admittedly a hastily prepared document. Ideologically, it was thoroughly normative and prescriptive about the future (Committee on Multicultural Education, 1979, pp. 8–9): 'Australia should seek to become a society where the preservation of the identity of cultural groups and interaction among them is encouraged . . . Australian society should promote a degree of cultural and social variation'. The Committee also adopted a view of the concept of culture similar to that of the Galbally Committee, based on the well known, but theoretically outmoded, definition of Tylor (1871). However, it is inherently limited for far-reaching policy-making to adopt '*the most common, popular usage* in education which equates culture with a social group's heritage, i.e. traditions, history, language, arts and other aesthetic achievements, religious customs and values' (Committee on Multicultural Education, 1979, p. 68, my italics).

Despite these theoretical weaknesses, the McNamara Report became the base document on which the Commonwealth Multicultural Education Program was subsequently developed. It proposed six major interrelated core elements to be incorporated into school curricula. They clearly show that the emphasis is on the lifestyles of children from ethnic backgrounds rather than on their life chances. General programmes are recommended to enable all students to appreciate the 'dignity' of cultures within Australian society, while special programmes should aim to provide opportunities for all to study the historical, social, cultural, aesthetic and literary backgrounds and traditions of particular ethnic groups. On a wider scale, international and intercultural studies are recommended as a way of appreciating something of the countries in which the ethnic groups originated.

Languages are emphasised, and have become subsequently the major thrust of multicultural education. Community languages should be taught in schools to give all children an opportunity to study a language other than English, and English as a second language should be provided for students from non-English-speaking backgrounds to enhance their capacities to participate in the activities of the school and the wider society. A more contentious recommendation, as subsequent events have shown, is for schools to set up bilingual programmes to enable students to learn school subjects in a language other than English.

Two further recommendations, among several others of a structural nature, are enhanced support for ethnic schools as a way of achieving linguistic and cultural maintenance and the appointment of ethnic schools liaison officers. These would have a number of responsibilities all designed to provide a variety of support and advice on educational matters for ethnic communities.

The Committee also conceptualised ethnicity solely in cultural terms in its definition of cultural pluralism, despite the recognised theoretical weaknesses of doing so (see van den Berghe, 1975, p. 72; Bullivant, 1984). However, a more theoretically respectable, if still normative, model was adopted by the Commonwealth Education Portfolio, set up in 1979 to discuss and clarify the idea of Multicultural Australia. In its view (Commonwealth Education Portfolio, 1979, p. 18), multiculturalism describes:

> . . . an ideal society where groups would co-exist harmoniously, free to maintain many of their distinctive religious, linguistic or social customs, equal in their access to resources and services, civil rights and political power and sharing with the rest of the society particular concerns and values, which have national significance.

However, immediately following this definition, this Committee also notes that 'Multiculturalism (multicultural society) is popularly used to refer to a nation state where there is a variety of ethnic groups, e.g. Australia, Canada, USA'. This latter view is typical of the tendency common at the time, and since, to confuse the *sociopolitical theory* of multiculturalism with a description of society, and to equate a multicultural society with a multiethnic one.

Regular government reports dealing with immigration and pluralism followed those already mentioned in an attempt to clarify the real nature of Australian society. The Australian Population and Immigration Council and Australian Ethnic Affairs Council (APIC and AEAC) published a joint statement in June 1979 with the title *Multiculturalism and its Implications for Immigration Policy*. Its purpose was to advise the Liberal Government Minister for Immigration and Ethnic Affairs on matters affecting his portfolio, and 'to stimulate community discussion on issues of public importance leading to a general community understanding and acceptance of the goal of a socially cohesive multicultural Australian society' (APIC and AEAC, 1979, Foreword). The paper was one of the first *official* documents to recognise the dangers of interethnic competition and conflict inherent in unrestrained development of *structural* pluralism as a concomitant of *cultural* pluralism, although attention had been drawn to this by academic writers (e.g. Martin, 1978, p. 216). This theme recurs in one way or another throughout the whole statement. Multiculturalism is acceptable provided it is confined to ethnic cultural diversity mainly in the areas of private lifestyles and local associations. It is not acceptable and should legitimately be curtailed if ethnic groups develop their own institutions and structures parallel with and independent of those maintained by the Australian nation-state, to improve their life chances.

Educational provisions favoured by these councils stressed English language teaching for immigrants, and the teaching of ethnic community languages 'to the extent that resources and other commitments permit' (p. 13), provided this does not detract from the primary aim of learning the dominant language of English. The councils also '*welcome* attempts to enhance mutual understanding of the values and customs of different groups and would *deplore* any prejudice or insensitivity that might disregard or devalue equally valid – but different – cultural traditions (APIC and AEAC, 1979, original italics).

The normative tenor of this document, albeit with a very rational and balanced presentation of the pros and cons of multiculturalism, is far exceeded by the two publications that followed it. In April 1981 under the Liberal Government auspices, the Australian Ethnic Affairs Council was merged with the Australian Population and Immigration Council and the Australian Refugee Council (this last being a symptom of the demographic realities of the late 1970s and 1980s) to form the Australian Council on Population and Ethnic Affairs. This body set up an Ethnic Affairs Task Force which met a number of times, held consultations with individuals and organisations around Australia, and received over 300 submissions. The results were published in May 1982 as a policy discussion paper *Multiculturalism for All Australians: Our Developing Nationhood* (ACPEA, 1982), edited by ACPEA Chairman, Professor Zubrzycki. It was widely circulated and made the basis of public forums and consultations held during the period 27 June–28 July 1982 in the eight capital cities and other population centres in Australia. The report of the second round of consultations was published as *National Consultations on Multiculturalism and Citizenship* in August 1982 (Department of Immigration and Ethnic Affairs, 1982).

Both publications are an advance on the majority of previous official views, especially in adopting more theoretically acceptable definitions of ethnicity and explicitly taking Australian Aborigines into consideration. However, the normative approach of *Multiculturalism for All Australians* is clearly stated by Professor Zubrzycki (Department of Immigration and Ethnic Affairs, 1982, p. 2): '[It] is not a survey of current social arrangements, but a model to be worked towards – a vision of the future'. Not unexpectedly this vision is far from shared by all Australians, to judge from the antagonism and opposition to multiculturalism, continued immigration of Asians and Aboriginal land rights which were evident at the public forums, and acknowledged as being present by Zubrzycki himself (Department of Immigration and Ethnic Affairs, 1982).

The three principles of the multicultural ideology – social cohesion, cultural identity, and equality of opportunity – have had to be bolstered by a fourth that is equally idealistic. This is 'equal responsibility for, commitment to, and participation in society' (ACPEA, 1982, p. 12). It would seem that proponents of multiculturalism have reached the stage where mounting challenges, or at least indifference, to it are forcing them to reformulate the ideology to negate claims by counter-ideologists and strengthen its legitimacy (Vaughan & Archer, 1971). The role of Professor Zubrzycki, like that of A. J. Grassby before him, assumes considerable significance in the process. Although he is a sociologist of some eminence, his views reflect the period of sociological theorising when 'grand theory' and holistic, consensus models of society and the world were in vogue, along the lines of his contemporary, Talcott Parsons. Maintaining interethnic consensus and cohesion may also have been politically desirable during the period between 1975 and 1982, when the Liberal Government under Prime Minister Malcolm Fraser held power. Added to Professor Zubrzycki's somewhat utopian vision of Australian society, such expediency would help to colour the publications for which he was responsible as Chairman of the AEAC in 1977 and the subsequent organisations and the Ethnic Affairs Task Force in 1982.

The Liberal Government was soundly defeated in March 1983, and the socialist Labor Government under Prime Minister Robert Hawke assumed power. Immigration became a major issue early in 1984 with the controversy generated by Professor Geoffrey Blainey, an eminent historian at Melbourne University. In a number of speeches and articles he warned, on the basis of past experience, that increased support for immigrants from Asian countries, most particularly Indochina, could generate antagonism from Anglo-Australians and longer-established immigrant settlers that could flare up into open conflict at a time when unemployment is high (Blainey, 1984). Reduced immigration from British and traditional European sources revealed by the statistics exacerbated the problem and made it appear that the Labor Government was giving preference to Asians. The matter threatened to become a major issue for the 1984 December Federal elections, but was defused by tacit consent of all political parties.

During the same period, Aboriginal land rights and increasingly insistent claims to former 'sacred sites' also became a contentious problem (see for background Bullivant, 1984, especially Chapters 1, 2 and 4). Together with the Asian immigration issue, it heightened the race awareness of many people to the point where opinion polls clearly indicated considerable Anglo-Australian antagonism towards Asians and Aborigines and support for Blainey's views (Gallup Poll, 1984). Official government attempts to reduce racial tensions invoked the multicultural ideology and allied it to the political 'consensus' ideology assiduously promoted by Prime Minister Hawke.

More direct pressure amounting to a form of 'sentimental censorship' was exerted over the mass media, especially radio and television. By a process of inverted racism and positive discrimination favouring Asians and Aborigines, even well-informed and rational academics and commentators were likely to be branded as racists if they ventured to comment on, let alone criticise, immigration and land rights issues. Radio and television announcers had perforce to fall into line and such matters virtually vanished from the airways: an ironical and disturbing example of Orwellian thought control coinciding with celebrations of the arrival of the year 1984 on the same mass media.

EDUCATIONAL DEVELOPMENTS IN THE 1980S

Education has thus had to come to terms with numerous, and often conflicting, social, political, cultural and ideological forces since the Galbally Report. The ideology of multiculturalism has been strongly attacked by academic conservatives (e.g. Chipman,

1978; 1980; Knopfelmacher, 1982) on the grounds that it is socially divisive and could lead to ghettoisation. Criticism has also employed Marxist analysis. Thus Jakubowicz (1984, p. 18) suggests that the ideology of multiculturalism is used by the Australian government as a means of hegemonic control: 'It is the invalidation of the class history of ethnic Australians and the reconstruction of their experience and histories in their countries of origin and in Australia as totally cultural . . . that is the effective outcome of multi-culturalism as ideology'.

Although the present writer also used a comparable analysis and concept of ethnic hegemony to arrive at a broadly similar conclusion (Bullivant, 1981b; 1981c), his recent work extending Banton (1983) and Parkin (1974) is an attempt to generate a more eclectic perspective (Bullivant, 1984). This proposes that Australian pluralism is *multi-faceted*. Processes of exclusion and inclusion involve groups in symbolically erecting 'boundaries' around those to be included and those to be excluded in attempts to maximise social rewards and economic resources. Reconstruction and mystification of historical experiences assist these processes.

Racial, cultural, ethnic, class and even gender differences can be adopted as boundary markers. However, they are not always used in this way, but become salient only as soon as some groups in a pluralist society become aware of their potential as boundary markers when they want to discriminate in some way against other groups. Race awareness, ethnic awareness and class awareness are necessary but not sufficient precursors for discrimination or prejudice against others to occur. They are triggered off by historical, social, economic and political situations and circumstances, as Schermerhorn (1970, p. 6) has suggested following extensive research.

In attempts to achieve a fairer share of power and maximise their advantage, minority groups use their own methods of inclusion and exclusion in the process of 'usurpation'. For such manoeuvres groups and individuals draw on the relevant knowledge and ideas about appropriate methods of inclusion, exclusion and usurpation encoded in their respective cultures. These can also include reconstructing history and mystifying the causes of their minority status – a strategy used successfully by Australian Aboriginal activists, for example.

The *situationality* of such processes must also be taken into account (see also Okamura, 1981). Members of both dominant and minority groups do not use ethnic or other distinguishing features all the time in processes of inclusion, exclusion or usurpation, let alone in the daily routines of making a living or carrying on normal social activities. Each of the distinguishing features is employed according to the situation, and this in turn changes according to historical circumstances. Variations between 'segments' within ethnic categories, and in degrees of accommodation across ethnic and class boundaries, must also be taken into account, to avoid treating ethnic or class groups as homogeneous entities or quasi-communities. The type of multicultural education to match this perspective must be much more power-sensitive and concerned with a survival curriculum for *all* children in Australian society (Bullivant, 1981a).

Conventional types of multicultural education cannot accommodate this type of analysis. For instance, the Australian theorist George Smolicz (1981) sees 'stable multiculturalism' as a desirable condition – the classical normative value judgement – and proposes that schools should teach the shared core values of Australian culture and the English language, and ethnic values. The latter are to include ethnic literature, ethnic community languages and literary criticism, religion, historical continuity and sense of peoplehood. Smolicz (1981, p. 137) places most emphasis on what he terms 'ethnic literacy', i.e. acquaintance with the more literary aspects of an ethnic group's 'high' culture, which will provide the 'cultural hinterland' that he claims is the necessary basis of a culturally complete ethnic identity. In such ideas one can clearly see the influence of European neo-idealist schools of thought drawn especially from Znaniecki (1968) and other Polish theorists, who have consistently informed Smolicz's views. Political issues are not confronted.

More recently Smolicz (1984) has warned against the continued growth of ethnic schools because they contribute to ethnic separatism. Their proliferation has been encouraged by recommendations of the Galbally Review and subsequent financial funding from the Schools Commission. This has been one of the notable developments of the 1980s. Smolicz now concedes that many state schools are not giving priority to 'ethnic literacy'; nor are they equipping children from ethnic backgrounds with enough survival knowledge to gain rewarding life chances when they leave school. In consequence, he warns (Smolicz, 1984, p. 36) that more ethnic schools could be developed to carry out this task, so that 'there is a danger of a head-on ethnic clash over allocation of funds, employment status and job opportunities in a climate of economic stagnation'.

In fact, this kind of development is taking place. According to evidence communicated to me, Greek ethnic schools in Melbourne, at least, are moving away from a traditionally nationalistic curriculum to helping children to acquire English language and other sociopolitical skills needed for survival in Australia. A 'Greek-Australian' culture is developing which incorporates elements from Greek tradition and modern Anglo-Celtic aspects.

On the broader educational front, major organisational and ideological developments have taken place in the 1980s. Each State has an official advisory committee on multicultural education or its equivalent, and the efforts of these kinds of bodies are co-ordinated at the federal level by the National Advisory and Co-ordinating Committee on Multicultural Education. An Ethnic Affairs Commission or equivalent is part of each State's bureaucracy.

The Schools Commission has assumed the major role as ideological pacemaker and funding body for multicultural education. Its views on multiculturalism have shifted ground from the simplistic cultural approach characteristic of the 1970s to a more realistic, even if theoretically confused, appraisal of Australian pluralism. In its *Report for the Triennium 1982–84* (Schools Commission, 1981, p. 112) the Commission warns against naive, romantic approaches to multicultural education and is at least prepared to concede that 'The specifics of what is needed to achieve equal opportunity for all of those people [ethnics] have yet to be worked out, but most groups realise that this will not be achieved without political action and struggle'.

However, in a changing economic, social and racial context, more pressing problems may yet claim the Schools Commission's attention and funds. In its *Report for 1985: Response to Government Guidelines* (Schools Commission, 1984), the Commission has foreshadowed a review of the concept of 'need' (an echo of the 1973 preoccupation), initiatives for improving educational outcomes for Aboriginal children, and several reviews or programmes to improve the quality of schooling through Commonwealth funding. A Participation and Equity Program (incorporating the former Transition from School to Work Program) was set up in 1984 and includes provision for Aboriginal education. Funding for a Computer Education Program established in 1984 is to continue, and is very much a sign of the times. 'The Curriculum Development Centre has been reactivated within the Schools Commission and will address improvements in basic areas such as mathematics, computer studies, Aboriginal studies and educational outcomes for girls' (Schools Commission, 1984, p. 58). These are also signs of the times.

Multicultural education does not feature in the agenda of this born-again organisation. However, it finds support through Schools Commission funding of $4.752 million, which includes $380 000 for 'projects of national significance' in the area of multicultural education. Ethnic schools will continue to be supported ($3.975 million), as will ESL teaching in both Government programmes ($50.188 million) and non-Government programmes ($18.203 million). Predictably, these last two gain the lion's share, and clearly indicate where the Schools Commission's priorities lie. In one sense they are quasi-assimilationist rather than really pluralist, as priority is clearly placed on learning the dominant language of English.

Meanwhile in most schools the teaching of multicultural education is generally confined to minor 'additive' courses about the *lifestyles* of major ethnic groups rather than there being a major reconstruction of the whole curriculum that might truly reflect a multicultural Australia, whatever that is. 'National days', family life, the more exotic customs, ethnic foods, costumes, religions and similar aspects are most commonly tackled. Some growth in the teaching of ethnic community languages in school-based language centres or ethnic schools is evident, especially those of the big groups, e.g. Greeks, Italians and Germans. Some Asian languages are also being taught. These developments have been accompanied by rapid expansion in the numbers of ethnic community language teachers, even though many have had no formal teacher training. The Victorian State Board of Education and Ministerial Advisory Committee on Multicultural and Migrant Education circulated a Discussion Paper in 1984 on *The Place of Community Languages in Victorian Schools*. The future direction of multicultural education at this State level seems predictable, in the stress being placed on ethnic community languages.

However, from evidence from practising teachers and researchers known to me, many schools have made only token efforts in other areas. Virtually nothing is being done to politicise multicultural education and make the curriculum more power-sensitive to the needs of ethnic children's life chances. If the logic of Anglo-Celtic ethnic hegemony holds, this might have been expected, multiculturalism being an ideal vehicle for mystifying ethnic relations (Bullivant, 1981b, Chapter 8).

CONCLUSION

It is not possible to arrive at a more accurate overall assessment of the situation regarding multicultural education in Australia, as there is considerable variation between states. However, some indication of the 'state of the art' can be gained from the proceedings of two Leadership Institutes on Multicultural Education which took place in May and September 1982 under the auspices of the prestigious but conservative and ideologically 'safe' Australian College of Education. They brought together people from a wide range of backgrounds in education – academics, educationists of all types, ethnic group spokespeople and, for the first time, Aboriginal representatives – for intensive discussions and analysis of current trends.

Two findings of the Institutes were clear. Firstly, there was a diversity of views on multicultural education and a 'variety of both political and educational stances which precludes arriving at consensus statements' (Falk and Harris, 1983, p. 2). Secondly, the multicultural nature of Australia cannot be taken for granted. Alan Kerr (1983, p. 118), one of the participants, suggested that the present social policy is one of 'social cohesion with cultural diversity'. This does not necessarily mean multiculturalism, despite its similarity to the official ideology, but could reflect a growing preference for the option of assimilation *with* accommodation. As Kerr puts it:

> Australian social policy thus still insists on some degree of assimilation, particularly through the adoption of certain core values, however badly they are defined. It also officially supports some degree of accommodation, as for example in official support for the preservation of ethnic languages and cultures. But . . . we are in a period of transition. We are, as a nation, in a holding position as we consider the options available to us.

A more recent picture of multicultural education in Australia is provided by the Review of the Commonwealth Multicultural Education Program carried out by a review team from the Language and Literacy Centre of the Melbourne-based Phillip Institute of Technology (Review Team of the Language and Literacy Centre, Phillip Institute of Technology, 1984). It found that all is not well with the programme despite some obvious achievements. An emphasis on community language maintenance by ethnic community leaders has worked against the aim of 'educating all children about tolerance, harmony and intercultural understanding'. Many school-based projects were unsuccessful for a variety of reasons, and there is little support among teachers for the aim that the school system should make pupils bilingual. There is widespread lack of understanding among teachers about ethnic groups and the concept of ethnicity. Lack of firm coordination of the programme at the national level is apparent and needs to be much improved. The Review Team concluded (Review Team of the Language and Literacy Centre, Phillip Institute of Technology, 1984, p. 318) that 'it is not convinced that, despite its many accomplishments, the Commonwealth Multicultural Education Program has during its initial growth stage brought about substantial and lasting change in the Australian schooling system and in the learning programs it offers'. A potentially contentious observation (p. 329) is that the name 'multicultural' is 'in some ways a misnomer for the program . . . A more suitable name . . . especially if the language aspect were parcelled out, would seem to be "intercultural", and its aim would be to create intercultural understanding'. Such an approach would not assist the life chances of children from ethnic backgrounds.

Together with the two statements from the Leadership Institutes, these findings are probably as accurate a summation of the current situation confronting multicultural education in Australia as can be obtained. As has happened so often in the nation's historical 'ideological transformations in the recreation of hegemony', there is no predicting where policy shifts and ideological developments will next take the multicultural debate.

NOTES

1. 'Immigrants' and 'migrants' are used interchangeably throughout this chapter.
2. Despite this criticism this is still the most usual method of TESL in the 1980s.
3. Changes have occurred since the Council was incorporated into a wider organisation, the Australian Council on Population and Ethnic Affairs, in 1981.
4. Since retired to Emeritus Professor status.

REFERENCES

Apple, M. (1979) *Ideology and Curriculum*. London: Routledge and Kegan Paul.

Australian Bureau of Statistics (1984) *Year Book Australia No. 68, 1984*. Canberra: Australian Bureau of Statistics.

Australian Council on Population and Ethnic Affairs (1982) *Multiculturalism for All Australians: Our Developing Nationhood*. Canberra: Australian Government Publishing Service.

Australian Ethnic Affairs Council (1977) *Australia as a Multicultural Society*. Submission to the Australian Population and Immigration Council on the Green Paper, *Immigration Policies and Australia's Population*. Canberra: Australian Government Publishing Service.

Australian Institute of Multicultural Affairs (1980) *Review of Multicultural and Migrant Education*. Melbourne: AIMA.

Australian Labor Party (1975) *Platform Constitution and Rules as approved by the 31st National Conference, Terrigal, 1975*. Barton: Australian Labor Party, National Secretariat.

Australian Population and Immigration Council (1977) *Immigration Policies and Australia's Population*. Green Paper. Canberra: Australian Government Publishing Service.

Australian Population and Immigration

Council and Australian Ethnic Affairs Council (1979) *Multiculturalism and its Implications for Immigration Policy*. Canberra: Australian Government Publishing Service.

Banton, M. (1983) *Racial and Ethnic Competition*. Cambridge: Cambridge University Press.

Berry, J. A. (1969) The stereotypes of Australian states. *Australian Journal of Psychology*, **21**, 227–33.

Blainey, G. (1984) *All for Australia*. North Ryde: Methuen Haynes.

Bourdieu, P. (1973) Cultural reproduction and social reproduction. In Brown, R. (ed.), *Knowledge, Education, and Cultural Change*. London: Tavistock.

Bullivant, B. M. (1970) Taking a cultural view of Asia through the social sciences. *Social Studies Journal*, **1**(1), 4–6.

Bullivant, B. M. (1972) The cultural reality of curriculum development. *Education News*, **13**(9), 14–16.

Bullivant, B. M. (ed.) (1973) *Educating the Immigrant Child: Concepts and Cases*. Sydney: Angus & Robertson.

Bullivant, B. M. (1974) *The Study of Cultural Change: A Classroom Approach*. Melbourne: Australian Council for Educational Research.

Bullivant, B. M. (1975) Implications of the

Australian Schools Commission for the education of immigrants. In Allwood, L. M. (ed.), *Australian Schools. The Impact of the Australian Schools Commission*, pp. 122–34. Melbourne: Australia International Press.

Bullivant, B. M. (1978) *The Way of Tradition. Life in an Orthodox Jewish School.* Melbourne: Australian Council for Educational Research.

Bullivant, B. M. (1981a) *Race, Ethnicity and Curriculum.* Melbourne: Macmillan Australia.

Bullivant, B. M. (1981b) *The Pluralist Dilemma in Education: Six Case Studies.* Sydney: George Allen & Unwin.

Bullivant, B. M. (1981c) Multiculturalism – pluralist orthodoxy or ethnic hegemony? *Canadian Ethnic Studies*, **XIII** (2), 1–22.

Bullivant, B. M. (1983) Cultural reproduction in Fiji: who controls knowledge/power? *Comparative Education Review*, **27**(2), 227–45.

Bullivant, B. M. (1984) *Pluralism: Cultural Maintenance and Evolution.* Clevedon: Multilingual Matters.

Calwell, A. A. (1972) *Be Just and Fear Not.* Melbourne: Lloyd O'Neil.

Chipman, L. (1978) Multicultural myth. *Quadrant*, **22**(3), 50–55.

Chipman, L. (1980) The menace of multiculturalism. *Quadrant*, **24**(10), 3–6.

Committee on Multicultural Education, Schools Commission, Australia (1979) *Education for a Multicultural Society.* Report to the Schools Commission. Canberra: Schools Commission.

Committee on the Teaching of Migrant Languages in Schools (1976) *Report.* Canberra: Australian Government Publishing Service.

Commonwealth Education Portfolio (1979) *Discussion Paper on Education in a Multicultural Australia.* Canberra: Department of Education.

Council of the Australian Institute of Multicultural Affairs (1984) *Looking Forward:* Report on Consultations Concerning the Recommendations of the Committee of Review of the Australian Institute of Multicultural Affairs Melbourne: AIMA.

Department of Immigration and Ethnic Affairs (1982) *National Consultations on Multiculturalism and Citizenship.* Canberra: Australian Government Publishing Service.

Falk, B. & Harris, J. (ed.) (1983) *Unity in Diversity: Multicultural Education in Australia.* Carlton, Victoria: The Australian College of Education.

Galbally, F. (1978) *Migrant Services and Programs.* Report of the Review of Post-arrival Programs and Services for Migrants. Canberra: Australian Government Publishing Service.

Gallup Poll (1984) 'Too tough' on Blainey, *Sun*, 28 August, p. 15.

Gould, J. (1964) Ideology. In Gould, J. & Kolb, W. L. (ed.), *A Dictionary of the Social Sciences*, pp. 315–7. London: Tavistock.

Grassby, A. J. (1973) *A Multicultural Society for the Future.* Canberra: Australian Government Publishing Service.

Grassby, A. J. (1984) *The Tyranny of Prejudice.* Melbourne: AE Press.

Harris, R. McL. (1979) Anglo-conformism, interactionism, and cultural pluralism: a study of Australian attitudes to migrants. In de Lacey, P. R. & Poole, M. E. (ed.), *Mosaic or Melting Pot. Cultural Evolution in Australia*, pp. 23–39. Sydney: Harcourt Brace Jovanovich.

Hill, B. (1977) *The Schools.* Ringwood, Victoria: Penguin Books.

Jakubowicz, A. (1984) State and ethnicity: multiculturalism as ideology. In Jupp, J. (ed.), *Ethnic Politics in Australia*, pp. 14–28. Canberra: George Allen & Unwin.

Johnston, K. (1983) Discourse for all seasons? An ideological analysis of the Schools Commission Reports, 1973 to 1981. *Australian Journal of Education*, **27**(1), 17–32.

Jupp, J. (1966) *Arrivals and Departures.* Melbourne: Cheshire-Lansdowne.

Jupp, J. (ed.) (1984) *Ethnic Politics in Australia.* Sydney: George Allen & Unwin.

Kerr, A. (1983) A national language policy. In Falk, B. & Harris, J. (ed.), *Unity in Diversity: Multicultural Education in Australia*, pp. 116–24. Carlton, Victoria: The Australian College of Education.

Knopfelmacher, F. (1982) The case against multiculturalism. In Manne, R. (ed.), *The New Conservatism in Australia*, pp. 40–64. Melbourne: Oxford University Press.

Kovacs, M. L. & Cropley, A. J. (1975) *Immigrants and Society: Alienation and*

Assimilation. Sydney: McGraw-Hill.

Lepervanche, M. de (1980) From race to ethnicity. *Australian and New Zealand Journal of Sociology*, **16**(1), 24–37.

Lunn, H. (1979) The willing workers. *The Weekend Australian Magazine 3*, 13–14 October.

Lynch, P. R. (1970) Australian House of Representatives, *Parliamentary Debates*, vol. 67, 1970, pp. 1521–2. Canberra: Australian Government Printer.

Martin, J. I. (1965) *Refugee Settlers*. Canberra: ANU Press.

Martin, J. I. (1972) *Migrants – Equality and Ideology*. Meredith Memorial Lecture. Melbourne: La Trobe University.

Martin, J. I. (1976) The education of migrant children in Australia. In Price, C. A. & Martin, J. I. (ed.), *Australian Immigration: A bibliography and digest, No. 3, Part 2, 1975*, pp. 1–65. Canberra: The Australian National University, Department of Demography.

Martin, J. I. (1978) *The Migrant Presence*. Sydney: George Allen & Unwin.

Menadue, J. L. (1981) *Language as a Neglected Resource*. Address to Future Directions Conference on Resource Management. Sponsored by Australian Frontier Inc. Canberra: Department of Immigration and Ethnic Affairs.

Minister of State Multiculturalism (1978) *Multiculturalism and the Government of Canada*. Ottawa: Ministry of Supply and Services, Canada.

Okamura, J. Y. (1981) Situational ethnicity. *Ethnic and Racial Studies*, **4**(4), 452–65.

Parkin, F. (ed.) (1974) *The Social Analysis of Class Structure*. London: Tavistock.

Passow, A. H., Goldberg, M. & Tannenbaum, A. J. (ed.) (1967). *Education of the Disadvantaged*. New York: Holt, Rinehart and Winston.

Price, C. A. (ed.) (1971) *Australian Immigration: A bibliography and digest, No. 2, 1970*. Canberra: The Australian National University, Department of Demography.

Price, C. A. (1976) Australian immigration: The Whitlam Government 1972–75. Pp. A1–A57 In Price, C. A. & Martin, J. I. (ed.), *Australian Immigration: A bibliography and digest, No. 3, Part 1, 1975*. Canberra: The Australian National University, Department of Demography.

Price, C. A. (1983) Multicultural Australia: demographic background. In Falk, B. & Harris, J. (ed.), *Unity in Diversity: Multicultural Education in Australia*, pp. 6–25. Carlton, Victoria: The Australian College of Education.

Price, C. A. & Martin, J. I. (ed.) (1976). *Australian Immigration: A bibliography and digest, No. 3, Parts 1 and 2, 1975*. Canberra: The Australian National University, Department of Demography.

Review Team of the Language and Literacy Centre, Phillip Institute of Technology (Victoria) (1984) *Review of the Commonwealth Multicultural Education Program*. Report to the Commonwealth Schools Commission, vol. 1. Canberra: Commonwealth Schools Commission.

Rooth, J. S. (1968) The Immigration Programme. In Throssell, H. (ed.), *Ethnic Minorities in Australia. The Welfare of Aborigines and Migrants*, pp. 57–72. Sydney: Australian Council of Social Service.

Schermerhorn, R. A. (1970) *Comparative Ethnic Relations. A Framework for Theory and Research*. New York: Random House.

School and Society Course Team (1971) *School and Society: A Sociological Reader*. London: Routledge and Kegan Paul and The Open University Press.

Schools Commission, Australian, Interim Committee (1973) *Schools in Australia: Report of the Interim Committee for the Australian Schools Commission* (The Karmel Report). Canberra: Australian Government Publishing Service.

Schools Commission, Australian (1975) *Report for the Triennium 1976–78*. Canberra: Australian Government Publishing Service.

Schools Commission, Australian (1978) *Report for the Triennium 1979–81*. Canberra: Government Publishing Service.

Schools Commission, Australian (1981) *Report for the Triennium 1982–84*. Canberra: Australian Government Publishing Service.

Schools Commission, Commonwealth (1984) *Report for 1985: Response to Government Guidelines*. Canberra: Commonwealth Schools Commission.

Smolicz, J. J. (1981) Cultural pluralism and educational policy: in search of stable multiculturalism. *The Australian Journal of Education,* **25**(2), 121–45.

Smolicz, J. J. (1984) Who's afraid of bilingualism? *Education News,* **18**(5), 36–9.

Snedden, W. (1969) *The Age,* 19 September.

Taft, R. (1965) *From Stranger to Citizen.* Perth: University of Western Australia Press.

Thompson, L. & Hostetler, J. H. (1970) The Hutterian Confession of Faith: a documentary analysis. *The Alberta Journal of Educational Research,* **16**(1), 29–45.

Tylor, E. B. (1871) *Primitive Culture.* London: John Murray.

van den Berghe, P. L. (1975) Ethnicity and class in Highland Peru. In Despres, L. A. (ed.), *Ethnicity and Resource Competition in Plural Societies,* pp. 71–85. The Hague: Mouton.

Vaughan, M. & Archer, M. S. (1971) *Social Conflict and Educational Change in England and France 1789–1849.* Cambridge: Cambridge University Press.

Victorian State Board of Education and Ministerial Advisory Committee on Multicultural and Migrant Education (1984), *The Place of Community Languages in Victorian Schools.* Melbourne: Department of Education.

Weber, M. (1968) In Roth, G. & Wittich, C., *Economy and Society.* New York: Bedminister Press.

Wynhausen, E. (1981) The survival of White Australia. *The National Times,* 13–19 September.

Yarwood, A. T. (1964) *Asian Migration to Australia.* Melbourne: Melbourne University Press.

Young, M. F. D. (ed.) (1971) *Knowledge and Control: New Directions for the Sociology of Education.* London: Collier-Macmillan.

Znaniecki, F. (1968) *The Method of Sociology.* New York: Octagon Books.

Zubrzycki, J. (1964) *Settlers of the Latrobe Valley: A Sociological Study of Immigrants in the Brown Coal Industry in Australia.* Canberra: ANU Press.

Zubrzycki, J. (1968) The questing years. In Australian Citizenship Convention, *Digest.* Canberra: Department of Immigration.

Zubrzycki, J. (1977) The formation of the Australian Ethnic Affairs Council. Speech to the Inaugural Meeting by Chairman, Professor Jerzy Zubrzycki, MBE, FASSA, Canberra, 23 March, 1977. *Ethnic Studies,* 1(2), 62–7.

BIBLIOGRAPHY

Australian Council on Population and Ethnic Affairs (1982) *Multiculturalism for All Australians: Our Developing Nationhood.* Canberra: Australian Government Publishing Service. This presents the most recent official government policy of multiculturalism and its intended consequences for education and other major institutions.

Banton, M. (1983) *Racial and Ethnic Competition.* Cambridge: Cambridge University Press. This book provides essential theoretical background for understanding rational choice theory and power relationships in pluralist societies.

Bourdieu, P. & Passeron, J.-C. (1977) *Reproduction in Education, Society and Culture.* London: Sage. One of the key expositions of Bourdieu's central contention that social and economic inequalities are reproduced through schooling and the curriculum.

Bullivant, B. M. (ed.) (1973) *Educating the Immigrant Child: Concepts and Cases.* Sydney: Angus & Robertson. A book, in advance of its time, that used case study data to develop multicultural and intercultural approaches to the curriculum and classroom practice.

Bullivant, B. M. (1981) *Race, Ethnicity and Curriculum.* Melbourne: Macmillan Australia. An anthropological analysis of the bases of discrimination, prejudice and inequalities in pluralist societies which provides the logic for a model of a survival curriculum to assist the life chances of ethnic minority children.

Bullivant, B. M. (1981) *The Pluralist Dilemma in Education: Six Case Studies.* Sydney: George Allen & Unwin. An influential comparative study of pluralist education in six countries, which argues that the multicultural approach is a concealed way of restricting the life chances of ethnic minority children by emphasising additive elements in the curriculum that focus on their lifestyles.

Bullivant, B. M. (1984) *Pluralism: Cultural Maintenance and Evolution*. Clevedon: Multilingual Matters. Develops a multifaceted model of pluralism and power in a pluralist society.

Committee on Multicultural Education, Schools Commission, Australia (1979) *Education for a Multicultural Society*. Report to the Schools Commission. Canberra: Schools Commission. One of the most influential official publications, which became the base document for the Government's Multicultural Education Program.

Falk, B. & Harris, J. (ed.) (1983) *Unity in Diversity: Multicultural Education in Australia*. Carlton, Victoria: The Australian College of Education. An informative review of the 'state of the art' at the school level in multicultural education based on two major symposia in 1982.

Galbally, F. (1978) *Migrant Services and Programs*. Report of the Review of Post-arrival Programs and Services for Migrants (the Galbally Report). Canberra: Australian Government Publishing Service. The seminal report which officially initiated the present multicultural ideology and policies underlying most Commonwealth and state provisions in Australia.

Jupp, J. (1966) *Arrivals and Departures*. Melbourne: Cheshire-Lansdowne. Of

major historical interest as one of the first critical analyses of the Australian immigration experience up to the mid-1960s.

Jupp, J. (ed.) (1984) *Ethnic Politics in Australia*. Sydney: George Allen & Unwin. A useful collection of essays from leading theorists focusing on the political issues involved in major institutions due to the pluralist nature of the society.

Martin, J. I. (1978) *The Migrant Presence*. Sydney: George Allen & Unwin. This book by a leading theorist is of major importance as an incisive critique of the discrimination towards immigrants that has been a feature of many institutions in Australia during the period after the Second World War.

Review Team of the Language and Literacy Centre, Phillip Institute of Technology (Victoria) (1984) *Review of the Commonwealth Multicultural Education Program*. Report to the Commonwealth Schools Commission, vol. 1. Canberra: Commonwealth Schools Commission. This report provides the most up-to-date and detailed analysis of all facets of multicultural education in Australia, showing both the achievements and the many weaknesses of the program.

Smolicz, J. J. (1979) *Culture and Education in a Pluralist Society*. Canberra: Curriculum Development Centre. A theoretical analysis of cultural pluralism by a leading advocate of multiculturalism and maintenance of ethnic community languages and cultures in Australia.

Chapter 6

Multicultural Education in Western Europe[1]

JAMES LYNCH

THE AETIOLOGY OF CULTURAL PLURALISM IN EUROPE

Historically, there would appear to be three major contextual influences which set the scene for current perceptions of cultural pluralism and an educational response to that pluralism in the continent of Europe. Two are longstanding and the other is, relatively speaking, recent. The first of these is the early patchwork settlement of Europe by different linguistic and in some cases ethnic groups and the second is the later equally varied religious overlay. Concerning the former, the pattern of settlement was such that, when they emerged, no nation-state in Europe was monolingual and some were, manifestly and boldly, officially bilingual, trilingual and in the case of Switzerland quadrilingual. Even in those cases where nationalistic nation-states tried to enforce a rigidly monolingual policy, as in Germany and France, large minorities retained their native language or dialect.

To this day, to give a few examples, there are large Alsation-speaking minorities in the east of France and Breton speakers in the west. There are German speakers in French Belgium and Danish speakers in northern Germany. There are Swedish speakers in Denmark and Wends in East Germany. There are French, Ladin, Friulian and German speakers in Northern Italy and Hungarian and Slovene speakers in Austria, Basque speakers in France and Spain and Gaelic and Welsh speakers in the United Kingdom, Albanians in Yugoslavia and Greeks in Albania.

In terms of religion, the Reformation superimposed on the linguistic, ethnic and political maps of Europe a further plane of cultural complexity, whilst in Southern Europe in particular, large areas already owed their religious allegiance more to Byzantium and Islam than to Rome or Geneva. The ethnic dimension can be equally diffused, as in the case of the Lapps of Scandinavia, nomadic groups such as the Romanies, the Irish travellers and the Quinquis of Spain (Ashworth, 1980). The profusion of overlying factors is never contained within one nation-state and the result is a kaleidoscope of confusing variety. And so one could continue, were the point not already made that ethnic, cultural, linguistic and religious boundaries almost never coincide with the boundaries of the modern European nation-state in the way in which they may do elsewhere. From the beginning such states were culturally pluralist, although structurally and often educationally monolithic.

The third major precursor has been brought about rather more by economic than by historical and political factors, although the latter (including political motivation) should not be underestimated as, for example, in the political agreement between the Netherlands and Indonesia in 1949 which led to the settlement of 12 500 Ambonese or South Moluccans in the Netherlands. Notwithstanding substantial immigration to some countries in the nineteenth century and later, for instance the emigration of Poles to Imperial Germany, where there was substantial educational provision (Szeloch, 1984), the period after the Second World War saw the major economies ever more hungry for workers as the post-war economic miracle of Western Europe 'boomed'. The 'white-hot' economic activity drew large numbers of migrant workers first from colonies and former colonies, from Southern Europe and then from round the globe. In some cases, these immigrants came from former colonial possessions, as in the case of the United Kingdom, France and to a certain degree Belgium and the Netherlands. In the case of the United Kingdom, large numbers of citizens of the Irish Republic continued to arrive throughout the post-war period, making them the largest immigrant group in the country.

In some cases, the migrant workers came from the poorer regions of Europe and were regarded as relatively easily assimilable. Later they came from further afield, the Far East, Africa, the Philippines, the West Indies, the Indian subcontinent, etc. Millions of 'migrant' workers arrived in the major economic centres of Western Europe in the decades up to 1980 and estimates place the numbers of migrant workers and their families in the European Economic Community countries at a peak of approximately 15 million in 1981, with countries such as France and West Germany each having in excess of 4 million (Ogden, 1982). Since that time numbers appear to have declined as a consequence of the recession and, in 1984, there were estimated to be 6 million migrant workers in the states of the European Economic Community. With their families, the figure rises to 12 million, of whom approximately 73 per cent were from outside the Community (Conservative Research Department, 1984, p. 211).

Whether or not, in the first stage of migration, they came with the intention of staying or bringing their families, as was often the case in the United Kingdom, where migration was always more permanent and family-based, those immigrant workers who came alone gradually wanted to settle down, bring their families to join them, marry and raise their families. Few of them wanted to return home, and this second stage of familial settlement led automatically to the maturation of the immigration process (Van den Berg-Eldering, 1983, pp. 215ff). In some countries, for instance the United Kingdom, nationality laws meant that they either were already, or could rapidly become, citizens of their new home country. A distinctly identifiable group was also formed by the successive influxes of refugees, often seeking political asylum.

In the early post-war period, millions of inhabitants of former German territories arrived in West Germany and many more came from the People's Republic of East

Germany. In the late 1960s millions of French North Africans of European descent emigrated from Algeria to France. Each political upheaval in Eastern Europe released its flood of refugees and more recently many have come from the Third World.

In a recent book considering general trends in migration to Europe in the post-war period, Castles has identified five major patterns, all of which are represented in the countries which we consider in this chapter (Castles et al., 1984):

(a) return migration of settlers from former colonies, such as the French North Africans of European descent from Algeria;
(b) immigration of ethnically distinct citizens of colonies and former colonies to the home territory of the colonial power, for example West Indians and Asians to Britain;
(c) labour migration, mainly of manual workers from Mediterranean countries, Finland and Ireland;
(d) migration of skilled employees between highly developed countries, for instance as part of work in international organisations and multinational companies;
(e) entry of foreign refugees seeking political asylum, including a high proportion from Third World countries in the period from the mid-1970s.

To this list must be added the 'indigenous' cultural minorities already referred to, both 'recognised' and 'unrecognised', and the already existing diversity of a linguistic, regional, religious, cultural and social-class variety. We are thus faced with an immense kaleidoscope of cultural pluralism, most of which has only very recently been perceived by the countries of Western Europe, and much of which remains unrecognised and unresponded to in broader social policies, let alone in the narrower field of education. This chapter will consider in outline the responses of five of the West European countries which have become 'multicultural societies', setting these responses in the context of broader international and bilateral policies.

EDUCATIONAL RESPONSES TO CULTURAL PLURALISM

The educational responses mounted to articulate to successive phases of migration are as varied as the reasons and sources of that migration. In some cases, settlers could easily be assimilated into existing provision: such was the case with the Irish and the *Volksdeutschen*. In other cases, parallel education systems were set up. In still others attempts at automatic assimilation were made and failed. Watson has suggested a three-part grouping of policy approaches to the provision of multicultural education: countries with a longstanding racial and cultural mix, such as the Soviet Union; countries with a cultural mix as a result of colonialism, e.g. the United Kingdom, France and Holland; and countries which have become multicultural and multiracial as a result of voluntary immigration, e.g. West Germany (Watson, 1981). These differences have resulted in different conceptualisations and apprehensions of cultural pluralism and therefore also different educational responses. In mainland Europe, for example, policies have been focused on the education of migrant children who are foreigners in their country of residence (see, for example, Mariet, 1980); in the United Kingdom, on the other hand, the migrant children are, in the majority, full British citizens or analogue British citizens in the case of the Irish.

In response to the complexity of the social and educational problems associated with the above picture, overarching educational initiatives have been attempted at three major levels: *international*, for instance through such organisations as the Standing Conference of European Ministers of Education, the Council of Europe and the European Economic Community; *national*, including *bilateral* country-to-country measures and agreements; and *local* and *regional*. Until the late 1970s such measures as were introduced were envisaged in most cases as relating to the needs of children of foreign migrant workers, who were regarded predominantly as temporary non-citizens who would eventually wish to return home to their country of origin. In the event, their labour has become a structural feature of the economies of the countries where they settled.

There was little linkage with the issues surrounding the so-called indigenous minorities referred to above, and only in the late 1970s and 1980s has a slightly broader conceptualisation, such as intercultural education in France, the Netherlands and West Germany, or multicultural education in the United Kingdom, been applied to the issue. The major assumption was that in so far as the migrants were citizens, for instance in the United Kingdom, they would be assimilated, and in so far as they were not citizens, they could be dealt with on a basis of cultural, social and educational special provisions, as in West Germany, Belgium and the Netherlands. In any case, the cultural adjustment was expected exclusively of the newly arrived minority, and little or no concession was made for their cultural traditions and values in the formal state system of education. Where dimensions from the minority culture entered the school arena, it was at the level of a folksy tokenism, of lifestyles rather than life chances.

The upshot of this 'tunnel vision' towards the new settlers was that few concessions were made to children with different languages and cultures: special instruction in the language of the host country in reception, or adaptation centres and schools, came into existence, sometimes also for adult workers, as did, more slowly, systems for the maintenance of links with the language and culture of origin (Mariet, 1980). Communities were gradually permitted to use school premises for home language instruction. Foreign teachers were recruited by the host countries for up to six years to teach children of their own nationality and language, either as part of the normal school curriculum or as a separate provision outside normal school hours, sometimes in school premises and sometimes not. Belgium, France, some West German states and, to a limited extent in the case of the consular-provided Italian teachers for outside-school classes, the United Kingdom adopted this approach. Some states in the Netherlands, Sweden and some parts of West Germany have recruited such teachers mainly from their own migrant communities. Only in Sweden has a right to such home language instruction been enshrined in public policy (Purnell, 1984a; 1984b).

Furthermore, the historical boundaries referred to earlier in this chapter, political, linguistic and religious, have acted as almost impermeable membranes to contain the way in which the issues surrounding the establishment and growth of new ethnic minority communities have been seen, conceptualised and responded to. The corollary of this approach has been that there has been little or no interchange of ideas, policies or findings across those boundaries except that developed recently by international organisations. Where it has commenced at all, conceptualisation of intercultural or multicultural education has taken place within a predominantly ethnocentric cocoon, and within states such as Belgium, where there is deep linguistic division woven into the very fabric of society, each linguistic group has adopted its own measures and there has been relatively little interchange, even of knowledge of how the other half has worked. This has probably impoverished developments and may have led to scarce resources becoming scarcer as each political, linguistic and religious host group has tended to 'rediscover the wheel'.

In the early 1970s a gradual change started to occur, partly, in the first instance, as a result of the oil crisis and economic recession. As long as labour demand had remained high, issues of the permanency of settlement, of the need to live together in cultural diversity and social harmony within the same nation-state, and of what kind of educational provision was now appropriate to the new pluralist cultural mosaic of society had remained masked. As a result of the economic upheavals of the early 1970s, however, the tide of immigration halted, as in France. In other cases, as in West Germany, it was actively stopped and even reversed for a few years, encouraged by payments to induce migrants to return to their country of origin. In some countries in these years, great damage was done to race relations by hasty policies on nationality and immigration, accentuated by the uneven social and economic settlement of the new arrivals, by the fact that they were politically and educationally naïve and by their often conservatively religious and frequently rural backgrounds.

INTERNATIONAL INITIATIVES

Into this scene a number of supranational initiatives began gradually to be injected. Already in 1972, the Council of Europe had commenced its support for experimental classes for the children of migrant workers aimed at *integrating* them into the school system and the general environment of the host country. A School Career and Health Record, on a simplified and uniform basis, was also designed, recommended to member countries and implemented on an experimental basis in some cases. In 1971 the Council for Cultural Co-operation launched a four-year programme for the training of teachers in charge of migrant children, and experts initiated pilot experiments in six member countries. Experimental INSET projects were offered in 1979–1980 and three pilot language projects were launched in 1978 (Standing Conference of European Ministers of Education, 1979). An ad hoc conference of the Standing Conference of European Ministers of Education, meeting in Strasbourg in 1974, met on the education of migrants and, in particular, opportunities for their vocational and technical training and education for adults and adolescents. Already in 1968, the Ministers' Deputies had adopted a resolution encouraging member governments to make greater efforts to enable migrant workers to learn the language of the reception country, and the Conference of European Ministers of Labour had resolved in Rome in 1972 to recommend further initiatives in the field of migrant workers' education and training to the Committee of Ministers of the Council of Europe, including pre-departure language instruction.

The ad hoc conference of 1974 focused on three main topics:

(a)   the situation of immigrants and their families on arrival in the host country;
(b)   measures to guarantee satisfactory education both before and during compulsory schooling in the host country;
(c)   action to give adult and teenage immigrants satisfactory opportunities for technical and vocational training and general education (Standing Conference of European Ministers of Education, 1974).

The Ninth Session of the Standing Conference of European Ministers of Education, meeting in Stockholm from 9 to 12 June 1975, endorsed the vast majority of the conclusions and recommendations of the Strasbourg meeting, and a group of experts was appointed to carry out a programme comprising a number of interrelated aspects. The consequent emphasis of what has come to be known as Resolution No. 2 (1975) on Migrant Education was then significantly tailored to:

(a)   promoting access to education and equality of opportunity;
(b)   guaranteeing continuing biculturalism in host and sending country culture and language;
(c)   moving forward from the phase of analysis to implementation and application of practical measures on behalf of migrants and their families (Standing Conference of European Ministers of Education, 1975).

The resolution and emphasis of the 1974 meeting were then echoed in subsequent meetings in Oslo (13–15 June 1976), for example Resolution 8, at the 1978 Athens Conference of European Ministers in Resolution No. 5, which encouraged participating countries to facilitate the maintenance of the national culture of migrant workers and their families, and in the annual experimental classes organised every year by the Council of Europe (Rey-van Allmen, 1979).

The work of the group, appointed after the 1975 meeting in Stockholm, had five major phases:

(a)   the analysis of a few significant pilot projects in several countries in the field of teacher training and the preparation of a consolidated report by M Louis Porcher, a member of the group (Porcher, 1979; 1981);
(b)   the production, for training centres and teachers, of a number of dossiers containing information about 'migrant-receiving' and 'migrant-sending' countries;
(c)   the launching of courses and pilot projects for the promotion of appropriate teacher training (e.g. training seminars in intercultural teaching);
(d)   the pilot production of teaching materials;
(e)   the compilation of a compendium of independent schemes, not directly related to the Council of Europe, but carried out using an intercultural approach (Council of Europe, 1983a).

Parallel to these initiatives, the Parliamentary Assembly of the Council of Europe and the Conference of Local and Regional Authorities of Europe (CLRAE) had begun to concentrate attention on second-generation migrants, advocating a series of specific measures in relation to them (Council of Europe, Conference of Local and Regional Authorities in Europe, 1978). Recommendation 841 of the Council of Europe Parliamentary Assembly recommended the preparation and implementation of a series of coordinated measures to provide better protection for second-generation migrants, including continuation of the periodic assessment of action taken, by the Standing Conference of European Ministers of Education, giving priority to pedagogic problems involved in the education of children and young people and promoting the training of teachers for the education of migrant children and young people (Parliamentary Assembly of the Council of Europe, 1978).

The efforts of the Conference of Authorities (CLRAE) emphasise the cultural policy of regions and municipalities and the teaching of language and bilingual education. In particular they have emphasised the role of practical measures, such as library provision, in the maintenance of links between migrants and their countries of origin (Council of Europe, Conference of Local and Regional Authorities in Europe, 1980).

The Council of Europe, through the working party mentioned above, has devoted a number of its European seminars for teachers at Donaueschingen in the Federal Republic of Germany to the training of teachers in the education of migrant children, for example, 24–28 September 1979, 22–27 September 1980, 19–24 October 1981 and 20–25 June 1983, and courses and symposia were organised at Lisbon in September 1981 and at L'Aquila in 1982 (Council of Europe and Ministero Pubblica Instruzione, 1982). A Teachers Guide to Intercultural Education was to be published at the end of 1984.

From 1980, Project No. 7 was launched with an expected duration of five years; it was committed to concentrating from an intercultural perspective on the relationships between:

(a) the school system and its immediate environment;
(b) the cultural activities in the school and outside the school;
(c) children's education and adult education (Rey, 1983).

The project group has adopted several different methods of work, including case studies and studies, visits to projects, the production of materials and colloquy meetings, of which there have been two, both in Strasbourg, one in December 1981 and one in January 1983. In addition, there have been a number of meetings of both the 'restricted group' and the full project group (Porcher, 1983).

In the Council of Europe's programme of activities and projects, 'multicultural' is seen as a factual description of the cultural situation and 'intercultural' as the pedagogic and other action which is taken in response to it. The main lines of such intercultural education are seen as follows:

1   It is the fundamental principle and aim underlying all school activity.
2.   Its field of reference is the real-life experience of children in the host country.
3.   It represents the broadening of existing concerns rather than the substitution of new educational targets for the basic functions of teaching in the school.

4. It involves an emphasis on the mutual influence of culture of origin and host culture on each other.
5. It embraces an acceptance of the new, dynamic and shifting cultural situation arising from migrants.
6. It implies a re-examination, revision and broadening of the sociocentric and ethnocentric standards of the school, going beyond its narrow framework.
7. It comprehends a broader scope embracing education and culture, children and adults.
8. It is a tool to evaluate life chances and to achieve an optimum of social and economic integration.

Interculturalism is seen by the group as possessing a common core of features universally accepted, comprising diversity as the overriding factor, identical features, the importance of interrelationships, theory and practice, values and outlooks, instrumental requirements, and migration as a total phenomenon.

Although not explicitly multicultural or intercultural, and only obliquely aimed at situations of racism, ethnicity and cultural conflict, the Council of Europe's work in the field of human rights education in schools, which dates from Resolution 41 of 1978 by the Committee of Ministers, is of importance for its commonality over areas of intercultural and multicultural education, which it provides both in principle and in substance. The Committee of Ministers has addressed this issue in a specific objective of its second medium-term plan and in its declaration of 14 May 1981 on intolerance (Council of Europe, 1983b).

The Council's work in this field has involved work with teachers, specialists and non-governmental organisations, and reports of meetings of experts and European teachers' seminars and dimensions in other reports, which culminated in the Vienna Symposium of May 1983 (Council of Europe, 1984). The central concept of the programme is that of co-existence, with an emphasis on education for countries where human rights are the basic ethic and the role of education is seen as highlighting abuses of human rights.

In this context it is also important to take note of the potential codification of the basic ethics for a multicultural society provided by international and European agreements such as the United Nations Declaration of Human Rights (1948), the European Convention on Human Rights (1950), the International Covenant on Civil and Political Rights (1966) and the International Covention on the Elimination of all forms of Racial Discrimination (1965), most of which have been ratified by the countries of Western Europe.

Apart from the projects described above, focused particularly on migrant workers and the approximately 2½ million 'foreign' children in Council of Europe countries (Council of Europe, 1981), the Division for Higher Education and Research of the Council of Europe approved a programme of activities on Multicultural Studies in Higher Education which commenced in April 1981. A preparatory workshop was held in Keele in October 1983 and modules were prepared, including one in the field of teacher education, for initial presentation in Fribourg, Switzerland, in November 1984, prior to implementation in Autumn 1985 and evaluation and revision in Malta in late 1986.

In the case of the European Economic Community (EEC) and with the exception of Council Regulation EEC No. 1612 of 1968, the major initiatives have also emerged from the mid-1970s. From that period come two major programmes concerned with, in one case, migrant workers and their families (a social action programme was embarked on in 1974), and in the other, education, including the publication of the influential Directive on the Education of the Children of Migrant Workers of 25 July 1977, coming into effect on 25 July 1981 (Commission of the European Communities, 1976; 1981, p. 1; Council of the European Communities, 1977).

The three objectives laid down by the Directive were:

(a)   to provide tuition to facilitate reception, including in particular intensive teaching of the language of the host country;
(b)   to provide training and further training of teachers responsible for the children of migrant workers;
(c)   to promote the teaching of the mother tongue and culture of the country of origin.

Directives are binding on member states, although the means and mode of implementation are a matter for national authorities, and in this case there is the qualification that it shall take effect 'in accordance with (the member states') national circumstances and legal systems' (Article 2). In spite of four years' notice of the Directive taking effect, it is clear that some countries, such as the United Kingdom, have been sluggish and tardy in planning action, whilst others, such as Belgium, may be in direct legal and practical conflict with the Directive.

In accordance with Article 5 of the Directive, and based on information provided by individual governments, a report on the progress of implementation up to March 1983 was presented by the Commission to the Council in February 1984 (Commission of the European Communities, 1984). Although the report indicates noteworthy progress in some areas in some countries, and there is no doubt that considerable progress has been achieved in the lifetime of the Directive, there are also areas of continued inadequacy which must be cause for grave concern. Exemplary cases of such lacunae are the lack of any formal provision of either initial or inservice training for teachers of the children of migrant workers in Belgium, the very high representation of migrant children in special education in France and the minimal provision of mother tongue teaching with the exception of Italian, the total lack of initial, further or inservice training for Italian teachers with foreign pupils in their classes, the manifest inadequacy of inservice training in Luxembourg and the fact that, in the United Kingdom, only 2.2 per cent of pupils whose first language is not English receive integrated tuition in their language and culture of origin.

In terms of action programmes, the Resolution of 21 January 1974 concerned migrant workers and their families, and the Council Resolution of 9 February 1976 defined measures adopted by the Ministers of Education in the field of education, in which member states undertook to develop reception education, including intensive teaching of the language or languages of the host country, to facilitate mother tongue teaching and to develop information for families on the training and educational opportunities available to them.

In the furtherance of these objectives, the Commission has organised exchanges of information through meetings of experts, conferences, seminars for representatives of national ministries and media experts, studies such as that conducted in 1975–1976 by AIMAV, an international association for applied linguistics and the adaptation of a language test for foreign children completed by an organisation called CITO in Arnhem. Five studies of educational and vocational guidance methods for foreign children have also been developed in Bradford, Brussels, Liège, Mönchen-Gladbach and Roubaix.

Then, in September 1976, the Commission launched a series of pilot schemes on teacher training, reception methods, teaching of the language and culture of origin and the presentation and distribution of teaching materials. Innovations in the field of teacher training took place in France, in collaboration with the Ministry of Education, CREDIF (Study and Research Centre for the Dissemination of the French Language) and the CEFISEM (Centres for the Training and Information of Staff involved in Teaching Migrant Children) at Douai, Grenoble, Lyons and latterly Metz; and in Brussels and North Rhine – Westphalia, the latter organised by the so-called ALFA Group (Training of Teachers for Work with Foreign Children) (Boos-Nünning, 1982).

In the field of teaching methods used in reception centres, projects were carried out in Holland, in Winterslag, from 1976 to 1979 and in Enschede from 1979; in Luxembourg from 1978; and in Denmark, in Odense, from 1978 to 1981. Concerning intercultural education, an initial pilot scheme was organised in the language and culture of origin in Paris from 1976 to 1979 and, as a follow-up to the Paris scheme, in Marseilles from September 1979. Similar projects were launched in Bedford, England, from 1976 to 1980, in Limburg from 1976 to 1979 and in London from 1980 to 1981. The work on the production and distribution of educational material has been conducted with Commission support by the Instituto del Enciclopedia Italiana (Commission of the European Communities, 1981; 1982).

Some of the work mentioned above has been evaluated by teams of international experts commissioned by the EEC. In 1978 the ALFA Group referred to above, comprising staff from the University of Essen and the College of Education in Landau, were requested to carry out a comparative study of the pilot schemes in Paris, Bedford, Hasselt and Leiden with particular reference to the approach to reception methods and the teaching of the language and culture of origins. The report was presented in 1980 and subsequently discussed by the Commission at a meeting of representatives of Ministries of Education and national experts (Boos-Nünning et al., 1980; 1983).

Other international organisations, with memberships less exclusively European, have also been turning their attention increasingly to issues concerned with the education of migrants and the development of multicultural education. In the spring of 1982, for example, the governing body of the Centre for Educational Research and Innovation (CERI) of the Organisation for Economic Co-operation and Development (OECD) approved a project on Education and Cultural and Linguistic Pluralism (ECALP), planned around two major aspects:

(a)   special educational problems posed by the children of migrants;

(b)   the problems arising in national education systems owing to the fact that cultural, linguistic and ethnic differences are permanent features.

The project will make a contribution to the appraisal of whether the aims thus far generally adopted with regard to migrants' children have continued validity. The work has included the examination of documentation submitted by member countries, a detailed national and international statistical analysis of the situation of the schooling of migrants' children in the school system, both nationally and comparatively, the preparation of a broad overview of the policy issues, and a critical analysis of multicultural education policies.

BILATERAL INITIATIVES

In addition to these international initiatives, bilateral agreements have been concluded between emigrant and immigrant countries concerning entry, residence and employment, but in some cases agreements also exist covering the provision of integrated instruction in the language and culture of origin: between Belgium and Italy, Greece, Turkey and Morocco; between Denmark and Yugoslavia; between Ireland and the Netherlands, Belgium, Greece, Norway and Spain; between Luxembourg and Italy, Portugal, Spain and Yugoslavia; between the Netherlands and Italy, Spain, Turkey, Yugoslavia and Morocco; and between France and the United Kingdom and several other countries. Joint committees have been established by several countries to assist in the education of migrant workers' children and the recruitment, training and, in some cases, supervision and inspection of foreign teachers, and individual embassies and consulates, e.g. in the United Kingdom and West Germany, are active in the provision of educational opportunities for their nationals and co-culturalists.

NATIONAL INITIATIVES

Apart from these bilateral and supranational initiatives, individual countries have also developed extensive repertoires of special provision for curriculum development and the training of teachers for the task of working with migrant children. Some, for example the United Kingdom, France, West Germany and the Netherlands, have even moved to the point where they are beginning to develop strategies of multicultural or intercultural education. Others, for example Sweden, have embraced principles of equality, partnership and freedom of cultural choice which are exemplary in their active expression of constitutionally and legally enshrined rights of equality, human rights, etc. (Purnell, 1984). A few examples may illustrate the trends and the distinctions, not least between the education of migrant children and intercultural education for all children.

The Federal Republic of Germany

The Federal Republic, with a population of approximately 61.5 million, has approximately 7.57 per cent 'foreigner' population (1982). A 'recruitment stop' was imposed in 1973 and the Federal Republic is currently adopting a series of restrictive measures and financial 'return home' inducements to stem the growth of this population. Approximately 17 per cent of the nursery school enrolments, 12 per cent of the primary enrolments and, at secondary level, 2 per cent of *Gymnasien* and 3.1 per cent of *Gesamtschulen* and *Realschulen* are of children of foreign nationality. Almost one in ten of the children in special schools are also of foreign nationality; approximately half of these are Turkish and one in five are Italian (Statistisches Bundesamt, 1981). Estimates vary, but approximately one-quarter of school-age children of foreigners are said not to attend school at all. Only approximately one in five foreign children obtain a school leaving certificate, as opposed to nine out of ten indigenous children. Whilst colloquially the term 'guest worker' has been replaced by 'migrant worker', the concept of *Ausländerpädagogik*, which might be loosely translated as theory about the education of foreigners (Ständige Konferenz der Kultusminister der Länder, 1981), still provides the dominant epistemological framework for the apprehension, processing and dissemination of issues and measures for their resolution in areas such as teacher education.

Intercultural programmes as such are relatively recent, but measures such as the inception of reception centres and classes, mother tongue lessons, including bilingual classes sometimes on a separate basis, the maintenance of cultural links with the country of origin, the establishment of mixed-culture learning groups, the preparation of bilingual materials, the preparation of suitable mother tongue textbooks and the overall revision of curricula are grouped together to indicate the breadth of commitment involved. More recently, proposals for making intercultural experiences an issue and topic of pupils' everyday learning, and extending intercultural experiences to all children, foreign and German, have received greater currency (Bundesministerium für Bildung und Wissenschaft, 1982). All provinces either have revised their examination regulations for teacher education or are in the process of doing so, in order that all initial teacher education includes a component on the education of migrant children, and some institutions of higher education, such as Oldenbourg in Lower Saxony, proposed, in 1983, the introduction of diploma-level studies with a focus on intercultural education.

An appraisal of the measures which have been adopted so far, and their effect, indicates that, against a background where demographic trends are tending to a rapid increase in the foreign population of school age, there is continued and marked inequality of educational opportunity and life chances between indigenous and foreign populations, with a lack of social, cultural and educational integration of some 'foreigner' groups. Proportional over-representation of certain foreign pupils (mainly from Mediterranean countries) in special education is complemented by the under-representation of these groups in academic, high-status secondary education and a low proportion of foreigners attending preparatory classes, where the quality of education provided is poor. The institution of special classes for foreigners is seen as a 'release valve' to reduce pressure on 'normal' classes, and bilingual classes tend to be isolated from the rest of the classes. Above all the fragmented and subject-based epistemology and organisation of schools and teacher education, and the immature theoretical development of concepts such as intercultural or multicultural education, reflect the intellectual conservatism of German teacher education and higher education in general and retard the development of more genuinely pluralist approaches (Essinger and Uçar, 1984).

France

France has roughly 2 million citizens from former colonial territories and over 4 million foreign nationals in a population of almost 54 million. Notwithstanding earlier agreements, such as Evian in 1964 and the Franco-Algerian of 1968, and an 'open-door' policy with regard to former colonies, immigration has effectively remained suspended since July 1974.

Approximately one in ten children in pre-school and primary education are foreign. Roughly 17 per cent of foreign pupils attend special education cycles and almost 70 per cent the first stage of secondary school only. A majority of foreign students are at least one year behind the grades of French children and a similar majority are on the short courses of secondary education. The major aim of reception classes and remedial teaching at primary and secondary level, together with the secondary adjustment classes, is to upgrade French language competence and to integrate children into school.

Circulars from the early 1970s have emphasised the development of linguistic competence, but it is with the establishment of the Centres de Formation et d'Information pour la Scolarisation des Enfants Migrants (CEFISEM), initiated by Circulars 76–397 and 77–310 from 1976 and 1977, that intercultural education was effectively commenced. These CEFISEM, the number of which has recently been brought up to fourteen, take account of the local and regional environment and have a particular and seminal role in the development of intercultural education. Additionally, the Ecole Normale Supérieure de Saint-Cloud (Higher Teachers College) and CREDIF (Centre de Recherche et d'Etude pour la Diffusion du Français) (Centre for Research and Study for the Dissemination of French) have played a particular role in the retraining of teachers in socio-pedagogical and didactic research and in the field of mother tongue instruction and pre-school education.

A few French scholars and researchers have begun to make a significant contribution to this area. Both nationally in France and internationally through organisations such as the EEC and the Council of Europe, Louis Porcher has done much to develop a more theoretically valid and empirically based intercultural education, and to define its limits, dilemmas and aims (Porcher, 1979; 1984), and attention has been given to conceptual and historical analysis of cultural pluralism in France (Mauviel, 1984). There are a number of projects currently in train at the National Institute of Educational Research in Paris, including human rights education, intercultural education and the acquisition of social behaviour by children engaged in a process of 'transculturation' and projects in provincial centres, such as the one against sexism situated in Nantes.

From January 1973, the Bureau de Documentation Migrants (Office for Documentation on Migrants) has been active in the publication and documentation of information about migrants, including the publication of a revue, *Migrants-Formation* (Ministère de l'Education Nationale, 1981, 1982, 1984). Through such individual, regional and national initiatives as these and through the activities of independent organisations such as the ones against racism and sexism, there is a rapidly increasing momentum towards the concept of intercultural education, appropriate for all pupils in all schools. This does not, of course, imply that the epistemological mould of French school curricula has yet been reshaped accordingly.

An appraisal of the French efforts in the field might show a number of marked parallels with the scene in the Federal Republic. There is, for instance, an increase in the foreign school population due to complementary demographic trends. Against this background, a proportionately higher representation of foreign children is to be found in special education, and there is proportionate under-representation of foreign children in academic and longer-cycle secondary education. This continuing inequality of educational opportunity between indigenous and foreign children leaves the Maghreb children most disadvantaged. The consequent educational marginalisation of foreign children has to be seen at the side of continuing ethnocentrism in French school and higher education curricula, a number of basic deficiencies in the provision of mother tongue instruction (except Italian), for instance in extra language provision in the first and second years of primary school and in reception and/or adjustment classes for 'new' older children, and a fundamental lack of impact of interculturalism in secondary teacher training and of racism- and prejudice-reduction pedagogies across the whole of teacher education.

The Netherlands

The Netherlands, with a population of just over 14 million, has approximately half a million citizens from former colonies and almost half a million foreign nationals. Approaching 80 per cent of foreign children in primary schools are following a course in the language and culture of origin, but there is in contrast continuing inadequacy of provision at secondary level, with approximately 10 per cent following such a course.

Four predominant forms of reception arrangements are currently found in the Netherlands:

(a)   *immersion*, where pupils are located in a normal class for their age and withdrawn in small groups for additional tuition in Dutch;

(b)   *national reception classes* which last for one to two years and aim at intensive learning of Dutch and social integration amongst other general education commitments and instruction in their home language;

(c)   *national schools*, which are schools following the normal syllabuses and methods of Dutch schools but comprising only one nationality;

(d)   *transitional bilingual classes*, which last for six years and have two phases: years one and two, where the two languages are used on a 50:50 basis linked with Dutch lessons, and the four subsequent years which have only one or two timetable units in the home language.

There is a certain fragmentation of reception methods and, in teacher education, methods and initiatives have included introducing courses for foreign teachers working in Dutch schools and courses for Dutch teachers in preparing foreign children in both primary and secondary education and with special reference to working with foreign girls (for women teachers and leaders) (Ministerie van Onderwijs en Wetenschappen, 1982a). An influential report has been published on mother tongue teaching by the Advisory Committee on Curriculum Development (ACLO) in 1982 (Batelaan, 1983). One project, the so-called PICOO-Project, is aimed at developing a model teaching plan for teacher education. It involves a joint venture by nine teacher training colleges with components in intercultural education amongst others (Ministerie van Onderwijs en Wetenschappen, 1982b). The project was evaluated by the Institute of Education of the University of Amsterdam (Leeman, 1982). Uniquely amongst European countries the Netherlands aimed, from 1 August 1984, to introduce intercultural education as a compulsory component of initial teacher training courses for all students.

A review of Dutch policies and practices might indicate a continuing inadequacy of provision for language and culture of origin at secondary level, and a rather outdated concept of teaching methods for immigrants offered by teachers' colleges. As in the case of the other countries reviewed in this chapter, there is also underprovision of appropriate inservice training. The continuing and marked underachievement of foreign children, particularly Turkish and Moroccan children, the over-representation of migrant children in lower types of secondary education, and the lower relative chronological class placement of migrant children in comparison with their ages also mirror similar phenomena in other European countries, and particularly as this has to be seen within the context of not enough account being taken of the role of teacher attitudes in underachievement, and an absence of fundamental reform in teacher education.

Sweden

In Sweden, and notwithstanding the immigration of refugees as a result of the Second World War, the major impetus to mass migration was given by the institution of the Nordic Free Market in 1954. During the 1960s, for example, Finns made up 50 per cent of all immigrants, although the proportion of Nordic immigrants has declined since the early 1970s as a proportion of all immigration. There is no restriction on Nordic immigration, and most other immigration is now refugee, adoptive or consequent (Council of Europe, 1981). None the less, although foreign nationals account for less than 5 per cent of the Swedish population of approximately 8.3 million, when all indigenous residents are included this figure rises to almost 1 million.

The year 1974 was a turning point in Swedish policy concerning migrants, with the publication of the *Invandrarutredingen*, which forsook the previous policy of assimilation and led to the adoption by the Swedish Parliament of a new policy in 1975 embracing the principles of *jamliket, valfrihet* and *samverkan*: equality, freedom and partnership (Willke, 1982). In turn, this led to the *hemspraksreformen* (Home

Language Reform) of 1977 which defined immigrant children as children having a 'home' language other than Swedish. That reform placed a responsibility on local authorities to provide mother tongue teaching if at least one parent speaks a language other than Swedish at home. By 1982–1983, 55 per cent of the 83 per cent eligible children were receiving instruction in one of sixty different languages (Purnell, 1984, p. iv). In 1978, 91 per cent of children at pre-school level recorded as having a mother tongue other than Swedish had at least four hours tuition per week in their mother tongue. In 1978, the proportion of migrant pupils in the compulsory school system ranged from 11.8 per cent in grade 1 to 98 per cent in grade 9. The forms of such instruction are available mainly according to numbers: in withdrawal, composite and home language teaching groups.

With the establishment of several more recent commissions, including in areas such as ethnic prejudice and discrimination and immigration policy, and the publication of the Report of the Commission entitled *Different Origins: Partnership in Sweden – Education for Linguistic and Cultural Diversity* (Swedish Commission, 1983), embracing a commitment to the inclusion of intercultural education in the training of all school staff, Sweden appears to have moved further than perhaps any other European country in responding to the newly perceived multiculturalism of its society, with policies founded in concepts of justice, equality and social cohesion unified with cultural diversity, which yet remain to be fully implemented. Notwithstanding that statement, there are continuing issues which centre around problems such as the persistence of racism and discrimination against adopted immigrants and the continued alienation, animosity and lack of sociacy in suburbia. The implementation of the high ideals of policy into practice heralds and points to the lack of overarching principles to resolve fundamental minority/majority value clashes other than on majority terms, in a context where conflict over resources at macro and micro levels is likely to become more rather than less acute.

Switzerland

In 1980, Switzerland had one of the highest proportions of 'foreigners' in Europe, approximately 14 per cent (exclusive of the 'saisonniers'), with a fairly constant 'foreign' school enrolment of approximately 15 per cent over the years 1976 to 1982. Restrictive immigration measures dating from 1964 and 1970 and the institution of a more recent change in the hereditary right of citizenship have both contributed to this relative stability, although internally within the school system there has been a shift, with decline in pre-school and primary enrolments and a marked increase in secondary enrolments (Mitter et al., 1982).

More than 20 per cent of the enrolments in special education (primary) are of foreign children and this proportion is increasing, despite the decline in primary enrolments referred to above. There is also an imbalance in the representation of foreign children in different kinds of secondary provision, dependent on whether a 'selection gate' has to be cleared or not, with the 'Mediterranean' children being the most under-represented.

Early educational responses tended to concentrate on the provision of additional teaching in French or German (e.g. the first declaration of the Swiss Conference of Cantonal Directors of Public Education (EDK) in 1962), but more recent declarations have recognised the importance of provision for the teaching of the language and civilisation of origin (Council of Europe, 1980). In spite of the publication of the LFMO Report on teacher education in 1975 and new recommendations by the Conference of Cantonal Directors of Public Education in 1978, recent regulations for teacher education at cantonal level have left Switzerland largely under-responsive to issues of migrant education, not to mention intercultural education, although Geneva was the setting in November 1984 for the establishment of a new francophone association for intercultural education.

Continuing problems may be seen as arising from the differing legal status of different migrants and the additional burden for foreign children which the national language policy represents. It is apparent that the more difficult 'cultural lock-on' problem is encountered by children from Mediterranean cultures, in the context of a general inequality of educational and broader economic opportunity. Once again, the over-representation of migrant workers' children of some nationalities in special education and the under-representation of some migrant workers' children from some nationalities in more economically and culturally potent forms of secondary education are key characteristics of the overall picture, with a similar cultural 'obduracy' on the part of teacher education and a cultural immobility by the host society in its response to a new and barely comprehended kind of cultural pluralism.

PATTERNS OF HOME TONGUE INSTRUCTION

Before we move to an analysis of overall policies, taking the Swedish tripartite approach of language, equality and partnership as our agenda, it may be enlightening to try to achieve an overview of the spectrum of policies in home tongue instruction, ranging from provision for indigenous and long-settled minorities to provision for newer migrant workers' children, whether they possess the nationality of the host country or not, for language policies have been the major means through which the countries concerned have attempted to respond to the arrival of large numbers of migrant workers and their children. There would appear currently to be six major patterns of such responses (Kodron, 1984):

(a) complete neglect in the normal school system of the language and culture of the minority, e.g. Frisians in West Germany and most ethnic minority children in the United Kingdom;
(b) neglect of language as part of the normal school system, but with lip-service to culture and opportunity to use school premises on a paid or unpaid basis for voluntary instruction, e.g. Kurdish in the Federal Republic of Germany, some languages in some local authorities in the UK;
(c) differential treatment of school and home language, home language sometimes being dealt with as an extended foreign language or used for a few hours a week,

e.g. Italian in French schools, home language in Sweden, Bedford and Bradford experiments in the United Kingdom;

(d)   bilingual instruction up to a certain age limit, with the school language gradually taking over and the home language relegated to an inferior position, e.g. Welsh in the UK, German–French grammar schools in the Federal Republic;

(e)   schools in countries with more than one national language, e.g. Switzerland and Belgium, where the territorial principle of the language of the area or region dominates but one or more of the other national languages is a compulsory first foreign language;

(f)   bilingual schools with a bilingual curriculum throughout the school life of the child and sometimes an opportunity to sit for several national qualifications or an international qualification, e.g. European schools, Unesco and international schools.

Such a diversity of approaches betokens substantially different assumptions and ideological orientations, and the next section of this chapter seeks to identify the major characteristics of policies and to categorise them accordingly.

MAJOR CHARACTERISTICS OF CURRENT POLICIES: AN OVERVIEW

Any attempt to summarise current policies must take account of the historical, political and structural pluralism of the selection of countries whose policies have been considered in this chapter. Not only do they have different compositions and national intellectual styles, but they also have different political aetiologies and contemporary administrative structures. Several European countries, for instance, have more than one central administration for education. In the Federal Republic of Germany there are eleven, in Belgium there are two and in Switzerland education is a cantonal responsibility. In some cases joint responsibility is exercised between national and regional governments or by two or more ministries.

Any educational generalisations have to be seen against this background and the broader societal context of measures on such issues as immigration, nationality, racism, sexism, etc. Nevertheless, with regard to the wider educational issues of language, equality and partnership, a cautious collation of the major characteristics of the educational response to cultural pluralism in Western Europe in the period since the end of the War elicits a number of characteristics shared by many of, if not all, the countries reviewed in this chapter. Thus, for example, in the wider society a number of common characteristics may be observed such as legal scapegoating in areas like immigration and nationality legislation, continued gross social, economic and cultural inequality, racial harassment and violence, and a process that one might term economic predestining by the educational system. The education systems bracket out minority cultures in a process of educational marginalisation of ethnic minority children by neglecting home languages, except for reasons of economic self-interest. Stereotyping and ability underestimation and minimisation lead to the structural over-representation of ethnic minorities in special education and the sedimentation of minority children into lower streams, paralleled by structural under-representation of ethnic minorities in academic and long (more prestigious, progression-facilitating) forms of secondary education. Given that there is differential deprivation according to different national and cultural backgrounds with, as a rule, the more culturally distant groups being most disadvantaged, there is substantial grade retardation (*sitzenbleiben; redoublement*) and under-achievement of school leaving certificates by minority children as a whole. It hardly needs to be observed that these phenomena lead to the under-representation of ethnic minorities in higher and teacher education.

However, structural discrimination, including racism, and a high level of cultural prejudice also have their effect on the majority population, with a state of ethnic captivity on the part of the dominant culture and cultural and social apartheid, and a consequent lack of 'potent' partnership with ethnic minorities in the regulation of education at school and system levels. Additive approaches to curriculum development which do not change fundamental epistemological moulds, and a lack of appropriate multicultural textbooks and materials, complement culture bias in control and selection mechanisms such as examinations in schools and higher education, and a cultural recalcitrance in teacher education as a whole, and lack of representation of ethnic minorities in the institutions of teacher education in particular. The picture is one of doing little and doing it inadequately.

A TYPOLOGY OF POLICY OPTIONS

If we survey these characteristics and look more closely at the spectrum of policies which are represented in the national and international initiatives described earlier, it seems apparent that differing underlying ideologies are at work. Some derive from the need to make sure that the productive process has, for as long as it needs it, but only for so long, sufficient labour to retain its efficiency, competitiveness and output. The early and dominant host-country language preoccupation encountered in all the countries reviewed comes into this category. Economic efficiency of worker and consumer is the major underlying driving force, with mother tongue language aims being added later in acknowledgement of the 'disposable component' nature of workers and their need to be re-integrated into their home countries when no longer needed.

Other measures have as their motivation the need to offer migrant workers and their children (now permanent members of society, if not yet full citizens) greater equality of opportunity in order to legitimate the rationale underlying the market economy. Second language provision, curriculum change and greater culture fairness in examinations and assessment would be examples of this underlying ideology, the fundamental aim of which is, through additive measures, to rationalise the existing social, economic, political and cultural hierarchy and value system.

Some countries, such as Sweden, are beginning to strive towards a greater community, mutuality and interdependence. The third of the Swedish principles, *samverkan* or partnership, is representative of this ideology, aiming at greater involvement and participation and pluralist democracy and discourse as a means of systematic, deliberate, shared and negotiated change.

Each of these ideologies has implications for the apprehension of issues involved in democratic pluralism and the aims envisaged by advocates and policy makers and, by means of these aims, for the conceptualisation of epistemological and structural issues on which policies depend. As with all social science models, there is overlap between categories, and the three ideologies which we might call purposive-economic, egalitarian and interdependent embrace a multitude of dimensions and nuances. These categories are simplificatory approximations to reality, intended for illustrative purposes, rather than exact replications of social and cultural facts, but they do enable us to trace through the policy options available in different social and cultural sectors under each ideology by means of a few exemplifications.

From such an analysis it is possible to say, as a generalisation, that the predominant response to cultural pluralism in the Western societies surveyed has been one based on an underlying ideology of economic efficiency, where migrant workers have been valued primarily as 'hands' and 'customers', and their children as future hands and customers in so far as they might be needed at all. A 1982 research report, prepared for the Commission of the European Community and concerned with three of the countries described in this chapter, graphically identifies and documents the vicious cycle of economic deprivation, social scapegoating and educational marginalisation, and subsequent economic predestination which is the lot of many ethnic minority communities (Gundara, Jones and Kimberley, 1982). Economic crisis has only served to sharpen their plight and to make legitimation impossible. A new rationalisation has, therefore, arisen, striving towards equality, and the word appears increasingly in policy statements, theoretical writings and curriculum development initiatives as a new means of additive adaptation to avoid fundamental change.

Gradually, however, there is increasing emphasis on human rights education, from which there is inevitable spin-off into issues of educational responses to democratic cultural pluralism. The Council of Europe initiative described above, and dating from the year 1978, is an early example of this trend, as are also the efforts of institutions such as the University of York in the United Kingdom in this direction. More recently, there has been the Report of the Swedish Government's Commission on Migrants' Languages and Culture in School and Adult Education in Sweden (Swedish Commission on Migrants' Languages in School and Adult Education in Sweden, 1983) which takes the word 'partnership' as its *Leitmotiv*. Emphases on education for co-existence and the role of education in combating abuses of human rights are gradually leading to the positive espousal of policies aimed not only at enhancing human rights and avoiding their abuse (as in the newer anti-racist movement in the United Kingdom) but at actively seeking interaction, mutual support, interlearning and social and cultural partnership. It goes without saying that few initiatives are currently addressed to this third ideology in the societies surveyed in Western Europe, except in the most embryonic form.

Table 6.1 seeks to illustrate the implications of these three ideological orientations in six major domains of human cultural and social existence: the underlying values, the aims which those values represent, the policies on language deriving from those aims, the structure of knowledge implicit in the aims and values, the structure of education, and the control of education. One or two brief examples are given to illustrate each ideology across each domain.

Table 6.1 *Typology of policy options for democratic cultural pluralism*

	Ideological orientation		
	Purposive-economic	Egalitarian	Interdependent
Implicit value orientation	Economic-led instrumental authority	Consensual but with weighted valuing of dominant groups	Norm-based and generative from a universal human rights baseline
Major aim	Cultural and social reproduction; educational marginalisation of minorities	Equality of opportunity from existing baseline; balance of pluralism and social cohesion	Intercultural development and behavioural change by negotiation and discourse
Language (a) host country	Main focus of attention: reception centres	Pre-school provision and additional support as long as needed	Dialectic with home language throughout pre-school and school span
(b) home language	Provision for return home	Lip service for legitimation; isolated experiments	Provision for all conceded as right facilitated by community support
Curriculum	Additive to existing subjects and folkloric; learning seen as competitive performance	Patchy, sometimes basic change in some subjects such as social sciences, religious education, etc.	Whole-curriculum approaches with community-linked options; interdisciplinary
Structure of education	Parallel and ad hoc	More links with supplementary schools, but main focus to make existing structure more fair and efficient	Whole school policy based on local and systemic guidelines; community schools
Control of education	No major changes to traditional locus of control	Examination reforms and token representation afforded; heightened democratic participation on inherently unequal basis	Interactive partnership with potent community involvement at all levels

SUMMARY

Even from this brief, incomplete and partial analysis, it will be apparent to the discerning reader that massive resources have been invested by national, international and local education authorities in the problems of migrant workers and their children. Most of this investment has been devoted to measures related to economic efficiency such as host-language provision and home language for re-integration purposes, leaving open the option of the eventual banishment of the 'foreigners', should the exigencies of the market economy so ordain. Relatively little of this investment nationally has been applied to issues of intercultural and multicultural education, with the notable exception of such countries as France, the Netherlands and the United Kingdom, and even there the amount is small and patchily distributed. Only in Sweden has the movement towards real partnership for democratic pluralism begun.

Our analysis shows little doubt about the continuing educational inequality and marginalisation suffered by migrant workers' children or the way in which their culture is 'bracketed out' from the normal school system, even in most cases – Sweden is one exception – in their home tongue. They tend to be over-represented in special education and under-represented in academic and long forms of secondary education, in teacher education and in higher education. In some cases alienation has caused them, in large numbers, to desert school altogether. The more distant their culture from the host culture, the less, as a rule, their life and education chances are, and their chances to achieve economically potent school-leaving credentials. Where they have access to home tongue instruction, it is either optional or on a parallel 'apartheid' basis.

The reasons for this deplorable situation in democratic societies are hard to perceive with clarity, but a provisional and speculative analysis might include the following points. One of the major difficulties would appear to be the way in which the issues were first perceived, i.e. as issues related to the immigration of foreigners, in response to the demands of industry and the service sector, rather than as issues of how the conditions might be brought about within a humane, pluralist society where different cultural groups live together in harmony and tolerance, creatively interlearning with each other, and planning their future through discourse and in partnership. In fact, far from interliving and interlearning, there is increasing evidence of cultural and social polarisation, alienation, animosity, scapegoating and symbolic and actual violence.

Some of the educational marginalisation and accompanying disadvantage and downright inequality may be attributed to the persistence of ancient curricular epistemologies, which are dysfunctional and obsolescent, if not obsolete. These 'knowledge-moulds' are locked in place by important social groups, including leading educational, political and economic groups, organisations and institutions which are as yet unconvinced of – perhaps even untouched by – the need for multicultural education.

In many cases, such groups and organisations maintain a cultural stranglehold on control mechanisms such as examinations and other processes and instruments of selection. Nowhere has this epistemological mould been broken; nor are there signs that this will occur in the future. While it remains, significant cultural groups find their culture excluded from the legitimately recognised culture of manifestly multicultural societies. This as yet unbroken mould determines in turn the content not only of school curricula but also of teacher education. Here the problem of archaic knowledge is compounded by the increasing cultural and social obsolescence of the practical experience of most teacher educators, contrasted with the parlous state of initial and inservice education – unrecognised as a major national priority in its new multicultural or intercultural form.

In the discipline of education itself, there are very few standard texts which recognise the problem of multicultural education, let alone adapt their epistemology to its values and ethical concepts. The disciplinary structure of education, *les sciences de l'éducation* and *Erziehungswissenschaften*, either resists the absorption of multi-cultural and intercultural education or fragments its problem orientation, or alternatively offers only a partial view. Often the focus is destroyed by being splayed across a dozen disciplines, the constellations of which are different political and linguistic entities, and the interchange of information, ideas and policies is imprisoned within still largely impregnable national and regional intellectual styles (Wirt, 1976).

But there are structural reasons too, deriving both from economic and from deep-rooted social phenomena, which in turn arise from ancient cultural apprehensions. In the universities and other institutions of higher education in Europe, ancient privilege, cultural self-dealing and a relative lack of social accountability, combined with distant, skewed and often inflated concepts of academic freedom, have significantly braked developments towards new concepts of economic and educational knowledge appropriate to a multicultural society. The answer to the ancient question 'What knowledge is of most worth?' is often the esoteric, the abstract, the non-applied, the socially irrelevant – and significantly, it is usually exclusive of the cultural capital of ethnic minority communities. Economic opportunity, on which it is based, derives more from birth and institutional appurtenance than from the provision of functional and relevant qualifications, experience and knowledge (Roizen & Jepson 1984).

The languages valued are often still those of idealised ancient societies or of a few immediate neighbours rather than those of the multiculture which makes up society at large and which could also provide the cultural powerhouse for changing the universities and institutions of higher education. The history studied is frequently not even Eurocentric but ethnocentric, exclusive and often charismatic and biased, sometimes even latter-day imperial. The modern languages are those dictated by political realities in the Europe of the nineteenth century. The curriculum is often a collection of subjects based on a similar historical location.

Very little effort and resource is being allocated to issues of interdependence, human rights, racism and prejudice reduction. The latter, in particular, is seen as a priority by visible minorities. Nor has the cultural bias of tests, examinations, assessments and teachers' observational and other judgements received a great deal of attention. It is in the context of such chronic and endemic problems that efforts towards intercultural and multicultural education in Europe have to be seen.

Whilst such problems remain, individuals and individual institutions may find enterprise in proposing and implementing curricula which are more appropriate to a multicultural society and speculating on the development of intercultural education. But in so far as, and for as long as, the overall mould and lack of potent political will remain and the task is seen as the socialisation of immigrants – or even ethnic minorities – to the dominant culture, and the perpetuation of an inherently unequal social hierarchy, the prospects for the development of an appropriate multicultural and intercultural education, reflecting the multicultural nature of European societies, concerned more with life chances than lifestyles, addressed to issues of educational equality in a culturally diverse society, desirous of the human rights of individuals and groups, committed to freedom from discrimination, and recognising the issues of power and access to rewards and resources involved, remain relatively bleak – to the impoverishment of all Europe's inhabitants and the detriment of its present and future citizens.

NOTE

1. An earlier version of this chapter was prepared for publication in the April 1983 issue of *Phi Delta Kappan*, and a revised version was given at the Second International Conference on Intercultural Curriculum at the University of London in September 1984. I am grateful to the Commission of the European Communities for the financial grant which made possible the study visit on which the original paper was based, and to staff at Headquarters in Brussels for the provision of information and publications.

REFERENCES

Ashworth, G. (1977, 1978, 1980) *World Minorities*, vols. I, II and III. Sunbury: Quartermaine House.

Batelaan, P. (1983) Four approaches to multicultural education. In Van den Berg-Eldering, L., *Multicultural Education: A Challenge to Teachers*. Dordrecht: Foris Publications.

Boos-Nünning, U. (1982) Ausbildung und Fortbildung von Lehrern für Kinder ausländischer Arbeitnehmer in Nordrhein-Westfalen: Aktivitäten und Konzeptionen der Forschungsgruppe Ausbildung von Lehrern für Ausländerkinder. *ATEE Journal*, 4, 171–90.

Boos-Nünning, U., Hohmann, M., Reich, H. H., Wittek, F., Kuhs, K. & Groenwold, P. (1980) *Vergleichende Evaluation von Modellversuchen zum Problem von Wanderarbeitnehmern in den Mitgliedstaaten der Europäischen Gemeinschaft: Abschlussbericht*. Essen/Landau: two volumes, mimeo.

Boos-Nünning, U., Hohmann, M., Reich, H. H. & Wittek, F. *Aufnahmeunterricht, Muttersprachlicher Unterricht, Interkultureller Unterricht*. Munich: R. Oldenbourg Verlag.

Bundesministerium für Bildung und Wissenschaft (1982) *Intercultural Education in the Federal Republic of Germany*. Bonn, 11 January, mimeo.

Castles, S. (with Booth, H. & Wallace, T.) (1984) *Here for Good: Western Europe's New Ethnic Minorities*. London: Pluto Press.

Commission of the European Communities (1976) *Bulletin of the European Communities*, Action Programme in favour of Migrant Workers and their Families, Supplement 3/76.

Commission of the European Communities,

Directorate General, Employment, Social Affairs and Education (1981) *Report on Activities for the Education and Vocational Training of Migrant Workers and their Families in the European Community*, 1975–81. Brussels: EEC.

Commision of the European Communities (1982) *Pilot Scheme on the Teaching of Language and Culture of Origin of Children of Migrant Workers attending Schools in the Marseilles Area*. Marseilles, 28 February, mimeo.

Commission of the European Communities (1984) *Report from the Commission to the Council on the Implementation of Directive 77/486/EEC on the Education of Children of Migrant Workers*, 10 February. Brussels: EEC.

Conservative Research Department, EDG Secretariat (1984) *Handbook for Europe*. London: Conservative Central Office.

Council of Europe, Conference of Local and Regional Authorities in Europe (1978) *Migrant Workers and Local and Regional Authorities*. Strasbourg: Council of Europe.

Council of Europe (1980) *Dossiers for the Intercultural Training of Teachers*: *Switzerland*. Strasbourg: Council of Europe.

Council of Europe (1981) *Dossiers for the Intercultural Training of Teachers*: *Sweden*. Strasbourg: Council of Europe.

Council of Europe and Ministero Pubblica Instruzione (1982) *La Formation Interculturelle des Enseignants*, L'Aquila, Italy, 10–14 May. Strasbourg: Council of Europe.

Council of Europe (1983a) *Compendium of Information on Intercultural Education Schemes in Europe*. Strasbourg: Council of Europe.

Council of Europe (1983b) Secretariat Memorandum on *The CDCC's Work on Human Rights Education in Schools*, April. Strasbourg: Council for Cultural Co-operation.

Council of Europe (1984) Symposium on Human Rights Education in Schools in Western Europe, Vienna, 17–20 May 1983. Strasbourg: Council for Cultural Co-operation.

Council of the European Communities (1977) *Council Directive of 25 July 1977*, 77/486/ EEC. Brussels: EEC.

Essinger, H. & Uçar, A. (1984) *Interkulturelle Erziehung in Theorie und Praxis*. Sulzberg, Allgäu: Pädagogischer Verlag Schneider.

Gundara, J. S., Jones, C. & Kimberley, K. (1982) *The Marginalization and Pauperization of the Second Generation of Migrants in France, The Federal Republic of Germany and Great Britain, Relating to the Education of the Children of Migrants*, Commission of the European Communities, Contract No. 82002. Brussels. European Economic Community (Research Report).

Kodron, C. (1984) Schule und Minderheiten in den Europäischen Gemeinschaften. *Zeitschrift für Erziehungs-und Sozialwissenschaftliche Forschung*, **1**(1) 55–67.

Leeman, Y. (1982) *Intercultureel Onderwijs* Amsterdam: Universiteit van Amsterdam, Sekretariat van de Vakgroep Onderwijs.

Mariet, F. (1980) *Maintaining Migrants' Links with the Culture of their Countries of Origin*. Strasbourg: Council of Europe.

Mauviel, M. (1984) 'Les Français et la diversité culturelle', *Education Permanente*, **75**, 67–82.

Ministère de l'Education Nationale-Direction des Ecoles: Centre National de Documentation Pédagogique (1981) l'Education Interculturelle. *Migrants Formation*, June, No. 45.

Ministère de l'Education Nationale-Direction des Ecoles: Centre National de Documentation Pédagogique (1982) *Scolarisation des Enfants Etrangers: Dossier d'Information*. Paris: Ministère de l'Education Nationale.

Ministère de l'Education Nationale-Direction des Ecoles: Centre National de Documentation Pédagogique (1984) L'école et les enfants d'immigrés. *Migrants Formation*. September, No. 58.

Ministerie van Onderwijs en Wetenschappen (1982a), *The Netherlands and Intercultural Teacher Training*, May. The Hague: Ministerie van Onderwijs en Wetenschappen.

Ministerie van Onderwijs en Wetenschappen (1982b) *Picoo-Projectplan*, 1 April. Amsterdam: Ministerie van Onderwijs en Wetenschappen.

Mitter, W., Döbrich, P., Kodron, C. & Lynch, J. (1982) *Lehrerbildung für Multikulturelle Schulen* (Abschlussbericht I des BMBW Projektes B4233, OOB), pp. 197–230. Frankfurt am Main: Deutsches Institut für Internationale Pädagogische Forschung.

Ogden, P. (1982) France adapts to immigration with difficulty. *Geographical Magazine*, **LIV** (6), 318–23.

Parliamentary Assembly of the Council of Europe (1978) *Report on Second-Generation Migrants* (Recommendation 841, 1978). Strasbourg: Committee on Population and Refugees.

Porcher, L. (1979) *L'Education des Enfants des Traveilleurs Migrants en Europe*: *l'Interculturalisme et la Formation des Enseignants*. Strasbourg: Counseil de la Co-opération Culturelle.

Porcher, L. (1981) *The Education of the Children of Migrant Workers in Europe: Interculturalism and Teacher Training* (French version 1979). Strasbourg: Council of Europe.

Porcher, L. (1983) *Interim Report of the Project Group to the CDCC*, CDCC (84) 10, Appendices I and II. Strasbourg: Council of Europe.

Porcher, L. (1984) *L'Enseignement aux Enfants Migrants*. Paris: Didier.

Purnell, P. (1984a) Multicultural education in Europe. *Education*, 13 April, pp. i–iv.

Purnell, P. (1984b) Multicultural education in Europe. In Greig, D. (ed.), *Learning from Europe*. London: Councils and Education Press.

Rey, M. (ed.) (1983) *Migrant Culture in a Changing Society*: *Multicultural Education by the Year 2000*. Strasbourg: Council of Europe.

Rey-van Allmen, M. (1979) *Assessment of the Method of Organising and Running the Experimental Classes of the Council of Europe*, Council of Europe Directorate of Economic and Social Affairs, Population and Vocational Training Division, CAHRS, 72 (79) revised. Strasbourg: Council of Europe.

Roizen, J. & Jepson, M. (1984) *Expectations of Higher Education: An Employer's Perspective*. Uxbridge: Brunel University.

Ständige Konferenz der Kultusminister der Länder (1981) *Zur Ausbildung und Weiterbildung von Lehrern für die Aufgaben des Unterrichts für Ausländische Kinder*. Bonn: Ständige Konferenz der Kultusminister der Länder.

Standing Conference of European Ministers of Education (1974) *Ad Hoc Conference on the Education of Migrants*, 5–8 November. Strasbourg: Standing Conference of European Ministers of Education.

Standing Conference of European Ministers of Education (1975) Tenth Session. *Migrant Education*. Stockholm: Standing Conference of European Ministers of Education.

Standing Conference of European Ministers of Education (1979) Eleventh Session, Committee of Senior Officials, February. *Migrants' Education*. Strasbourg: Standing Conference of European Ministers of Education.

Statistisches Bundesamt (1981) *Bildung und Kultur* (Fachserie 11, Reihe 1.1). Wiesbaden: Statistisches Bundesamt.

Swedish Commission on Migrants' Languages in School and Adult Education in Sweden (1983) *Different Origins: Partnership in Sweden – Education for Linguistic and Cultural Diversity*. Stockholm: Utbildnings-departementet.

Szeloch, Z. (1984) Das Polnische Schulwesen in Deutschland: Abriss der Problematik. In Döbrich, P., Kodron, C., Lynch, J. & Mitter, W., *Lehrerbildung für multi-kulturelle Schulen in ausgewählten Ländern*. Cologne: Böhlau Verlag.

Van den Berg-Eldering, L. (1983) Moroccan and Turkish women and girls in the Netherlands: Is education interested in them? In Van den Berg-Eldering, L. et al. (ed.), *Multicultural Education*: *A Challenge for Teachers*. Dordrecht, Holland/ Cinnaminson, USA: Foris Publications.

Watson, K. (1981) Education policies in multicultural societies. *Comparative Education*, **18**, 17–31.

Willke, I. (1982) Die Bildungssituation von Einwandern in Schweden. In Bartwerwerfer, H. (ed.) (1982), *Erziehung für Ausländerkinder*, pp. 13–35. Frankfurt: Gesellschaft zur Förderung Pädagogischer Forschung.

Wirt, F.M. (1976) *Ethnic Minorities and School Policy in European Democracies: Theory and Case Studies*. Paper presented at the American Political Science Association Annual Meeting, Chicago, September, mimeo.

BIBLIOGRAPHY

Ashworth, G. (1977, 1978, 1980) *World Minorities*. Sunbury: Quartermaine House. This three-volume publication contains basic information on the economic, political, social and human conditions of many of the world's minorities and their position within their host countries.

Baetens-Beardsmore, H. (1982) *Bilingualism: Basic Principles*. Clevedon: Tietco Ltd. The nature of and basic concepts associated with bilingualism and the problems of bilingual speakers are examined in this important and well-written book.

Batelaan, P. (1983) *The Practice of Intercultural Education*. London: Commission for Racial Equality. Issues of how educational services and those who work in them can influence change are considered in this publication, which arises from a conference held in November 1982 which eventually led to the foundation of a new international association for intercultural education (IAIE) in 1984.

Bullivant, B. M. (1984) *Pluralism: Cultural Maintenance and Evolution*. Clevedon: Multilingual Matters Ltd. The concept of culture and some of the principles and models of pluralism in modern Western societies are perceptively examined by the author as a means of understanding the pluralist dilemma, which arises from tensions between ethnic minorities and the state.

Castles, S. (with Booth, H. & Wallace, T.) (1984) *Here for Good: Western Europe's New Ethnic Minorities*. London: Pluto Press. This well-researched book examines and analyses the post-war migratory movements into Western Europe and includes a study of the responses of seven countries, including Britain and West Germany, to the arrival of millions of migrant workers.

Corner, T. (ed.) (1984) *Education in Multicultural Societies*. Beckenham: Croom Helm/British Comparative and International Education Society. The contributions to this book are grouped in four sections: perceptions and identities, education and pluralism in the developed countries, education and development in the developing countries, and comparative analysis in multicultural education.

Craft, M. (ed.) (1984) *Education and Cultural Pluralism*. Lewes: Falmer Press. This symposium includes original contributions on multicultural education, including such aspects as bilingualism, assessment and evaluation, pupil progress and community–school relations.

Greig, D. (ed.) (1984) *Learning from Europe*. London: Councils and Education Press. The papers contained in this collection derive from visits by educationists to European countries, funded by the British Association of Education Committees, and aimed at studying aspects of educational policy.

Husen, T. and Opper, S. (ed.) (1983) *Multicultural and Multilingual Education in Immigrant Countries*. Oxford: Pergamon Press. This collection of papers derives from an international symposium held in Stockholm in 1982 and contains differing perspectives on multicultural education.

Neave, G. (1984) *The EEC and Education*. Trentham: Trentham Books. This book represents the first authoritative study, undertaken with official support, of the full range of educational activities of the multinational European Economic Community. It is essential reading for all scholars of education in Europe.

Porcher, L. (1981) *The Education of the Children of Migrant Workers in Europe: Interculturalism and Teacher Training*. Strasbourg: Council of Europe. This is an important and unique contribution to multicultural education, based on the work of the Council of Europe, and presenting a distinctively 'mainland' European perspective on the issues and their resolution.

Sweden, Utbildningsdepartamentet (1984) *Intercultural Education* (with multicultural education and a global perspective – a way to partnership and peace). (DsU 1984:17). Stockholm: Allmänna Förlaget. This publication is a discussion paper about the goals, opportunities and methods of intercultural education. It derives from the work of the Commission on Migrant Languages and Culture in School and Adult Education in Sweden, and was published in conjunction with the main report of the Commission: *Different Origins: Partnership in Sweden – Education for Linguistic and Cultural Diversity*.

Van den Berg-Eldering, L., de Rijcke, P. J. M. & Buck, L. V. (ed.) (1983) *Multicultural Education: A Challenge for Teachers*. Dordrecht, Holland/Cinnaminson, USA: Foris Publications. This book contains most of the papers presented at a US–Dutch bicentennial conference held in the Netherlands in September 1982 to explore basic issues and concepts concerning education in a culturally diverse society.

Verma, G. K. & Bagley, C. (ed.) (1984) *Race Relations and Cultural Differences*. Beckenham: Croom Helm. This collection of key papers, given at an international conference, is grouped into three sections: race relations, cultural differences and ethnocentrism; language, education and minority groups; and minority group children in multicultural contexts.

PART III

Guidelines and Strategies for Change

The chapters in this part focus on important themes and topics in multicultural education that have not been treated comprehensively in Parts I and II. The final chapter summarises the book and proposes a tentative agenda for action.

Most theorists and researchers in multicultural education believe that the classroom teacher is the most important of the variables that influence the knowledge, attitudes, values and skills that students acquire related to ethnic and cultural diversity. Despite this realisation, most teachers within Western nations are not having educational experiences – either pre-service or inservice – that prepare them to function effectively in multicultural classrooms and to help all students to become culturally literate. In Chapter 7, the author reviews policies and practices related to multicultural teacher education in the major Western nations, and concludes that these practices are inadequate. She advances a synergetic proposal for teacher education that can be used to guide effectively theory, research and practice in multicultural teacher education. The proposal includes four fundamental dimensions: theory, philosophy, cognition and pedagogy.

In the final chapter Lynch, drawing upon the information and insights presented in the previous chapters, summarises some of the key ideas, insights and generalisations in the book, discusses advantages and disadvantages of an international approach to multicultural education, and formulates an agenda for educational and broader social action, based on his analysis of the previous chapters in the book.

Chapter 7

Multicultural Teacher Education

GENEVA GAY

> The degree to which multicultural education becomes a reality in our schools depends largely upon the attitudes and behaviors of classroom teachers.
>
> (Rodriquez, 1983)

INTRODUCTION

Many different factors account for the progress, prospects and perils of multicultural education in elementary and secondary schools. Essential among these are the attitudes, values, skills and commitments of classroom teachers (Rivlin, 1977; Hillard, 1974). To a large degree teachers' effectiveness, or the lack thereof, with ethnically different students and multicultural content is a direct reflection of the quality of their professional preparation.

Efforts to implement multicultural education in teacher preparation programmes have been fragmented and haphazard, and have proceeded largely without the legal incentives of teacher certification laws and mandates of colleges of education. Only a few of the fifty United States specify multicultural education in their laws governing teacher licensure (Burks, 1984). Few Canadian provinces have comprehensive multicultural education policies that indicate basic principles and content to be included in teacher training (McLeod, 1984). In the UK and Western European nations some exemplary practices in multicultural teacher education are evident in local education authorities (LEAs), but, overall, systemwide success has not been achieved (Craft, 1981). In Australia policies and programmes of multicultural education vary markedly from state to state (Bullivant, 1981a).

Throughout the United States, Western Europe, Canada, the UK and Australia multicultural theoretical developments are far more advanced than classroom practice. Curriculum developments for use with elementary and secondary school students are more numerous and varied than advancements in teacher education.

Efforts in both multicultural teacher education and curriculum for students have been prompted more by political crises than by pedagogical foresight. These fragmentary trends suggest the need for more conceptual coherence and deliberately planned intervention strategies to prepare teachers to work more effectively with ethnically diverse students and multicultural content in elementary and secondary schools.

WHY MULTICULTURALISE TEACHER EDUCATION?

'Teachers Can't Teach What They Don't Know'

Competence and *accountability* are quick responses to the question of why teachers in the ethnically and culturally pluralistic societies of Western Europe, North America, Australia and the United Kingdom need multicultural education. Aragon (1973) argues that 'the true impediment to cultural pluralism is that we have culturally deficient educators attempting to teach culturally different children' (p. 78). The failure to include multicultural education in preparatory programmes for teachers is largely responsible for these inadequacies. In 1981 the Rampton Committee in the UK reported 'an overwhelming picture of the failure of teacher training institutions to prepare teachers for their role in a multiracial society. In very few institutions is a grounding given in how to appreciate and understand the experiences and cultures of ethnic minority pupils' (Department of Education and Science, 1981, p. 60). Rather, the multicultural experiences that are available for pre-service and inservice teacher training tend to be sporadic, fragmentary and 'optional extras' (Klassen & Gollnick, 1977; Craft, 1981).

Generally, school practitioners and teacher educators have tried to accommodate teachers' needs for multicultural education in teacher training by appealing to the spirit of voluntarism and altruism in their staffs and students, rather than making multicultural training mandatory for employment in multiethnic schools. Some schools have even operated on the assumption that personal caring without any professional preparation is sufficient to teach ethnically different students successfully. However sincere and genuine, personal caring is no substitute for professional competence, and voluntarism has proved to be an ineffective approach for recruiting those teachers who need training the most into multicultural training programmes.

Teachers cannot be expected to be effective in teaching multicultural content and working with ethnically diverse students without having had professional preparation for these tasks. To attempt this compromises a legal precedent of the teaching profession, and some conventional wisdom of what we know about the instructional enterprise. It violates the regulation that demonstrated subject-matter competency, through completion of an approved programme of study, is a non-negotiable condition of certification or licensure to teach. It is contradictory to the principle that knowledge competency is a minimum condition for teaching. While mastery of subject-matter content is no guarantee that one will teach it well, most certainly teachers cannot teach what they do not know. We also know that many classroom teachers are reluctant to change what they are accustomed to doing. The more a proposed change departs from prevailing norms, the more reluctant some teachers are to embrace it. The absence of real incentives to change, such as mandates, fiscal rewards, ease of implementation and adequate training, exacerbates this reluctance.

The concepts and principles of multicultural education depart markedly from how schools and societies historically have dealt with ethnic and cultural pluralism. Few teachers have had the kind of education, experiences or training in multiculturalism that create feelings of confidence in their ability to work well with ethnic diversity. Feelings of inadequacy, coupled with few persuasive incentives or strong and convenient programmes of professional development, result in severe shortages of competent multicultural teachers. These conditions suggest that teacher educators, education policy makers and state school leaders should not leave multicultural teacher training to choice or happenstance. Just as licensure laws and professional preparation programmes do not allow prospective and inservice teachers to determine whether they need special training to teach English, mathematics, science or social studies, this should not be the case with education for multiculturalism. If it is genuinely accepted as a legitimate and worthy component of the educational process in ethnically and culturally pluralistic societies, then the rules governing multicultural teacher training should have the force of law and mandate.

'Individual Commitment is Necessary but not Enough'

Administrative and policy-making units of government, teacher education institutions, local education authorities and professional organisations are officially recognising the need for multicultural teacher education. In the UK the Rampton Report (DES, 1981), the 1981 Schools Council report on *Multiethnic Education: The Way Forward*, the 1981 Report of the House of Commons Home Affairs Committee (Craft 1981) and the 1985 Swann Report (*Education for all*, DES, 1985) are notable policy statements on multiculturalism that have serious implications for teacher education. Indicative of these is the Swann Report's declaration that 'all schools and all teachers have a professional responsibility to prepare their pupils for life in a pluralist society and the wider world' (DES, 1985, p. 560). In the United States the 1977 Multicultural Standard for the Accreditation of Teacher Education has national prominence (NCATE, 1977), and state regulations requiring teachers to have some training in multiculturalism, combating racism, and ethnic pluralism are gradually increasing. The Official Languages Act announced by the Canadian Parliament in 1971 establishes a national policy of multiculturalism within a bilingual framework (Canadian House of Commons, 1971). The 1976 report of the Committee on the Teaching of Migrant Languages in schools acknowledges Australia as a cultural mosaic of ethnic diversity, and the 1978 Galbally Report establishes multiculturalism as the official ideology of the Australian government (Bullivant, 1981a). Common emphases of these statements include: recognition of the reality of ethnic pluralism and cultural differences within their respective societies; dissatisfaction with sporadic, fragmentary treatment of multicultural education in teacher preparation; and recognition of the significance of ethnic pluralism in students' lives and school cultures.

While these policies give official recognition to ethnic diversity, and even encourage schools, teachers and colleges of education to respond favourably to these realities, too often they lack the power of practical enforcement. Multicultural education practice in both schools and teacher education lags behind theoretical and policy formulations. In fact, the implementation of policy statements continues to be limited by conceptual confusion, ethnic illiteracy, and the lack of technical competence of educational planners, teacher educators and classroom teachers; by the self-serving manipulation of the concept by non-ethnic interest groups; and by resistance from those educators who wish to perpetuate monoethnic status quo standards (Bullivant, 1981a; Banks, 1984). Fortunately, some educators who are in positions to influence teacher preparation directly are beginning to rethink the long-held belief that teachers who can teach any students well can teach *all* kinds of students equally well (Eggleston, 1981; Gay, 1981).

Thus, one of the first 'accountability' reasons for revising teacher training to include multicultural education is a very *pragmatic* one. In this era of demands for educational excellence, increased teacher competence in pluralistic school settings, and equality of opportunities for ethnically diverse students, more concerted and systematic attention must be given to multicultural teacher education. We cannot afford to gamble students' school success on the pretentious assumption that untrained or ill-trained teachers can teach that which and those whom they neither know culturally nor value unprejudicially. Nor can we speak reasonably and validly about teacher accountability for quality performance in multiethnic, multiracial and multilingual schools unless teachers have been specifically trained to perform in these contexts.

Legal and quasi-legal mandates constitute a second set of accountability commitments to multicultural teacher education. Legal policies are legislative enactments, judicial decisions and executive orders at the federal, state or local levels of educational governance. They include such direct and general regulations as human relations training for teachers and sensitivity to ethnic group cultures as conditions for teacher certification or licensure. An example of a legal regulation that has indirect implications for teacher education is policy guidelines for the inclusion of ethnic pluralism in instructional materials. The effective use of these criteria by teachers who serve on textbook selection committees requires some basic competency in knowledge about ethnic pluralism and multicultural education, as well as their methodological application in instructional materials.

Other examples of legal mandates about ethnic pluralism in society and schools which indirectly evoke multicultural teacher education are the Canadian Charter of Rights and Freedoms (Samuda, Berry & Laferrière, 1984), the 1974 *Lau v. Nichols* Supreme Court decision in the United States (Baker, 1979) and the 1978 Galbally Report in Australia (Bullivant, 1981a). These documents have the rule of law, but their influence on teacher education is indirect. The primary issue of contention of each is recognition of the right of ethnically different populations to practise their cultures without compromising their educational opportunities. For example, in adopting the Galbally Report, the Australian government made a commitment to encourage the development of a multicultural attitude in society, to foster the retention of ethnic groups' cultural heritages, to promote intercultural understanding, to research multicultural issues, and to encourage the introduction of information on ethnic groups' cultural backgrounds in professional preparation programmes (Bullivant, 1981a). The inferential message of these policies is that for teachers to provide equal educational opportunities to ethnic students, they must understand and appreciate the cultural heritages and sociopolitical life experiences of different ethnic groups.

Similar inferential messages about multicultural teacher competence are embodied in several other policy statements. The 1979 Ontario Ministry of Education policy statement states that 'the responsibility for preparing all Ontario students to live in Canada's multicultural society has significant implications in terms of general approaches to education' (p. 23). Title IX of the Elementary and Secondary Education Act (1972) in the United States declares that 'all persons in the educational institutions of the Nation should have an opportunity to learn about the different and unique contributions to the national history made by each ethnic group' (Giles & Gollnick, 1977, p. 117). The 1977 policy statement of the Australian Ethnic Affairs Council states that multicultural education programmes are intended for all children, not just non-English speakers, and that these programmes have ramifications for all school curricula (Bullivant, 1981a). The Consultative Committee on Curriculum of Scotland suggests that multicultural education is relevant to all Scottish primary and secondary schools, whether or not they contain ethnic minority students, and it should be undertaken within an international perspective (Grant, 1979).

The policy statements of state and local education authorities are another significant source of legal support and accountability for multicultural teacher education. The *Wisconsin Administrative Code* (1973) is illustrative of the kind of multicultural provisions that some of the states in the USA have issued. The code states that training in human relations, including intergroup relations, must be a part of teacher education leading to the initial certification and continuing education. The training has to include: attitudes, skills and techniques for translating human relations knowledge into learning experiences for students; analyses of racism, prejudices and discrimination in US life; the study of the values, lifestyles and contributions of different ethnic, cultural, social and economic groups; and analyses of instructional materials and teachers' own attitudes to and feelings about racism, prejudices and discrimination. Four Canadian provinces – Ontario, Manitoba, Saskatchewan and Alberta – have official policies of multiculturalism that endorse similar emphases. These policies provide guidelines for promoting bias-free textbooks and curriculum materials, outlines for implementing intercultural studies in schools, teacher training in multiculturalism, stipulations that multicultural education should permeate the entire educational process, and resource materials for classroom use (McLeod, 1984; Wilson, 1984).

Quasi-legal regulations on multicultural teacher education are directives, policy statements, and resolutions which gain their influence from the power of professional persuasion rather than rule of law. Frequently, they are products of professional organisations, commissions, study groups and research reports. Examples of these are the 1977 Standards of the National Council for the Accreditation of Teacher Education in the United States, the 1981 Rampton Report and the 1985 Swann Report in the UK, resolutions of the Standing Conference of European Ministers of Education and the 1977 European Economic Community Directives on the Education of Children of Migrant Workers (Lynch, 1983a), and various reports of the Schools

Commission in Australia, such as *Education for a Multicultural Society* (Australian Schools Commission, 1979), prepared by its Committee on Multicultural Education.

The National Council for the Accreditation of Teacher Education (NCATE), an agency of the American Association of Colleges for Teacher Education (AACTE), stimulated a flurry of activity when it included multicultural education in its 1977 revised standards for the accreditation of teacher education programmes. The member institutions of AACTE (about 80 per cent of all colleges of education in the United States) hastened to modify, at least minimally, their curricula in anticipation of NCATE accreditation visits so that they could receive favourable ratings on the multicultural standard. The standard stipulates that teacher education institutions must become more responsive to the cultural and ethnic pluralism present in the nation by including in their programmes of study 'competencies for perceiving, believing, evaluating and behaving in differential cultural settings' (*Standards for Accreditation of Teacher Education*, 1977, p. 4). In 1975 the Australian Schools Commission proposed that, since multiculturalism is a reality of Australian society, it should be reflected in the school curricula, instructional processes, staffing and organisational structure (Australian Department of Education, 1975). This proposal has produced several committees and reports on strategies needed, including teacher training, to translate this ideology into school practice. The 1983 report of the Swedish Commission recommended that intercultural education be included in the professional training of all school staff (Lynch, 1983a). Teacher unions in both Manitoba and Nova Scotia have enacted resolutions and implementation provisions which emphasise staff development, curriculum reform, support services and information dissemination about multiculturalism (McLeod, 1984). These standards and policy statements have the influence of professional sanction, but not the rule of law. Yet they are a major source of accountability commitment to multicultural teacher education.

An even more compelling accountability justification for multicultural teacher education than pragmatic survival and legalistic mandates is *professional ethics*. This claim argues that teachers should receive multicultural education training because it is the right and reasonable thing to do. It is humanistic and humane; it is consistent with some of the most universally accepted principles of good education and democratic living; and it is personally enriching and professionally enabling for teachers in multiracial and multicultural societies.

The philosophical ideals of equal educational opportunities for all, 'educating the whole child', accommodating individual differences, and maximising the human potential of all students imply the need for multicultural teacher education (Gay, 1983c). As Burke (1984) suggests, 'commitment to the maintenance of basic human rights and fundamental freedoms provides a natural reinforcement . . . the nature of the society provides a philosophical rationale, and the characteristics of learning and teaching provide an educational basis' (pp. 5–6) for developing an educational policy of multiculturalism in schools.

The impact of ethnic experiences and cultural conditioning on the classroom behaviours and expectations of students and teachers, along with the pedagogical principle that knowledge of students' backgrounds and orientations increases the potential for effective teaching, imposes a specific obligation upon teacher education in pluralistic societies. That obligation is the need to incorporate multiculturalism in all aspects of teacher preparation programmes. To this end, William Hunter (1974) has observed that 'if education in the United States is to meet the needs of its people . . . it must have a life blood of multicultural content in order to be sociologically relevant, philosophically germane, psychologically material, and pedagogically apropos' (p. 11). The same can be said about education in Western Europe, the UK, Canada and Australia.

PRESENT MULTICULTURAL PROVISIONS IN TEACHER EDUCATION

'Variability, Fragmentation and Imbalance Abound'

Generally, much more activity around inservice curriculum planning and staff development for teaching about different ethnic groups' histories and heritages has been generated in state schools than in college teacher education programmes. Inservice multicultural teacher education has been most prominent in those school communities, usually urban, which have substantial ethnic minority student enrolments. It has covered a wide range of experiences: compulsory one-time lectures for all staff; optional, single-topic discussions over a period of time; multiple-topic, multiple-session seminars for select staff; and full courses of study, endorsed and licensed by LEAs and teacher certification laws. Conceptually, these experiences have emphasised either supplementary, compensatory ethnic instruction, arrangements for mediating the special needs of ethnic minority students, or school-wide changes for all students, whether or not they are ethnic minorities.

   We do not know nearly as much as we need to know about the content, structure, methodology and effect of pre-service multicultural teacher education. Yet personal experiences, anecdotal evidence and the few research reports available (Cherrington & Giles, 1981; Craft, 1981; Gollnick & Chinn, 1983; Ray, 1984) suggest several general trends. Among these are: (a) the tendency for any college courses or experiences beyond introductory surveys to be optional rather than compulsory; (b) a continuing decline in the number of specific course offerings available in multicultural education within teacher education degree programmes; (c) a continuing decline in enrolments in the courses offered; (d) shifts in the conceptions of multicultural education away from separate and specific emphases on *ethnic* pluralism to integrating more eclectic notions of *cultural* pluralism throughout all teacher education curricula; and (e) an increasing tendency of college instructors to claim 'we are already doing that' when invited to revise their course content to incorporate multicultural education.

   Craft's (1981) review of research on inservice and pre-service multicultural teacher education in the UK led him to conclude that the provisions are fragmentary and incomplete, often superficial and inconsequential, and highly varied from region to region; they are non-existent in many areas, and in none are they wholly adequate. The Inquiry into the Education of Children from Minority Groups, finding similar results, concluded that 'the great majority of students are thus entering teaching having received little or no guidance in how to adopt a broadly-based approach to education which takes full account of the presence of ethnic minorities in our society' (DES, 1981, p. 61). With a few modifications the same observations can also be made about the status of pre-service and inservice multicultural teacher education in the United States, Canada, Western Europe and Australia. Yet the need for systematic and substantial teacher training in ethnic pluralism and multicultural education continues to be of paramount importance.

SUGGESTED MODELS FOR MULTICULTURAL TEACHER EDUCATION

Conceptual Similarity within Structural Diversity

Some general consensus exists among international scholars and practitioners of multicultural education about what should be included in teacher preparation. These agreements prevail regardless of whether the training models advocate separate ethnic education courses or infusing ethnic information into the content of all other teacher education experiences. However, specific details of the models are configurated differently.

These educators agree that professional preparation programmes should help pre-service and inservice teachers to: (a) understand the concept of multicultural education; (b) acquire some basic cultural knowledge about ethnic pluralism; (c) learn how to analyse their own and students' ethnic attitudes and values; and (d) develop different methodological skills for implementing multicultural education in classrooms. They also agree that these experiences should be compulsory for *all* teacher education students. Sullivan (1974) suggests further that the challenge of multicultural teacher education is to develop teachers who have the commitment, competence, confidence and content necessary to teach effectively in culturally pluralistic contexts. These competences and experiences are imperative. Nothing less than a multidimensional perspective on multicultural teacher education is adequate to meet the challenge of quality education for students in ethnically and culturally pluralistic societies.

The major components suggested for multicultural teacher education have been arranged in a variety of ways to create structurally different, though conceptually similar, models. Watson (1979) believes that specific models of multicultural teacher education are influenced, in varying degrees, by five general policy approaches to the overall education of ethnic minorities. These are: legal recognition of ethnic pluralism; unification of ethnic minorities with the dominant population; integration of ethnics into prevailing institutional and cultural structures; separation of ethnics from the mainstream social system; and non-recognition of or a *laissez-faire* attitude to ethnic minorities.

Of the several models of multicultural teacher education that have been developed by educators in the United States, those proposed by Gwendolyn Baker, Tomas Arciniega, Carl Grant and Reyes Mazon are summarised here to illustrate that some consensus of emphasis and similarity of purpose exist among different proposals on multicultural teacher education. Grant (1977) proposes that both pre-service and inservice teacher training for multicultural education include three phases of development. These are: self-awareness and understanding of ethnic attitudes and values; appreciation and acceptance of racial, cultural and ethnic differences which derive from acquiring knowledge of human diversity; and affirmation of ethnic and cultural differences through mastery of tools and techniques for designing, implementing and evaluating multicultural educational experiences. The Baker model (1983) also includes three stages of professional growth. The *acquisition* stage focuses on establishing a core of cultural information about ethnic pluralism. *Development* emphasises creating a personal philosophy of and commitment to multicultural education. *Involvement* concentrates on implementing multicultural instruction in classrooms with students. Arciniega (1977) believes that the specific knowledge, skills and orientations essential for effective multicultural teaching must stem from *personal, professional* and *community* needs and perspectives. The major components of Mazon's (1977) model are: multicultural conceptual and philosophical understanding; sociocultural sensitivity to ethnic communities; cultural knowledge; culturally relevant diagnosis and assessment techniques; and appropriate strategies for instructional reform.

The similarities of conceptual design and curriculum content among US models of multicultural teacher education are also evident in models suggested by British and Canadian educators. Most of the US models are *prescriptive* in that they grew out of the authors' personal involvement with actual programmes designed around their conceptual ideals. In Britain Cherrington and Giles (1981) used their survey of multicultural content in teacher education programmes at British colleges, universities and polytechnics to create a *descriptive* model of prevailing trends. They report that multicultural education in teacher training programmes is offered either as a *separate course* of study or as *elements* included in other courses within the overall programmes of study. In either case, the content is designed to: (a) prepare teachers to understand and teach about Britain as a multicultural, multiracial society; (2) help teachers to develop the special competencies needed to teach in racially or culturally diverse schools; and (c) help teachers to learn how to address social and academic needs of specific racial groups and, ultimately, to facilitate equal educational opportunities for minorities. Gaffikin (1981), speaking from the perspective of a British practitioner, proposes that teachers in a multicultural society should have three kinds of training. These are: factual knowledge of cultural and ethnic pluralism; the development of attitudes appropriate for multicultural curricula and ethnically different students; and personal exposure to and experience in different ethnically and culturally pluralistic communities.

The British Commission for Racial Equality in a publication entitled *Further Education in a Multi-Racial Society* (1982) recommends that, since teacher attitudes and skills are crucial to the effectiveness of multicultural education in schools, all teachers should have *compulsory* training in five areas. These are: (a) awareness of the extent and influence of racism in societal institutions and the personal lives of individuals and groups; (b) sensitivity to the ethnocentricity of existing school curricula, instructional resources and classroom practices; (c) understanding of and respect for the cultural backgrounds of different ethnic groups; (d) knowledge of the process of language acquisition, and how it applies to second-language and dialect speakers; and (e) knowledge of current research on race relations.

In Canada, Paul Collins suggests a four-part model (as summarised by H. Tomlinson, 1981) that includes emphases similar to those proposed in the United States and the UK. For him the essential elements of multicultural teacher education are: self-knowledge and analysis; analysis of multicultural interpersonal interactions; abilities to facilitate interactions among students in multicultural settings; and ability to teach ethnic content.

These various approaches to training teachers to work better in multiracial schools and with multiethnic student populations suggest a stronger consensus and continuity of purposes across them than may appear to be the case at first glance. All of them endorse the idea that knowledge of and sensitivity to different ethnic groups and cultures are necessary, but alone are not sufficient. These abilities and attitudes must be complemented by pedagogical skills which provide teachers with opportunities to practise translating their knowledge and sensitivity into instructional behaviours. The ability to communicate with ethnically diverse students and communities without debilitating stress, fear or prejudice is as important to facilitating effective multicultural teaching as are cultural knowledge and sensitive pedagogy (Pusch, Seelye & Wasilewski, 1979). Hence, all of the models emphasise some combination of content and process, knowledge and skills, cognition and affect, personal growth and professional development (Hillard, 1974).

A SYNERGETIC PROPOSAL FOR MULTICULTURAL TEACHER EDUCATION

A cross-national review of multicultural needs, programmes, policies and practices reveals several recurrent characteristics. These common features are compiled here to recommend some general essential elements of multicultural teacher education. The model proposed represents a synergy of ideas about the realities of ethnic pluralism in contemporary societies, the significance of multicultural education in school programmes for children, the significant role teachers play in formulas for school success, and the kinds of skills and processes teachers need to master in order to be effective multicultural instructors.

The curriculum emphasis of this model is not intended to suggest that other dimensions of multicultural education reform, such as instruction, administration and evaluation, are not essential in teacher training. They are imperative, but they are also more susceptible to the particular political exigencies of the communities in which they exist and are therefore more transient, variable and idiosyncratic. As such, these dimensions of educational change are less conducive to valid abstract conceptualisations across international boundaries. By comparison, curriculum ideology and theory are driven more by principles of planning and mandates of disciplinary knowledge that transcend geopolitical boundaries. They are therefore more transcendent over time and place, and capable of cross-national application.

Whether designed as elements of other courses or as separate courses, as core requirements or degree specialisations or as pre-service or inservice experiences, multicultural teacher education should include four fundamental dimensions. These are *theory, philosophy, cognition* and *pedagogy.* As suggested by Figure 7.1, these components are closely interrelated, and studying any one of them invariably evokes the others. Where teacher training programmes begin the sequence of teaching these elements is not a critical issue, as long as all of them are included.

Effective performance of teachers in classrooms presupposes cognitive competence of the subject-matter they teach, sensitivity to the unique characteristics of their students, commitment to a value system which prizes human diversity, and mastery of techniques for maximising curriculum relevance and student learning. Professional development programmes are expected to help teachers to acquire these attitudes and skills. It seems reasonable, then, to use these general expectations as conceptual contours in this proposal for multicultural teacher education.

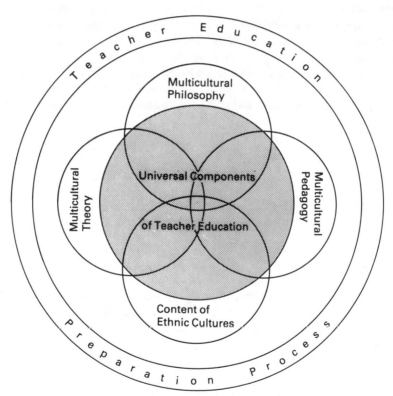

Figure 7.1 *A synergetic model of multicultural teacher education.* The shaded area represents the universal components of the teacher preparation process. The four overlapping circles represent the basic elements of multiculturalism in teacher education. They are interrelated and should be integrated throughout the universal components. The outer circle implies that the teacher preparation process is an interactive system in which the interrelationship of universal and multicultural elements is a central influence.

'Conceptual Principles Should Guide and Direct Classroom Practice'

Teachers of multicultural education and ethnically diverse students need, first of all, to become conversant with the conceptual language, theoretical ideas and philosophical beliefs of the field. Instructional efforts cannot be maximised, either in focus or effect, in the absence of a clear understanding of the theory of multicultural education. Therefore teachers need to know what multicultural education means, the different ways it is conceptualised, and the implications of these for classroom instruction. For instance, teachers need to understand what Gay (1977b; 1983a; 1983b) and Sally Tomlinson (1981) mean when they contend that the conceptions of multicultural education have changed in several ways since the movement began. These conceptions have evolved from perceiving multicultural education as separate mono-minority ethnic studies to integrated polyethnic studies; from primary focus on curriculum content to reforming the entire educational system; from an educational alternative intended for racial minorities to an educational essential for all students; from additive, supplementary units of study in selected subjects to content, perspectives and sensitivity that permeate all school subjects; from content emphasis to process priorities.

As part of their conceptual training teachers also need to study the accommodationist, assimilationist, cultural pluralist, structural pluralist and Marxist radical ideologies of multiculturalism (Martin, 1978; Bullivant, 1981, 1984; Martin & Encel, 1981; Banks, 1984; Lynch, 1983b; Jeffcoate, 1984; Mullard, 1980, 1982). In analysing these ideologies they should examine how each considers the role of class and culture, economics and ethnicity, racism and pluralism, intellectual understanding and political action in its theoretical and practical conceptions of education in and for a multiethnic society and world.

An impressive body of literature now exists on ethnic pluralism and its implications for education in multicultural societies. It includes anthropological, sociological, psychological, historical and political perspectives on different ethnic group cultures, experiences and lifestyles in both historical and contemporary times; ethnographic descriptions of ethnic group cultures; interdisciplinary dialogues about the relationships between education and ethnicity, cognition and culture, opportunity and experience; and pedagogical principles for educating the ethnically and culturally different student. Pre-service and inservice teachers should become familiar with the major ideas that the different sources of information offer with respect to building a theory of multicultural education.

To understand the theory of multicultural education, teachers should examine the works of authors who have made major contributions to the fields of ethnic pluralism and multicultural education. These include social and behavioural scientists, policy statements of school governing bodies and administrative units, and professional organisations and individuals concerned primarily with the pedagogy of multicultural education (see, for example, resources and bibliographies in Lynch, 1983b; Banks, 1984; Smolicz, 1979; Lee, 1980; Bullivant, 1981a; Samuda, Berry & Laferriere, 1984).

Other important sources of information which contribute to multicultural theory-building are governmental laws, and books and professional journal articles which specify the definitive components of multicultural education. Teachers should search these sources for information about major content and methodological concepts related to ethnicity, and the implications of these for school practice. Such concepts as culture, ethnicity, pluralism, identity, power, racism, politics, assimilation and biculturalism are critical to understanding the theory of multicultural education.

Conceptual models for planning curricula and instruction for ethnic pluralism are another dimension of multicultural education theory that is essential in teacher preparation. Banks' (1984) four models for designing multicultural curricula for students are distinguished by their primary content emphases and structural organisations. He identifies them as Anglo-centric, ethnic additive, multiethnic and ethno-national. Sizemore (1979) recommends a 4M curriculum, which she characterises as being multilingual, multicultural, multimodal and multidimensional. Williams (1979) proposes a three-perspective curriculum for ethnic students. The perspectives are: basic educational skills development; moral learning to diminish prejudices and discrimination; and a sociopolitical approach to teaching which emphasises knowledge as power, political action skills, holistic analyses of identity issues, and multicultural permeation of all school learning.

The conceptual framework for multicultural curricula suggested by Lynch (1983b) has six different strategies which can be used in teacher education or public classrooms. These are: (a) *parallelism*, where separate ethnic courses exist along with the rest of the school curricula; (b) *additive* units, modules or components on various aspects of ethnic cultures or groups included in existing courses; (c) *permeating* of ethnic information throughout the entire structure of other courses; (d) *a materials production approach* which emphasises changing instructional materials to make them more accurate in their treatment of ethnic pluralism; (e) a *consultancy* model for changing teachers' personal attitudes and instructional behaviours; and (f) an *action research* approach to determining the appropriate ethnic content to be taught to students. Bullivant (1981b) offers still another conception of multicultural education in his notion of a polyethnic survival curriculum. This approach to instructional planning is intended for ethnically diverse students only. Its five core elements are communicative competence, political and economic education, numeracy, moral and social education, and environmental awareness.

'Genuine Commitment to Multicultural Education Demands Value Investments too'

A second essential component of multicultural teacher education, and one closely related to theory, is *philosophy*, that is, the values, beliefs and assumptions which constitute the ideology of multicultural education. Invariably, teachers, students, the public and politicians want to know the what, why and how of multiculturalism in the education of elementary and secondary school youths. Knowledge of its abiding philosophy provides a basis for responding to these questions. Therefore teacher education programmes should include comparative analyses of the different ideologies of multiculturalism (Bullivant, 1981a; Smolicz, 1979; Lynch, 1983b; Banks, 1984; Mallea, 1984) so that teachers can: (a) become familiar with the different ideological foundations and possibilities for conceptualising multicultural education; (b) understand how and why ideology influences practice; and (c) establish a basis from which they can fashion their own personal philosophy of multicultural education.

Teachers need to understand and accept why multicultural education advocates believe it is, at once, compensational, enriching, essential and potentially conspiratorial. It is compensational because it corrects the oversights and omissions concerning ethnic pluralism that school programmes have made in the past. It is enriching because it enhances one's humanity, and provides opportunities for societies to better cultivate their most valuable natural resource – the human potential of its diverse peoples (Smolicz, 1979). It is essential because it deals with reality: ethnic pluralism is a fact of life; its influence is ever-present; it has the potential to be both vital and volatile; it significantly affects the lives of individuals, groups and societies. It is potentially conspiratorial because some people may use multicultural ideology to camouflage their continuous subjugation of dominated ethnic minorities. In pointing out this danger, Bullivant (1981a) explains that:

> ideologies of pluralism . . . are expressed in a symbolic 'political language' which enables people's behavior to be manipulated, their fears assuaged, and the provisions of the government to be seen as beneficent . . . In this way government both structures people's expectations of what it provides and their acceptance of what is provided, while at the same time legitimating its claim to authority and having people take that for granted. In the field of multicultural education and multiculturalism . . . symbolic political language . . . structures ethnic perceptions of their inequality in terms of cultural or identity deficits, that can be remedied by education, rather than in terms of structural aspects of the political system that deny them access to knowledge/power (pp. 238–9).

Martin (1981) expresses a similar viewpoint. She concludes that the predominance of theories of cultural, as compared with structural, pluralism in many current conceptions of multicultural education 'obviates the need to face uncomfortable questions of pluralism in relation to order, power and conflict' (p. 148). These perceptions underscore the need for teacher education and school programmes for children to deal with the acquisition and use of power, politics and economics, as well as cultural understanding, to improve opportunities and the quality of life for different ethnic groups.

Another assumption of multicultural education is that ethnicity, self-image, self-concept and school achievement are closely interrelated. Teachers who hold certain ethnic groups in low esteem tend to behave negatively towards students who are members of those groups. These negative attitudes create self-fulfilling prophecies. Teachers practise instructional discrimination, and ethnic students experience academic failure because of low performance expectations, unequal educational opportunities and culturally skewed diagnoses and evaluation. Informed insights into ethnic cultures and lifestyles can mediate this cycle. Teacher education programmes should help their students to understand the bases of these beliefs by examining research on ethnic prejudices in the classroom, ethnic psychology, school performance patterns of ethnic groups, and teachers' classroom behaviours with different ethnic groups.

Much of the theory of multicultural education is founded on the beliefs that ethnic heritage and cultural conditioning influence how teachers and students behave in instructional settings. Conflicts between these different cultural orientations are inevitable in ethnically pluralistic schools and societies. When left unmediated, these conflicts can jeopardize the instructional process and exacerbate the potential for school failure of ethnically diverse students.

The problem of ethnic students' failure in schools is a complex one that defies simple, unidimensional solutions. But there is a strong belief among multicultural advocates that it is caused as much by sociocultural, environmental factors as by the academic abilities of individuals. They believe, further, that school leaders can make the learning environment more hospitable to ethnic students, and thereby increase their school success, by incorporating ethnic content and sensitivity into school climates, curricula and instruction.

Many multicultural education theorists believe that schools have a moral and ethical obligation to teach youths how to live in ethnically and culturally pluralistic societies. This belief suggests several other related ones: (a) that ethnicity is socially and personally pervasive and persistent; (b) that ethnic understanding enhances one's capability to be human; (c) that individuals and groups should be encouraged to praise and promote their ethnicity; (d) that ethnic pride and national loyalty are not mutually exclusive; and (e) that multicultural competence is not an automatically acquired skill; it has to be learned. Implicit in these beliefs is the idea that multicultural education is a reform movement, the ultimate goal of which is educational equity for all students (McCormick, 1984). It is of such importance that its implementation should be neither incidental nor dependent upon teachers and other school leaders who are not specifically trained for the task.

'Multicultural Instructional Competence Requires Cognitive Knowledge'

The beliefs and values that are embedded in the theory and philosophy of multicultural education imply a necessary body of *cognitive content* about ethnic groups' cultures and sociopolitical life experiences, as well as instructional skills for teaching these, to be included in teacher education programmes. So does the pedagogical argument that multicultural education involves both teaching the ethnically different students and teaching about ethnic pluralism. Both require teachers to know, and to know how to know, ethnic cultures and life experiences. Just as the effective teaching of a given body of subject-matter presupposes teacher knowledge of the subject and the students, so does teaching multicultural content, and teaching students from different ethnic backgrounds.

Several components of ethnic groups' cultures and life experiences are particularly important for teachers to know. The cultural components include core values, interactional and relational styles, socialisation patterns, communication styles, learning styles, and patterns of ethnic identification. As part of their multicultural training teachers should also study the effects of racism, the distribution of economic resources and the allocation of political power on the opportunities and experiences of different ethnic groups. They should examine the research and scholarship of the social and behavioural sciences, history, the humanities and the arts to obtain the information needed to understand ethnic life experiences and cultural processes. This means that teacher education students will need to take courses outside their own college to acquire the necessary substantive content about ethnic pluralism. Information provided by professional educators which explains the educational implications of different ethnic cultural characteristics and life experiences is essential.

If teachers are to make better, more accurate sense of many of the social and academic classroom behaviours of ethnically different students they must apply *informed cultural perspectives* to their analyses. These analyses are possible only after teachers know more about the cultural specifics and perspectives of different ethnic groups. Even greater insights into the sociocultural dynamics of ethnically pluralistic schools can be acquired by contrasting school cultural components and expectations with those of different ethnic groups.

In addition to knowledge about ethnic cultures teachers need to know how to process cultural and ethnic information. Frequently, teachers use caveats like stereotyping, labelling and overgeneralising as excuses for not accepting some basic descriptions about ethnic group cultures. Or they impose impossible criteria of validity upon these descriptions as conditions for acceptability, such as demanding that the descriptions apply equally to all individuals within the groups, or exclusively to one group (Gay, 1977b). While they may be well-intended, these attitudes show a basic lack of understanding about how to process information about human cultural behaviours, and they are counterproductive to changing teachers' ethnic attitudes and practices.

Professional preparation programmes should help teachers to develop more adequate processes and orientations for dealing with cultural information. Those offered by anthropology and sociology can mediate these abortive attitudes. Teachers, therefore, need to know that:

> the key to understanding cultural characteristics of [ethnic] groups is to seek out *patterns* of human behavior, *sets* of beliefs and values most members of the group ascribe to, different *configurations* of values, attitudes and behaviors by ethnic groups; and [know that] laboratory (classroom) descriptions of human behavior are, at best, only approximations of how that behavior is likely to be expressed in 'living use'.
>
> (Gay, 1977b, p. 17)

These 'ways of knowing' ethnic cultures can be used subsequently by teachers with their own students.

Thus, factual, reference and process knowledge about ethnic group cultures and sociopolitical life experiences should make up the 'cognition' component of multicultural teacher education. From these emphases teachers learn: (a) 'what to know', 'from where to learn', and 'how to know' specific information about the fundamental characteristics of different ethnic groups' cultures and experiences; and (b) which of these have the most direct implications for teaching ethnic puralism, and ethnically different students, more effectively.

'Teacher Knowledge Alone Does Not Guarantee Instructional Effectiveness'

Effective instruction presupposes mastery of the subject-matter content, but it does not guarantee it. To achieve instructional success in classrooms, teachers have to do more than merely share their knowledge. They must *translate* their knowledge of the discipline into a *delivery system* that is meaningful to students. In fact, for any curriculum to be successfully implemented, 'the "what" and the "how" are both indispensable and . . . in practice they are usually symbiotic' (Lynch, 1983b, p. 46). We cannot assume that the skills required of instructional translation are acquired automatically; rather they must be taught deliberately and systematically. These facts speak to the significance of the imperative to include *pedagogy* in multicultural teacher education.

If we give any credence to Benjamin Bloom's taxonomy of objectives in conceptualising the major components of teacher training for multicultural education, then theory, philosophy and cognition, as described in it, should precede pedagogy in the sequence. While the emphases of the first three components are knowledge acquisition and comprehension, *pedagogy* is a translation process which requires teachers to synthesise and apply their knowledge about ethnic pluralism to the context of teaching multicultural content in ethnically pluralistic contexts. It also requires teachers to configurate their knowledge about ethnic pluralism differently from the way they learned it in order to achieve certain objectives for students. Furthermore, 'pedagogy', as the art or science of teaching, means instructional action directed toward others. This action implies the need for planning, and planning requires the use of informed decision-making. The pedagogical elements of multicultural teacher education, then, should focus on planning for and practising multicultural teaching (Gay, 1977b; 1981).

At least five 'operative' aspects of the multicultural teaching process should be included in teacher education programmes. First, teachers should have some supervised practice in developing multicultural instructional plans for use with students in primary and secondary schools. They should learn how to select appropriate content and teaching strategies for use with different ethnic students and school subjects, to achieve a variety of multicultural objectives. Instructional plans for multicultural curricula must pass the tests of quality, accuracy, appropriateness and feasibility. To produce plans which meet these criteria, or to determine if others already in existence meet them, teachers will need to apply their factual knowledge about ethnic cultures and experiences, and understand the generic principles of curriculum development. These principles include: (a) writing objectives for specific learning tasks and student populations; (b) choosing content that is compatible with the learning tasks and the objectives to be achieved; and (c) using instructional strategies and evaluation techniques that are congruent with the content and the objectives, and are relevant to the students for whom they are intended. In practice, designing multicultural curricula for students in multiethnic schools requires cultural context teaching (Gay, 1977b).

Second, skills training for multicultural teaching should involve teachers in practising, analysing and evaluating different instructional strategies and teaching styles. These analyses should focus on actual. teaching behaviours as opposed to proposed ones. The objective should be to get teachers to become sensitive to their own instructional styles in multicultural contexts. This sensitivity should make them aware of the attitudes and behaviours they exhibit toward ethnic groups, issues and experiences that are encouraging, facilitative, reinforcing and debilitating. Once awareness is acquired, teachers should then develop techniques for changing some aspects of their instructional styles to make them more accommodating to ethnic diversity. From these analyses teachers will acquire skills in assessing the feasibility of alternative teaching styles and strategies with different multicultural content and ethnic student populations. They also allow teachers to begin to expand their own personal repertoires of multicultural teaching techniques for future use with students.

A third pedagogical need in the multicultural training of teachers is learning how better to diagnose ethnic students' educational needs and assess their academic performance. This may mean developing alternatives to existing standardised tests and experimenting with novel techniques to achieve a better match between diagnostic and evaluative tools, and different ethnic groups' learning styles and cultural ways of demonstrating competence.

Developing diagnostic and evaluation competence for multicultural education also means that teachers must know how to assess students' readiness to learn different kinds of content about ethnic pluralism, how to determine how students are responding to or are being affected by the ethnic information being taught; and how to use information about ethnic group cultures to better understand the classroom attitudes and behaviours of different ethnic students. These assessments require both cognitive and affective abilities. When properly applied these dimensions of multicultural pedagogy can lead to changes in the teaching processes and school climates that embrace multicultural perspectives for the ultimate improvement of ethnic understanding and academic performance for all students.

Fourth, since instructional materials have such an important influence upon how teachers teach, and textbooks are known for their inadequate treatment of ethnic issues, groups and experiences (Hicks, 1981; Pratt, 1984a; 1984b), learning how to evaluate textbooks and other instructional materials is imperative for multicultural teacher education. It is not enough to merely encourage teachers to be sensitive to ethnic bias in instructional materials. They must be taught how to identify and correct these biases.

Several scholars of multicultural education, local education authorities, professional organisations and commercial publishers have developed guidelines for evaluating textbooks and writing multicultural education materials. Examples of these guidelines can be found in the authors' manuals of major publishing companies, State Education Authority (SEA) and Local Education Authority (LEA) style manuals for writing curriculum materials and evaluating textbooks, and the writings of Banks (1984), Lynch (1983b), Hicks (1981) and Pratt (1984b). Teachers should become familiar with the sources, content and capability of these guidelines, and practise applying evaluative criteria to samples of instructional materials.

Although different sets of criteria may vary somewhat in details, given their specific purposes, there are some general evaluation components that all teachers should know. They need to know how to evaluate textbooks' and other instructional materials' content, language and visuals for equity of treatment across ethnic groups, for factual accuracy and authenticity, and for the quality of their tone or 'contextual messages' about ethnic pluralism. In particular, teachers should be taught how to determine whether instructional materials: adequately reflect the ethnic pluralism of their society; present ethnic pluralism as a pervasive and positive feature of society;

include a wide variety of ethnic groups, experiences, issues and contributions; portray ethnic individuals in positions of authority; use complimentary language to present ethnic pluralism; present ethnic pluralism without undue attention to the exotic and the exceptional; and examine social and political issues associated with ethnic pluralism honestly and openly.

A fifth aspect of pedagogical training for multicultural teacher education is helping teachers learn how to establish positive rapport with ethnically different students, and with multicultural content. This skill is essential, since pedagogical confidence and good interpersonal relations with students are prerequisites for effectively teaching the formal curriculum.

Some of the insecurity that teachers feel about ethnic pluralism will be negated by their increased knowledge; other uncertainties need to be abated through skills of cross-cultural communication, or what Lynch (1983b) calls engaging 'cultural diversity in creative dialogue' (p. 26). Three aspects of cross-cultural communication or interaction are crucial. One has to do with knowing how to 'connect' instructionally with students from different ethnic and cultural backgrounds, so that what is taught has personal meaning for them. A second involves the moral right and professional obligation of teachers to teach multicultural content. Some teachers experience great uncertainty about their credibility to teach about an ethnic group experience that is not their own. There is no place for this kind of insecurity or misplaced modesty in multicultural education. All teachers need to understand and accept this professional obligation, and explore different ways of overcoming their insecurities. A third aspect of cross-cultural communications among students and teachers in multicultural schools is being fully aware of the values, attitudes, behaviours, nuances and expectations in human interactions that are culturally determined. It also involves knowing how cultural conditioning is manifested in behaviour by different ethnic groups, knowing how to anticipate potential conflicts among these different ways of behaving, and engaging in deliberate actions to minimise these conflicts. Teacher education programmes can help facilitate the development of these skills by teaching teachers how to do cultural analyses of the social and structural protocols which surround teaching and of the dynamics of the teaching act itself, and then developing strategies for remedying conflicts which occur.

CONCLUSIONS

Teachers who feel inadequate about their knowledge of ethnic pluralism are not likely to be very effective in their efforts to teach ethnically diverse students and multicultural content. And, while we know that knowledge competence alone is neither sufficient for, nor a guarantee of, effective teaching, the lack of it most certainly ensures the inability to teach. The simple fact is that teachers cannot teach what they do not know. Nor should they be expected to function well in multicultural teaching situations with handicaps of 'context illiteracy' and 'cognitive incompetence', when they are not expected to do likewise in other school subjects, programmes or contexts. We also know that teachers tend to teach as they have been taught. If they have not been exposed to carefully designed ethnic content and multicultural methodologies in their training programmes, in turn they will not incorporate multiculturalism in their own classroom instruction. These facts suggest an indisputable mandate for teacher education in any society where ethnic pluralism exists and is accepted as a worthy feature of life. Teachers must be taught how to teach multicultural content and ethnically different students.

Whether multicultural education is conceptualised as teaching content about the lifestyles and cultures of different ethnic groups or the political socialisation of ethnic minorities, or using cultural perspectives and materials to make school experiences more meaningful for ethnically different students, the dictum for the multicultural preparation of teachers is equally valid. For teachers to be held reasonably accountable for implementing multicultural education in any form, they must have some basic knowledge about ethnic pluralism and some pedagogical competence for translating ethnic knowledge into instructional plans for use with students.

At least, teacher education programmes should include four multicultural components. First, teachers need to understand the different theoretical conceptions and ideologies of ethnic pluralism and multiculturalism, and the implications of these for classroom instruction. From these theories teachers will learn different ways of thinking about how ethnicity affects the life experiences and opportunities of ethnic groups, and what content should be taught in schools, and to what ends schools should promote ethnic pluralism. Second, teacher training should include the study of the philosophical assumptions, values and beliefs about the worth of multicultural education to schools and societies. Teachers need to understand how and why multicultural education has the potential to be enriching, enpowering and manipulative simultaneously, and why it involves the dialectics of content and process; consensus, conflict and compromise; similarities and differences; culture and economics; power and politics among ethnic groups and the institutional superstructures of nations. Third, multicultural teacher education should include substantive content about the cultural characteristics and sociopolitical experiences of different ethnic groups in pluralistic societies. Essential to this are such cultural components as ethnic value systems, learning styles, communication patterns, socialisation, and interactional styles. Teachers also need to understand the facts and effects of social and political experiences like racism, political disenfranchisement, imperialism, economic inequality and social activism which shape the life chances of ethnic groups in schools and society. Fourth, training programmes should help teachers to learn skills and techniques for teaching ethnically different students, and for teaching multicultural content to all students. Fundamental to this component of teacher education are learning how to: plan and implement multicultural curricula; diagnose and evaluate different teaching and learning styles; differentiate instruction to accommodate various student populations and learning objectives; evaluate instructional materials; and develop effective interpersonal relations and communication skills with ethnically diverse students.

Without some training in all of these components – theory, philosophy, substantive content and pedagogy – teachers cannot be considered adequately prepared to teach ethnic pluralism and/or to teach ethnically different students. The quality of teacher preparation for multicultural teaching is a serious indication of the extent to which the educational opportunities of ethnically diverse students will improve substantially and the potential for all students to learn to live more fully in pluralistic societies. We must begin now to implement training programmes that are designed, with foresight and deliberate intent, to incorporate multiculturalism into all aspects of pre-service teacher education and inservice staff development. Without such training, teachers cannot be held accountable for incorporating ethnic pluralism and multicultural education into their classroom instruction.

REFERENCES

Administrative Code Requirement in Human Relations, PI 3.03 (1973) Madison: Wisconsin Department of Public Instruction.

Aragon, J. (1973) An impediment to cultural pluralism: culturally deficient educators attempting to teach culturally different children. In Stent, M. D., Hazard, W. R. & Rivlin, H. N. (ed.), *Cultural Pluralism in Education*, pp. 77–84. New York: Appleton-Century-Crofts.

Arciniega, T. A. (1977) The challenge of multicultural education for teacher educators. *Journal of Research and Development in Education*, **11**, 52–69.

Australian Department of Education (1975) *Report of the Inquiry into Schools of High Migrant Density*. Canberra: Department of Education.

Australian Schools Commission (1979) *Education for a Multicultural Society*. Canberra: Schools Commission, Committee on Multicultural Education.

Baker, G. C. (1979) Policy issues in multicultural education in the United States. *The Journal of Negro Education*, **XLVIII**, 253–66.

Baker, G. C. (1983) *Planning and Organizing for Multicultural Education*. Reading, MA: Addison-Wesley.

Banks, J. A. (1984) *Teaching Strategies for Ethnic Studies*, third edition. Boston: Allyn & Bacon.

British Commission for Racial Equality (1982) *Further Education in a Multi-Racial Society*. London.

Bullivant, B. M. (1981a) *The Pluralist Dilemma in Education: Six Case Studies*. Sydney: George Allen & Unwin.

Bullivant, B. M. (1981b) *Race, Ethnicity and Curriculum*. Melbourne: Macmillan.

Bullivant, B. M. (1984) *Pluralism: Cultural Maintenance and Evolution*. Clevedon: Multilingual Matters.

Burke, M. E. (1984) Educational implications of cultural diversity: dilemma and direction. In Samuda, R. J., Berry, J. W. & Laferriere, M. (ed.), *Multiculturalism in Canada: Social and Educational Perspectives*, pp. 3–17. Toronto: Allyn & Bacon.

Burks, M. P. (1984) *Requirements for Certification for Elementary Schools, Secondary Schools, Junior Colleges*, 49th edition. Chicago: The University of Chicago Press.

Canadian House of Commons (1971) *Debates*, 8 October.

Cherrington, D. & Giles, R. (1981) Present provisions in initial training. In Craft, M. (ed.), *Teaching in a Multicultural Society: The Task for Teacher Education*, pp. 75–85. Lewes: Falmer Press.

Craft, M. (ed.) (1981) *Teaching in a Multicultural Society: The Task for Teacher Education*. Lewes: Falmer Press.

Department of Education and Science (1981) *West Indian Children in Our Schools*. Interim Report of the Committee of Inquiry into the Education of Children from Ethnic Minority Groups (Rampton Report). London: HMSO.

Department of Education and Science (1985) *Education for All*. The Report of the Committee of Inquiry into the Education of Children from Ethnic Minority Groups (Swann Report). London: HMSO.

Eggleston, J. (1981) Present provisions in in-service training. In Craft, M. (ed.), *Teaching in a Multicultural Society: The Task for Teacher Education*, pp. 87–105. Lewes: Falmer Press.

Gaffikin, J. (1981) Multicultural teaching and future education. In Craft, M. (ed.), *Teaching in a Multicultural Society: The Task for Teacher Education*, pp. 141–5. Lewes: Falmer Press.

Gay, G. (1977) Changing conceptions of multicultural education. *Educational Perspectives*, **16**, 4–9.

Gay, G. (1977) Curriculum for multicultural teacher education. In Klassen, F. H. & Gollnick, D. M. (ed.), *Pluralism and the American Teacher: Issues and Case Studies*, pp. 31–62. Washington, DC: American Association of Colleges for Teacher Education.

Gay, G. (1981) Multiculturalizing teacher education. *Urban Education*, **5**, 12–20.

Gay, G. (1983) Multiethnic education: historical developments and future prospects. *Phi Delta Kappan*, **64**, 560–3.

Gay, G. (1983) Retrospects and prospects of multicultural education. *Momentum*, **14**, 4–8.

Gay, G. (1983) Why multicultural education in teacher preparation programs? *Contemporary Education*, **LIV**, 79–85.

Giles, R. H. & Gollnick, D. M. (1977) Ethnic cultural diversity as reflected in state and federal educational legislation and policies. In Klassen, F. H. & Gollnick, D. M. (ed.), *Pluralism and the American Teacher: Issues and Case Studies*, pp. 115–60. Washington, DC: American Association of Colleges for Teacher Education.

Gollnick, D. M. & Chinn, P. C. (1983) *Multicultural Education in a Pluralistic Society*. St Louis: The C. V. Mosby Co.

Grant, C. A. (1977) The teacher and multicultural education: some personal reflections. In Gold, M. J., Grant, C. A. & Rivlin, H. N. (ed), *In Praise of Diversity: A Resource Book for Multicultural Education*, pp. 27–32. Washington, DC: Teacher Corps.

Grant, N. (1979) Education policies in multicultural societies. *Comparative Education*, **15**, 17–32.

Hicks, D. W. (1981) *Minorities: A Teacher's Resource Book for the Multi-Ethnic Curriculum*. London: Heinemann Educational.

Hillard, A. G. (1974) Restructuring teacher education for multicultural imperatives. In Hunter, W. A. (ed.), *Multicultural Education Through Competency-Based Teacher Education*, pp. 40–55. Washington, DC. American Association of Colleges for Teacher Education.

Hunter, W. A. (1974) Antecedents to development of and emphasis on multicultural education. In Hunter, W. A. (ed.), *Multicultural Education Through Competency-Based Teacher Education*,

pp. 11–31. Washington, DC: American Association of Colleges for Teacher Education.

Jeffcoate, R. (1984) Ideologies and multicultural education. In Craft, M. (ed.), *Education and Cultural Pluralism*, pp. 161–87. Lewes: Falmer Press.

Klassen, F. H. & Gollnick, D. M. (ed.) (1977) *Pluralism and the American Teacher: Issues and Case Studies*. Washington, DC: American Association of Colleges for Teacher Education.

Lee, M. (1980) *Multicultural Teacher Education: An Annotated Bibliography of Selected Sources*. Washington, DC: American Association of Colleges for Teacher Education.

Lynch, J. (1983a) Multiethnic education in Europe: problems and prospects. *Phi Delta Kappan*, **64**, 576–9.

Lynch, J. (1983b) *The Multicultural Curriculum*. London: Batsford Academic and Educational Ltd.

McCormick, T. E. (1984) Multiculturalism: some principles and issues. *Theory Into Practice*, **23**, 93–7.

McLeod, K. A. (1984) Multiculturalism and multicultural education: policy and practice. In Samuda, R. J., Berry, J. W. & Laferriere, M. (ed.), *Multiculturalism in Canada: Social and Educational Perspectives*, pp. 30–49. Toronto: Allyn and Bacon.

Mallea, J. R. (1984) Cultural diversity in Canadian education: a review of contemporary developments. In Samuda, R. J., Berry, J. W. & Laferriere, M. (ed.), *Multiculturalism in Canada: Social and Educational Perspectives*, pp. 78–98. Toronto: Allyn and Bacon.

Martin, J. I. (1978) *The Migrant Presence: Australian Responses 1947–1977*. Sydney: George Allen & Unwin.

Martin, J. I. & Encel, S. (1981) *The Ethnic Dimension*. Sydney: George Allen & Unwin.

Mazon, M. R. (1977) Community, home, cultural awareness and language training: a design for teacher training in multicultural education. In Klassen, F. H. & Gollnick, D. M. (ed.), *Pluralism and the American Teacher: Issues and Case Studies*, pp. 205–15. Washington, DC: American Association of Colleges for Teacher Education.

Mullard, C. (1980) *Racism in Society and*

Schools: History, Policy and Practice. London: University of London, Centre for Multicultural Education.

Mullard, C. (1982) Multiracial education in Britain: from assimilation to cultural pluralism. In Tierney, J. (ed.), *Race, Migration and Schooling*, pp. 120–33. London: Holt, Rinehart and Winston.

NCATE (1977) *Standards for Accreditation of Teacher Education.* Washington, DC: National Council for the Accreditation of Teacher Education.

Ontario Ministry of Education (1979) Special populations in education. *Review and Evaluation Bulletins*, **1**(3).

Pratt, D. (1984a) Bias in textbooks: progress and problems. In Samuda, R. J., Berry, J. W. & Laferriere, M. (ed.), *Multiculturalism in Canada: Social and Educational Perspectives*, pp. 154–66. Toronto: Allyn and Bacon.

Pratt, D. (1984b) The social role of school textbooks in Canada. In Mallea, J. R. & Young, J. C. (ed.), *Cultural Diversity and Canadian Education: Issues and Innovations*, pp. 290–312. Ottawa: Carleton University Press.

Pusch, M. D., Seelye, H. A. & Wasilewski, J. H. (1979) Training for multicultural education competencies. In Pusch, M. D. (ed.), *Multicultural Education: A Cross Cultural Training Approach*, pp. 85–103. La Grange, Ill: Intercultural Network.

Ray, D. W. (1984) Cultural identity and education. In Samuda, R. J., Berry, J. W. & Laferriere, M. (ed.), *Multiculturalism in Canada: Social and Educational Perspectives*, pp. 50–61. Toronto: Allyn and Bacon.

Rivlin, H. N. (1977) Research and development in multicultural education. In Klassen, F. II. & Gollnick, D. M. (ed.), *Pluralism and the American Teacher: Issues and Case Studies*, pp. 81–113. Washington, DC: American Association of Colleges for Teacher Education.

Rodriquez, F. (1983) *Education in a Multicultural Society*. Washington, DC: University Press of America.

Samuda, R. J., Berry, J. W. & Laferriere, M. (ed.) (1984) *Multiculturalism in Canada: Social and Educational Perspectives*. Toronto: Allyn and Bacon.

Sizemore, B. A. (1979) The Four M Curriculum: A way to shape the future.

Journal of Negro Education, **XLVIII**, 341–56.

Smolicz, J. J. (1979) *Culture and Education in a Plural Society*. Canberra: Curriculum Development Centre.

Sullivan, A. R. (1974) Cultural competence and confidence: a quest for effective teaching in a pluralistic society. In Hunter, W. A. (ed.), *Multicultural Education Through Competency-Based Teacher Education*, pp. 56–71. Washington, DC: American Association of Colleges for Teacher Education.

Tomlinson, H. (1981) Multicultural teaching and the secondary school. In Craft, M. (ed.), *Teaching in a Multicultural Society: The Task for Teacher Education*, pp. 133–40. Lewes: Falmer Press.

Tomlinson, S. (1981) The research context. In Craft, M. (ed.), *Teaching in a Multicultural Society: The Task for Teacher Education*, pp. 55–72. Lewes: Falmer Press.

Watson, K. (1979) Educational policies in multicultural societies. *Comparative Education*, **15**, 17–32.

Williams, J. (1979) Perspectives on the multicultural curriculum. *The Social Science Teacher*, **8**, 126–33.

Wilson, J. D. (1984) Multicultural programmes in Canadian education. In Samuda, R. J., Berry, J. W. & Laferriere, M. (ed.), *Multiculturalism in Canada: Social and Educational Perspectives*, pp. 62–77. Toronto: Allyn and Bacon.

Wisconsin Department of Public Instruction (1973), *Wisconsin Administrative Code*.

BIBLIOGRAPHY

Banks, J. A. (1984) *Teaching Strategies for Ethnic Studies*, third edition, Boston: Allyn and Bacon. A useful resource for teachers on understanding the concept, philosophy, assumptions and goals of multicultural education; acquiring some basic cultural information about major US ethnic minority groups; and designing curriculum and instruction strategies for teaching multiethnic studies.

Bullivant, B. M. (1981) *The Pluralist Dilemma in Education: Six Case Studies*. Sydney:

George Allen & Unwin. This book examines the effects of different multicultural ideologies on the educational policies and provisions in Britain, Canada, the United States, Hawaii, Fiji and Australia. It describes what ideologies and models of society are held in each case study, and how these affect school programmes designed to deal with the challenges posed by pluralism.

Bullivant, B. M. (1984) *Pluralism: Cultural Maintenance and Evolution*. Clevedon: Multilingual Matters. This book uses the ethnic presence in Australia as case study information in its analysis of different ideologies of pluralism and multiculturalism. Such ideologies as democratic pluralism, cultural pluralism, dynamic pluralism, pluralistic integration and structural pluralism are analysed.

Craft, M. (ed.) (1981) *Teaching in a Multicultural Society: The Task for Teacher Education*. Lewes: Falmer Press. This is a collection of papers presented at a multicultural teacher education seminar at Nottingham University, under the auspices of the Advisory Group on Teacher Education of the Commission for Racial Equality. It includes a combination of research, theory and practice perspectives to discuss the 'what', 'why', and 'how' of multicultural education in Britain and to assess its status.

Hunter, W. A. (ed.) (1974) *Multicultural Education Through Competency-Based Teacher Education*. Washington, DC: American Association of Colleges for Teacher Education. This book uses a competency-based conceptual model to propose and discuss general multicultural competencies for teacher education, as well as specific teacher competencies for three major US ethnic minorities: Afro-Americans, Spanish-speaking populations, and native American Indians.

Klassen, F. H. & Gollnick, D. M. (ed.) (1977) *Pluralism and the American Teacher: Issues and Case Studies*. Washington, DC: American Association of Colleges for Teacher Education. This is a collection of papers and reports prepared for the Leadership Training Institute of the American Association of Colleges for Teacher Education. It includes five papers discussing issues and experiences essential to conceptualising multicultural teacher education, and case study descriptions of multicultural teacher education programmes at six different US universities.

Lynch, J. (1983) *The Multicultural Curriculum*. London: Batsford Academic and Educational Ltd. This book draws upon research in the UK and Australia to discuss major principles, policies and practices for multicultural teacher education, curriculum planning and classroom instruction in socially, politically and ethnically pluralistic societies.

Martin, J. I. (1978) *The Migrant Presence: Australian Responses 1947–1977*. Sydney: George Allen & Unwin. This book uses data from original research to examine the changing trends in official policies and governmental services for Australian migrants in the areas of education, health and trade unions.

Samuda, R. J., Berry, J. W. & Laferriere, M. (ed.) (1984) *Multiculturalism in Canada: Social and Educational Perspectives*. Toronto: Allyn and Bacon. This collection of articles represents a compilation of the various trends, perspectives, strategies and programmes in multicultural education in Canada. The articles discuss such issues as policies, attitudes, assessments, strategies and adaptations needed to implement multiculturalism. The book is intended for use in increasing the awareness and knowledge of pre-service and inservice teachers about the ethnic diversity in Canadian society, and to improve their skills for teaching this diversity in schools.

Smolicz, J. J. (1979) *Culture and Education in a Plural Society*. Canberra: Curriculum Development Centre. This book analyses the concept of culture and the practice of education from the perspective of humanistic sociology and in relation to different structures and policies in ethnically pluralistic societies. Its primary emphases are theoretical and conceptual. It could serve as a very useful textbook in teacher education programmes on the sociological implications of cultural pluralism for educational practice.

Chapter 8

Multicultural Education: Agenda for Change

JAMES LYNCH

In Chapter 1 of this volume, Banks portrayed and analysed the varying conceptualisations of multicultural education current in major Western societies, and appraised the contemporary critiques of the field. Synthesising these two elements, he derived a coherent and developmental theory of multicultural education and identified its implications for school reform and educational practice. He argues that the acknowledgement of the existence of institutionalised racism is a necessary preliminary to the development of more holistic, complex, pluri-dimensional and multifactor paradigms for the problems faced by victimised ethnic groups and the development of realistic strategies of multicultural education for all. Such paradigms will need to conceptualise the school, and indeed the education system, as an interrelated whole, in order to assist in the formulation of school reform, which can both help minority students, improving their achievement, and develop democratic attitudes and values in all. The active dimension of such reforms would be a process of mutual and pluralist acculturation for children and teachers, providing the knowledge, skills and attitudes necessary for full participation in their community cultures, their nation-states and the global society of humankind.

Taking up Banks' challenge, the chapters in Part II of this volume have variously described, analysed and appraised the ways in which several Western democratic multicultural societies have responded, through their educational provision, to new and still emerging perceptions of cultural pluralism. Basing their judgements on a historical overview, the authors have sought to identify the current legal and political context and the competing theories informing both the debate and contemporary practice in the field, before proceeding to a critical assessment of the present state and direction of that debate. It will be clear to the discerning reader how far each society is from the goals proposed by Banks and also how little each nation has seemed able to learn from the others in their common odyssey to resolve the 'pluralist dilemma' (Bullivant, 1981).

Banks, for example, charts the development of multiethnic education in the United States through the ethnic revitalisation movement, and acknowledges the influence of both pluralists and biculturalists on the school curriculum and educational policies in the educational reforms of the 1960s and 1970s. Whilst he sees assimilationism as having won the day in the battle to control education, his judgement is that there has been a gradual institutionalisation of elements from the reform movement into the educational system, its structure and content, principles and procedures.

For her part, Moodley highlights the ambiguity of much that passes for multicultural education in Canada and pinpoints its crucial weakness in overlooking the prime goals of equality of opportunity and of condition. She castigates exponents of the field for the static conception of culture inherent in most views of multicultural education and many official pronouncements, which is itself often causative of stereotyping: the opposite of what is intended. Uncritical attempts at heritage maintenance only seem to reinforce this weakness. She draws our attention to the analogous difficulty arising for teachers if they are to gain purchase on the implications of cultural diversity for their work and yet avoid trivialisation, reification and stereotypical representation. To this process, teacher attitudes and pedagogies are central contributors.

Craft charts the pragmatic and legislative process of cultural pluralism in the United Kingdom. He perceptively and clearly identifies current controversies surrounding multicultural education in the United Kingdom as located around similar issues of underachievement, racism, cohesion and diversity, but covering a broad spectrum of approaches and perspectives. He casts doubt on the factual accuracy of some of the generalisations and assumptions concerning such issues as underachievement and anti-racism and envisages the further progression of policies motivated by a commitment to cultural pluralism including issues such as the negotiation and transmission of core values by schools.

Bullivant describes the complex and chequered history of multicultural education in Australia, and the rich diversity of its contemporary form and application. As in the case of other contributions, he emphasises the variety of both political and educational stances which precludes overall consensus. Once again he points to undoubted achievements as well as persistent institutional and systemic malfunctions and inadequacies.

The chapter by Lynch presents the background of cultural diversity in Europe. In drawing on cameo descriptions of the response in several European countries, he seeks to identify the commonalities and differences in their approaches. With the notable exception of Sweden, he sees the other nations of Western Europe as pursuing simultaneously policies of social exclusion and cultural assimilation, cloaked by an expressed commitment to an innocuous intercultural education to salve their continued commitment to democratic values. Once again, issues of the underachievement of migrant workers' children and the inadequacy of teacher preparation are highlighted at the side of wider social phenomena such as economic and legal marginalisation and discrimination.

In the third part of this book one of the core areas for action identified continually by the contributions in preceding chapters is examined: teacher education. Drawing on Part II and on a broad summary of the literature, Gay makes coherent proposals for necessary reforms and renewal, based on a synergetic model of teacher education.

In this chapter, a brief attempt is made to draw together the strands of the other contributions and to focus them on the sharp edge of political and educational action. First, however, a brief explanation is given of the limitations of the approach adopted in this book and of the selection of countries included. Next, some of the more important commonalities which they share are described. Equally, some of their differences, those things which separate them, are referred to briefly, prior to the identification of desirable strategies for change.

It is important to make clear the limited parameters of this book. Whilst, for example, all the societies described in this volume are Western societies, this is not intended to imply that there are not other nation-states, amongst the socialist countries and in the Third World, which face similar issues of how the educational system may respond to newer perceptions of society as being culturally pluralist. (See, for example, Young, 1976.)

This volume has attempted to develop an international overview and analysis of the responses to cultural pluralism of countries which share a similar sociopolitical and economic structure and ideological commitment to democracy and equity, in order to achieve a sharper focus on issues of democratic pluralism. It remains for subsequent volumes to attempt to look at such issues in a more global way and to include in the analysis evidence and descriptions from other countries and socioeconomic systems. Thus, the selection of countries is neither accident nor caprice, but a deliberate decision to recognise the modest state of our theoretical and conceptual progress in the field and, by limiting the parameters for analysis to what could be realistically and rigorously included within one volume, to focus firmly on industrialised Western countries committed to democratic forms of government and egalitarian ideals and values.

SOME ADVANTAGES OF AN INTERNATIONAL APPROACH

It will be apparent that a number of advantages arise from the adoption of an international view of initiatives in multicultural education. The first of these is the additional element of detachment which can be levied against the phenomena as they are perceived within an individual country. All countries, for instance, are faced with decisions about those aspects of their value systems which are essential to all citizens and those which might be the prerogative and privilege of particular groups and minorities, and the way in which these two domains of values may be educationally represented. They all need to define the particulars and universals of their value systems and to work out their frontiers of cultural acceptability. The same applies to the perceptions and interpretations of democratic cultural pluralism and to the definitions and theories which are currently and differently emerging in each country in the formulation of educational responses to such pluralism. Seen in the context of an international scenario, they all achieve a sharper focus.

Their differences in values are reflected in the terminology used by different countries to gain purchase on issues of pluralism in education. Some of the countries described in Part II of this volume, for example, refer to the minority target group as ethnic minorities, as immigrants, as guest workers, as seasonal workers, as black citizens or as the children of migrant workers. Often, the nomenclature used for minority communities is so deeply encapsulated within national epistemologies as to be barely transferable. In some cases, minorities are citizens, new or old; in other cases they have no hope of ever achieving nationality. Their access to justice and equality is similarly and differentially circumscribed and marginalised.

Yet equality of educational opportunity is not a new slogan in Western societies, and certainly not in the case of the countries which have been described in this volume. Not without prior historical location, the concept has experienced since the Second World War successive reinterpretations, from a concern with sponsored mobility, striving through utopian attempts to offer all pupils an opportunity to experience the same, to the introduction of structural changes such as comprehensive systems of education and an appreciation that equality may reside in the provision of different opportunities within an overall unified system, and that it must address conditions and outcomes as well as inputs. Further, these opportunities relate as much to curricular issues as they do to the organisational structure within which education takes place. All the countries in this volume have begun to scrutinise what equality for all *and* members of ethnic minority communities may mean, regardless of whether those people are citizens or foreigners, and to recognise them as human as well as workers and 'hands'. But the developments are neither contemporaneous nor equally balanced in all of the countries.

A further major advantage of an international overview may be seen in the way in which similar social and cultural phenomena appear in different geographical areas at different historical times and are differently perceived by policymakers, academics and teachers. The United States, for example, has, for most of its history, experienced the kind of immigration which countries in Western Europe had to respond to, although not for the first time, in the decades after the Second World War. What policy responses have been adopted in these different geographical locations and at these different historical times? An international analysis enables us to see whether each nation is successively and stubbornly rotating the same wheel of policy options considered appropriate to cultural pluralism, or whether there is a maturing of thought and action leading to one nation being able to build on the experience of the other, to learn from the other, even indeed, through international agreement and covenant, to jointly attack some of the problems.

With all the differences of view and approach of the individual contributions to this book and their different judgements of the relative weight to be attributed to varying cultural and social phenomena, the chapters express two things: multicultural education, with all its immaturity and diversity, has had an impact on schools and education in those societies; and there is a long and enduring agenda of continuing tasks for education as the cultural composition changes dynamically in the future.

A further advantage afforded by international treatment of this field is the opportunity to view contrasting perceptions arising from the same issue, the maturation of different policy responses developed in articulation to the same phenomena. Racism, for example, is at present the subject of heated debate in the United Kingdom, whilst in the United States it has entered a more quiescent phase and in other countries, such as West Germany, it is hardly on the agenda except amongst the cognoscenti. Some Western countries have extensive legal and structural supports for racial equality: the USA, Canada and the United Kingdom are cases in point. Others, most notably some of the European nations represented in this volume, have few, if any. Thus, in spite of the fact that all countries in this volume come within the broader international consensus embodied in international agreements, treaties, covenants and contracts concerned with human rights protection and the elimination of racism, there is a wide variety of different legislative and organisational responses manifested by the Western democratic nations (United Nations, 1983a; 1983b). The civil rights embodied in an explicit charter such as is the case in Canada have no analogue in other countries such as the United Kingdom (Canada, House of Commons, 1982), though European counterparts exist.

As democratic societies, all the countries represented face important human and moral dilemmas with regard to such policy areas as their nationality and immigration legislation and the criteria against which the acceptability of behaviour of both majority and minority communities can be appraised in secular societies. There are, for example, in all the countries concerned, important clashes of values between such areas as the right to freedom of speech and the right to freedom from defamation and discrimination on the basis of race, sex, religion, ethnicity, language, social class, caste and name. The locus of that discrimination is different within each society and it defeats attempts at simplistic generalisations and resolution (Whitaker, 1985).

There is, too, advantage in such an international overview of policy responses to newly perceived cultural pluralism, in the collective reinforcement of issues such as human rights within a democratic society, for all of the countries represented within this volume are at least ideologically committed to equality and justice for all members of their societies, within a maturing concept of democratic discourse. It is apparent from the contributions to Part II of this volume how far each is from having achieved the discourse in practice, with dominant groups sharing power with oppressed ethnic groups. It is precisely because they are democratic societies that the problems of pluralism which countries in this volume face cannot be solved by authoritarian diktat, but have to be legitimated with ethnic groups and the population at large, through creative discourse, in order to support and achieve their intended effect. The ways in which these countries have variously, but so far only marginally, sought, through the introduction of new structural measures, to achieve greater involvement and participation as a basis for policy formulation is one of the most fascinating but discouraging aspects of this volume.

SOME COMMONALITIES

The commonalities of the countries in this volume include the fact that all are Western democracies committed to a pluralism of political views and cultural perspectives within certain agreed limits and that they espouse an ideological commitment to human rights for their citizens. They thus share similar liberal Western ideals, as they share a disarray in making them actual for all their members. They face issues of diversity in unity, such as how newly arrived or resurgent ethnic minorities may achieve full inclusion in political and economic life, enjoying the same life chances as other groups in society, whilst, at the same time, creatively retaining their own cultural identities and characteristics. All face dilemmas and contradictions between their overall ideological tenets and their treatment of minorities, either as individual groups or structurally, within a context where the overt reality of their democracy and cultural pluralism is to be found in racism and discrimination, in sexism and chauvinism, in prejudice and social and cultural hierarchies and in the marginalisation of many ethnic minorities in educational, political and economic sectors.

In some cases too, their historical record in the field is deeply blemished: a source of shame rather than pride. Yet all seem to be seeking ways to begin the long march of social movement from a new perception of the cultural pluralism of their societies to *democratic pluralism*, where both social and cultural diversity may exist within common political, economic and legal institutions, as part of the process of emergence of the ethnic group as a new social and political, not solely cultural, phenomenon. They share common problems of immigration and linked issues of nationality as a means of controlling that immigration, and some seek to solve them by measures inimical to their political ideology and values. Whilst the United States, for example, may have abolished the national origins quota system in 1965, and has created a fair and just immigration policy consistent with democratic ideals, this is far from being the case in other societies, such as the United Kingdom (Commission for Racial Equality, 1985). Even in the United States, however, issues surrounding mass illegal immigration remain to be resolved.

Indeed, all the countries represented in this volume face difficult human rights decisions concerned with both legal and illegal immigration and how to make congruent with their values their own ectopic political responses in social sectors such as health, social welfare, industry and education. They all confront problems in the ecology of urban settlement, in the extent of economic specialisation amongst ethnic minority groups, which have an impact on and may often frustrate the thrust of their ideals in educational policy. They seek harmony in society and education, at the same time as inequality, discrimination, prejudice and, in some cases, endemic violence are regularly encountered by visible minorities, who are increasingly vociferous in expressing their dissatisfaction at these infringements of their democratic rights and at their continued exclusion from the full benefits of participation in democratic society and decisions about its core values.

SOME DIFFERENCES

These commonalities, however, should not blind us to the fact that there are important differences in the historico-cultural make-up and political and social structures which may pre-empt the policy responses of each of the countries concerned. Not all countries share the same historical continuities and discontinuities.

Not only are there different languages and different histories of domination and submission, shaping different individual, group and national self-perceptions, but there are differing world views and self views, dependent, for example, in some cases, on previous colonial empires, or on role ascription through fundamental religious and moral tenets, or on differing economic specialisation and political awareness and experience on the part of both majority and minority communities. Different, too, are the external political systems; in some cases the societies are republics, deriving from ancient revolution, or phoenix-like from recent traumatic catastrophe; in other cases they are kingdoms deriving from even more ancient lineage, and based on religious privilege and domination and the subjugation of minorities.

There is a wide spectrum of approaches to the language issue in different nations and variable legislation on matters such as nationality, discrimination and immigration, as on the status of minorities and women. In some cases, Janus-like, contradictory policies are processed simultaneously. In West Germany, for example, there is legally endorsed commitment to the continued existence and cultural independence of the Danish minority in Schleswig Holstein, and the status of that minority and its educational provision are secured in international treaty. Notwithstanding bilateral agreements, no such functional position is afforded to more newly arrived migrants or their children. A similar paradox could be perceived in the treatment of Welsh and other mother tongues in the United Kingdom, for, although the special role and status afforded Gaelic and Welsh should not be ignored as a possible model for alternative approaches to nations' linguistic pluralism within unified nation-states, the United Kingdom and other countries are far from achieving a just policy of biculturalism for all home languages. In France and Germany in particular, with regard to language, the national tongue has been seen as the major political forge to unify the country, and rigorous measures have been taken historically to exclude all other languages. The same applies at different times but in different ways to Australia, the United States, Canada and the United Kingdom.

The dominance and submission of minority groups in society have been different at given historical periods of time in the various countries. Slavery was a legal part of the structure of the United States and Great Britain until the nineteenth century. More recently, enslavement has been suffered by whole populations under totalitarian regimes such as that in Germany from 1933 to 1945. The systematic extinction of the Australian Aborigines and their more recent continued economic and cultural enslavement make it apparent that similar phenomena have emerged in dynamically different ways in the different countries at different periods of time and that the enslavement of humans by humans is not something that has been outgrown in humankind's dubious ascent.

In addition to cross-national differences, there are also intergroup ones within the same countries: differences deriving from such phenomena as religion, race, language, social class, urban and rural habitation and current existence and perceptions of sex roles. Indeed, even within those intergroup differences there are intra-group differences within a generalised category. Not all West Indians, for example, have the same religion or values or come from the same island or have the same social class or even the same mother tongue, and this comment applies equally to Hispanics in the United States, Asians in the United Kingdom, and North Africans and Turks, whether Christian or Muslim, in West Germany and France. Yet as Moodley points out for Canada – and it applies to the other nations too – there is a predominantly static concept of ethnic culture which underlies many contemporary policies.

The urge to gain purchase on complex issues of cultural pluralism has led in all countries to stereotypical approaches which mask the dynamic nature of pluralism and culture. Differences have been created by the varying national intellectual styles and histories which have influenced very deeply the way in which the ethnic groups have been perceived and the way in which those perceptions have been processed first into policies and then into action. Moreover, definitions based on those national intellectual styles are themselves unstable across time and often incompatible across language and culture, let alone national boundaries. To speak, for example, of the ethnic revival is an appropriate generalisation for the United States, but one which does not entirely cover the explosive dynamic of post-colonial France and the United Kingdom, West Germany after the Second World War or long-pacific Sweden and Switzerland.

SOME CONCERNS

In spite of, or perhaps because of, these commonalities and differences, what one might term an agenda of common concerns is beginning to emerge. The contributions to Part II of this book give enduring testimony of the continuity of issues such as racism, discrimination and violence, of prejudice and stereotyping, of academic and social exclusion, of economic and educational marginalisation and of educational predestining. All of these infringements of civil rights are seen by minorities, but particularly by visible minorities, as barriers to their full participation in the benefits, structures and processes proclaimed by the ideals of democratic Western societies, and as major problems for urgent resolution by dominant groups (Katz, 1978). The shifting ideological parameters within which current discourse takes place, where prevailing and countervailing ideologies are subject to sudden change and reaction to each other, as portrayed by Banks at the beginning of this book and endorsed in a different form in Craft's description of current British controversies, are more than just a backcloth to otherwise disengaged policy and action. Ideologies are the stock-in-trade of the democratic pluralist climate, in the values and attitudes which they pollinate, and the action which they may legitimate. They are, in that sense, the unpredictable agenda-makers of a democratic society, with which any strategies for change have to reckon, but by which they do not need to be stultified.

Their effect may equally be to make taboos and proscribe issues. Worrying issues, for example the rights of women, continued relationships with homelands and, in particular, the matter of arranged marriages, evoke deep misgivings and on occasion antipathy, not to mention doubts concerning the fullness of commitment of participants to their newly adopted countries. But how may the issues be rationally judged rather than rhetorically proscribed? In all countries there is to be observed a creeping apartheid of parallel school systems, public and private, indigenous and migrant, bilingual and unilingual, religious and lay, maintained and supplementary, ordinary and special, which vies against the avowed commitment to social cohesion and the espousal of democratic equality based on equal provision for all. The little studied relationship between vertical economic and political structures on the one hand and horizontal ethnic and cultural group appurtenances on the other highlights the paucity of resource and research and the meagre state of knowledge of the field at present, as much as it illuminates the tortuous responses of dominant groups to escape the educational consequences of their own nation's diversity (Bullivant, 1984). Where there is no commitment to democratic pluralism by dominant groups, can there be any effective reform? Banks has argued that an acceptance of the existence of institutionalised racism – and the same could be said of sexism, credism and ethnicism – is essential to the emergence of multi-factor theories of multicultural education, and most of the nations in this volume have made that acknowledgement in their recent legislation. But where norms of custom and morality inherent in the behaviour of majorities and dominant groups deny this commitment, in practice the ideal of the legal goal is frustrated, for legal norms cannot possibly regulate more than a small part of human interaction. This slippage between legal goal and customary action is one powerful reason why the agenda for change has to commence with broader educational, not solely school, initiatives, addressed to the normative re-orientation of the majority and dominant groups as a supplement to essential legal baselines.

Deep misgivings have arisen about how far definitions of equality, currently being canvassed, are practicable within a society which maintains a commitment to the freedom of the individual and, particularly, freedom to dispose of economic wealth in legitimate but not unconstrained ways. Would a new commitment to equality of outcomes achieve a levelling down which might 'legitimately' exclude capable people on the basis of their ethnic derivation? Would a headcount approach to participation, achievement, employment and success in society offend against the principles of meritocratic progression and human rights, because any positive discrimination may involve parallel negative discrimination (Glazer, 1983)? Should some cultural groups exercise freedom of choice by not wishing to pursue certain kinds of careers and restricting themselves voluntarily, or female members of their communities by social pressure, from access to certain opportunities freely enjoyed by other communities? Should members of some cultural groups be able to maintain traditions of marriage inimical to international agreements to which the host society is signatory? On the other hand, would a new definition of equality shatter the deeply entrenched patterns of cultural and social reproduction within all the Western states represented in this volume and interrupt the economic and cultural self-dealing of dominant groups? Would destructive revolution be the result rather than mutually supportive evolution towards greater liberty and equality?

Similarly, what is the balance of linguistic diversity which a society may sustain, whilst maintaining a nationally valid lingua franca for its legal, economic and political organs and processes? Is a national policy, intercommunally secured, a viable proposition for all languages within the nation-state, when some home languages do not pertain to an identifiable national or political context? Where do the limits of justice and practicability lie? Such issues are within the indistinct area of the relationship between social cohesion for national survival and freedom to diverge within accepted bounds for creative cultural survival, including linguistically. Current injustices such as the disproportionate presence of ethnic groups in all the countries in this volume in disadvantaging forms of education, their relative exclusion from appropriate credentialism, and their weaker participation in elite and social mobility-inducing forms of education are only strengthened by policies of linguistic homogenisation which ignore the cultural and economic benefits of diversity.

Finally, there are major concerns about current policies and practices in the field of immigration and nationality. With the ease and speed of travel in the modern world and the manifest inequalities – economic, social, political and cultural – which exist between different nation-states around the globe, Western nations such as those in this volume have deemed it necessary to surround themselves with legislation addressing these twin issues. Whilst completely open-door policies for all are utopian, completely closed ones will inevitably infringe human rights cherished by democratic societies, and ultimately undermine their democratic practice for all. The as yet unreached ideal is somewhere in between. But where and what are the principles on which criteria for decision may be based? Most countries represented in this volume have as yet found no satisfactory resolution to this dilemma which is congruent with their ideals, and the problem of undocumented immigrants to the United States is a case in point.

Such issues pose once again questions of economic, social and cultural interdependence (Brandt, 1980; 1983) in the modern world and of how far multicultural education, of necessity, not only requires a global dimension, but demands the pursuit of its ideals beyond the boundaries of the nation-state. No nation can hermetically seal its cultural development, and so much of modern ethnicity relates to contexts beyond the boundaries of the nation-state.

TOWARDS THE IDENTIFICATION OF AN AGENDA FOR ACTION

An agenda of concerns leads us, in turn, to the identification of a common agenda for action, deriving from the international descriptions and analyses contained within this volume. Such an agenda needs to take account of the commonalities and differences, but also to address areas of policy where nations may combine their expertise and historical insights to gain purchase on their own and shared problems. Bearing in mind the limitations of schools and indeed education, it may be useful to think of such an agenda for change as residing at three different levels, that of the nation-state (societal), that of the education system (systemic) and that of the educational institution (institutional).

The Societal Agenda

At the societal level there can be little doubt that ethnic groups feel, and in most cases in reality are, excluded from participation in the formulation and implementation of those overarching ideals, philosophies and values by which they, as all other members of society, are regulated in their behaviour and relationships. The result is exclusion from true equality, social disintegration, and even violence. But as the experience of some longstanding minorities shows, this need not be so, if elite and dominant groups are willing to share power with oppressed groups to achieve greater equality.

One response to the current crisis of democratic pluralism may be found in the increasing flight to decision by experts: a kind of technocratic dictatorship. But a response to current legitimation crises could, alternatively, be located in an explicit, structural recognition of the fundamental role of discourse as a prerequisite to legitimated and functional *democratic pluralism* (Habermas, 1976; 1979). Such discourse, based on balanced interrelationships between groups, could be the means to the identification and reconciliation, through negotiation rather than coercion, of often conflicting *universal* and *particular* issues within pluralist society. In this way, members of ethnic minority communities involved in the 'ethnic revival movements' of the 1980s might be seen as the outriders of a new democracy, in helping to test out the outer reaches of democratic diversity and freedom which will not cause social disintegration, rather than fulfilling their present role of 'outsiders' of those same democratic societies. In that sense, human and minority rights can be isotropic.

Such discourse implies the need for an acceptance of the existence of differing ideologies, not just as mechanisms for political orientation and action, but as mechanisms for discourse and social action by which legitimate purchase is achieved on negotiated change in a democratic diversity. The corollary of this acceptance of alternative legitimate ideologies is the periodic and systematic shared review and continual openness of the negotiated criteria for judgement – and the competence on the part of all groups to make the discourse actual. Further, and as pointed out by Banks in this volume, such discourse for pluralism can commence only when the nation-state itself acknowledges the historical and contemporary injustice of institutionalised racism (and credism) and when dominant groups meaningfully share power with oppressed groups.

Such a discourse can flourish only against a background of more concerted action on the legal and political front in all of the countries concerned, if disastrous social and economic consequences are to be avoided. Minorities currently require broader entitlement programmes to achieve their rights than do majorities, because they are minorities and they tend to be weak and under-represented in the legal and political 'power-stations', where laws and 'rules' of custom and morality are generated and where access to economic rewards is forged. Put simply, minorities cannot usually win elections.

There is, too, a need for the legal recognition of the overlapping and interacting multiple senses of peoplehood and manifold identities with which individuals and groups within an economically and culturally diverse society are concerned and the consequent diverse occupational and cultural reference groups to which individuals may equally belong without detriment to the nation-state. The individual's option to belong to a cultural group or not is surely a part of democratic freedom and essential to the avoidance of the current predestining ascription of status by education and other sectors of society. Democratic pluralism must fully support the extension of domains for personal choice, as part of a covenant of human rights, into the area of occupational and cultural reference group membership.

The Systemic Agenda

Such a new covenant for democratic pluralism can be achieved, however, only by secular update of the instrumental bases on which intergroup relations are conducted, including the minimum conformity essential to the continued existence of the nation-state for individuals and groups. Schools do not need to be used by nation-states as mere slaves of a passé 'melting-pot' ideal, or to passively accept their role as calibrators of life chances at the behest of dominant groups. They may express community culture and human values at the same time as they are transmitting agreed and overarching universal values of society as a whole and, preparing for change, they may change themselves, creatively altering, not just maintaining, democracy for all.

For this new role, a differentiated curriculum, but one centred on common values and competences, with a strong community dimension, is required. A local curriculum within a nationally agreed framework may assist the rejuvenation and re-invigoration of the membership of leading groups in society, so that they do not become intellectually sterile and self-serving. Within the context of a new curricular ideal for schools, however, it has to be recognised that multicultural education can only ever be one dimension of a societal response to cultural and democratic pluralism and that it and the school are limited as vehicles of social change. For disillusion will surely ensue if an attempt is made to harness the insufficiency of schools as the sole means of reforming the multitude of problems arising from cultural diversity with which societies are currently faced. Whilst the school cannot be expected to solve such problems as those associated with segmented housing policies in major urban areas, educationists and teachers can take the initiative in coordinating education *with* other policy areas to achieve greater justice.

A movement too from the deficit concept of education to one based on cultural diversity may be necessary, but it can hardly be sufficient alone, for the dilemma of how to reconcile equality and diversity has to find its resolution in the arena of different needs and entitlements, and those needs and entitlements are generated by a dynamic of relationships and definitions, ranging far beyond the schools, which are themselves constantly changing. A person may not remain within the same cultural group for the whole of his or her lifespan. Nor may that person embrace the same *particular* values on exit at death as on entry at birth. Such changes are not only multidimensional, they are also multifaceted, and they arise from the continuing process of multiple acculturation which is co-existent with life in a democratic pluralist society and an essential mechanism for peaceful change.

Within the educational system there needs to be a firm commitment to the fact that the compensatory phase was transitional in Western societies. A new, more dynamic cultural era has opened up to which schools both institutionally and systematically have to respond. As indicated at a societal level earlier, cultural diversity implies a negotiated epistemology and control mechanisms, including procedures for testing, examinations and assessment in the schools. The processes by which knowledge is given status and value in education and by which it is transmitted also need, therefore, to be opened up to more democratic discourse and control. Not every student needs to study the same curriculum, and the implication of democratic pluralism is quite clearly that there will be commonalities which represent a core for all students, with legitimated and equal options which represent different kinds of vocational and cultural particulars and aspirations.

Similarly, each nation, whilst having a firm policy for the lingua franca within its society, will also need to have an explicit policy for mother tongue, negotiated and agreed at national level and differentiated for implementation at the school level. Not all schools have the same cultural biography and the same is true of their linguistic one.

There is a need, too, for a conceptual clarification of the relationship of multicultural education to issues of global and international citizenship. Students in all the countries contained in this volume are, in a sense, standing on the economic shoulders of the Third World's poor whilst preaching cultural and social equality. But where do the frontiers of such a commitment lie? Democratic pluralism cannot exist within impermeable economic and cultural membranes. Partnership, in the sense of shared culture across territorial boundaries, already exists in all countries in this volume. The concept of economic supremacy on which all these nations feed needs to be subjected to more critical appraisal and made more attentive to that ideal of partnership, their own democratic and humanitarian values and their declared commitments to human rights and democracy for all.

Finally, several contributors have made reference to the difficult task facing teachers if they are to come to terms with and overcome their own ethnocentrism and make creative their own value-incongruence with their pupils. Even given the introduction of criteria for teacher education, by the National Council for the Accreditation of Teacher Education in the United States and the British analogue in the United Kingdom, teachers are not well served in the countries in this volume with the vital means of updating and upgrading their professional competence to prepare pupils for democratic cultural pluralism. As Gay indicates, the central importance of teacher education in multicultural education enforces on policy makers the need to recognise teacher education, initial and inservice, as a central and priority concern of any effective multicultural education, for neglecting it will reinforce prejudice acquisition.

The Institutional Agenda

The need for holistic policies for schools and educational institutions is manifest in the pages of this volume, as it has been urged by many advocates of multicultural education elsewhere (e.g. Banks, 1981). Schools socialise and allocate life chances through their curriculum, their organisation and their assessment procedures. They express their commitment to the democratic values referred to above in those features, as in their governance, their staffing and the effectiveness of their dialogue with their communities. In their approach to assessment, and in particular in the use of tests for the allocation of life chances, new initiatives are urgently needed in order to derive more criterion-reference-based, cross-culturally valid means of appraisal which are fair to all cultural groups. This implies a policy of recognising different cultural norms in the standardisation of tests and validating all future means of assessment on all cultural groups represented within the nation-state. Such a cultural validation process is particularly required in the area of examinations, which have the function of giving access to social and economic mobility, if the continuation of current injustices is to be avoided and educational practice is to be legitimated. A societal commitment to discourse and negotiation means, within education, that such issues as that of culturally fair assessment must be legitimated on the basis of greater dialogue, openness and accountability, where criteria, judgements, scores and records, and their transmission, are equally open to parents and children (Samuda, 1975; Lynch, 1986).

If schools are to develop a more reflexive interaction with their communities, holistic policies for institutional evaluation will need to develop from current emphases on narrower student performance assessment and teachers will have to be encouraged individually and collegially to study their own practice and attitudes, extending both their criteria for judging their own performance and their cultural reference groups, for teachers cannot encourage students to throw off their ethnic encapsulation whilst themselves still residing in cultural captivity. The lockstep in the propagation of prejudice is obvious.

With all its limitations in bringing about greater equality for excluded cultural groups (Jencks, 1972), the school's task in a democratic society is to extend, complement and facilitate the initial stages of a lifelong process of multiple and mutual acculturation of students and teachers. This effect takes place as part of the differing socialisation patterns and social learning of individuals, groups and the wider society, as a basis for preparation for participation in ethnic and vocational cultures as well as in the wider national and global cultures. For such tasks, teacher preparation is indispensable, if schools are manifestly to espouse pluralistic norms and values.

Yet programmes of teacher education have a remarkable blind spot in this respect, as they have had for so long in any deeper commitment to multicultural education and prejudice reduction, drawing on cross-cultural insights and inventories (Schermerhorn, 1970). At the systemic level greater energy, resource and priority will have to be allocated to retraining and normatively re-educating teachers, and especially those who train the teachers. Already, in some cases, desperation at the lack of change in this area has provided the seedbed for proposals for coercive approaches to staff development for teachers, which fail to understand that democratic pluralism cannot be sustained by coercion – only by genuine discourse and negotiation, with a baseline of state-mandated requirements. Such discourse does not, however, obviate the need for leadership. At the institutional level, teachers need to express and espouse a firm commitment to the national covenant, representing both unity and diversity under which the schools and the teachers colleges work. At the moment, the balance is too much towards unity and too little towards (comm)unity, and there is too little willingness to break through from the provision of a curricular gloss to the deeper epistemological structure and its relationship to issues of organisation, participation and governance. Such issues of involvement are directly related to the legitimation of control in a pluralist education system, whether at systemic or institutional levels, implying a rolling programme of self- and system-evaluation for all, against publicly available criteria. The continual mapping of the cultural bibliography of the teachers' colleges and schools involves, in turn, a more central role for educational research in supporting the necessary cultural cartography, as has been indicated by the various contributions to this book.

Staff development for teacher educators and teachers in schools is in a very real sense an indisputable fulcrum to progress on educational policies addressing democratic cultural diversity, and each institution needs a comprehensive staff development programme subject to continuing monitoring and review against negotiated criteria. The individual and institutional isolation from which teachers and schools currently suffer, the 'boxed-in' nature of much contemporary teaching, calls for the acceptance of a greater role for collegiality and communality in professional decision and action and for networking schools and educational institutions with contrasting cultural biographies in the pursuit of new and extended criteria for professional judgement by teachers. Teachers have to learn to articulate in their pedagogy and personal styles learning and value patterns from a diversity of cultures and to accept that pupils also will increasingly fulfil teaching and leadership roles in collaborative patterns of learning. But they cannot be expected to do this unless those who train them are equipped to do this as well.

Values underlying such areas as library acquisition policies, materials and supplies procedures and textbook writing and acquisition all need to be subjected to clarification and renegotiation, as do also the choice of means and message of non-verbal expression such as festivals, displays, parents' evenings, school examinations and records and their communication to parents and prospective employers. Stronger connections will have to be achieved and common commitment expressed, reflecting closely the particulars of the local community and its children, and responding to the 'core' competences necessary for effective social action in a culturally pluralist democracy. Conceptual coalitions need to be forged with existing and emerging commitments to human rights and global and development education as much as political coalitions to pave the way by democratic social action for the necessary reforms.

Already in each of the societies, writings have portrayed the need for the school to reflect the basic ethic of multiculturalism in its curriculum, as also in its organisation, materials, staffing and evaluation. Schools must come to see ethnicity as an important acculturation point in education, where personality-enhancing, norm-encouraging and satisfying human interaction takes place and counters the social alienation of those who in the past were educated for a vocational activity and an economic location which no longer exists: an alienation resulting from a culturally and economically inappropriate education, neglectful of newly extended dimensions of human activity and commitment.

Western societies are now facing something more significant than a diversity necessitating ad hoc, piecemeal responses: a new and unprecedented challenge to interpret and reform their democratic ideals and structures to capitalise on cultural diversity. If the rise of a 'new ethnicity' can be seen as an opportunity and a challenge, rather than a threat, it can be a means of achieving a more satisfying and meaningful social identity for more members of society and of disengaging from the current ratchet of decline in community relations. Ethnicity can be a new means of sustaining democratic commitment to cultural pluralism, to political freedom, to human rights for all and to democracy. If the opportunity is not seized, however, and the challenge of cultural diversity is not faced, the failure will be likely to prove a source of successive legitimation crises, political unrest and disintegration, with devastating economic and social consequences.

Based on the analyses presented in this book, Western societies have no alternative but fruitless recourse to coercive and authoritarian, dysfunctional and ultimately destructive and crisis-deepening means, if they do not respond positively and creatively to the opportunity presented by the ethnic revivals and cultural dilemmas with which they are now convulsed. For this task, they need to recognise new ways of forging creative coalitions across issues and groups in society and, through intensified discourse, to foster, re-interpret and expand continuing and fundamental commitments inherent within a democratic way of life. Such coalitions in turn afford a means of achieving a greater equality of discourse as a means of resolving the contradictory impulses at the heart of democratic pluralism: change and continuity, idealism and realism, freedom and necessity, and individual and group justice. In that sense, the new ethnicity is a pathfinder to a new democracy, and multicultural education remains a potentially efficacious means of achieving that new democracy.

REFERENCES

Banks, J. A. (1981) *Multiethnic Education: Theory and Practice*. Boston: Allyn and Bacon.

Brandt, W. (Chairman) (1980) *Report of the Independent Commission on International Development Issues (North–South: A Programme for Survival)*. London: Pan.

Brandt, W. (Chairman) (1983) *Report of the Brandt Commission (Common Crisis: North–South: Co-operation for World Recovery)*. London: Pan.

Bullivant, B. (1981) *The Pluralist Dilemma*. Sydney: George Allen and Unwin.

Bullivant, B. (1984) *Pluralism: Cultural Maintenance and Evolution*. Clevedon, Avon: Multilingual Matters.

Canada, House of Commons (1982) *The Canadian Constitution 1981*. Ottawa: Minister of Supply and Services.

Commission for Racial Equality (1985) *Immigration Control Procedures: Report of a Formal Investigation*. London: CRE.

Glazer, N. (1983) *Ethnic Dilemmas 1964–82*. Cambridge, Massachusetts: Harvard University Press.

Habermas, J. (1976) *Legitimation Crisis*. London: Heinemann.

Habermas, J. (1979) *Communication and the Evolution of Society*. London: Heinemann.

Jencks, C. et al. (1972) *Inequality: A Reassessment of the Effects of Family and Schooling in America*. New York: Basic Books.

Katz, J. H. (1978) *White Awareness: Handbook for Anti-Racism Training*. Norman, Oklahoma: University of Oklahoma.

Lynch, J. (1986) *Multicultural Education: Principles and Practice*. London: Routledge and Kegan Paul.

Samuda, R. J. (1975) *Psychological Testing of American Minorities: Issues and Consequences*. New York: Dodd, Mead.

Schermerhorn, R. A. (1970) *Comparative Ethnic Relations*. New York: Random House.

United Nations (1983a) *Human Rights: International Instruments*. Geneva: UN.

United Nations (1983b) *Human Rights: A Compilation of International Instruments*. Geneva: UN.

Whitaker, B. (ed.) (1985) *Minorities*. Oxford:

Pergamon.

Young, C. (1976) *The Politics of Cultural Pluralism*. Madison, Wisconsin: The University of Wisconsin Press.

BIBLIOGRAPHY

Allport, G. W. (1950) *The Nature of Prejudice*. Reading, Massachusetts: Addison-Wesley. This book has now become an essential baseline for all students of race relations.

Banks, J. A. (1981) *Multiethnic Education: Theory and Practice*. Boston: Allyn and Bacon. This book is a highly readable and indispensable basic text for the student of multiethnic education. It is helpfully and attractively laid out and contains a wealth of information on the theory and practice of multiethnic education.

Bullivant, B. M. (1981) *Race, Ethnicity and Curriculum*. Melbourne: The Macmillan Company of Australia. This challenging book argues the weakness of approaches to multicultural education and seeks to link theory and practice by substituting modern, realistic theories of culture, race and ethnicity.

Centre for Contemporary Cultural Studies (1982) *The Empire Strikes Back*. London: Hutchinson. This collection of papers attacks the racism of contemporary Britain, points to this as part of a long-term political and economic crisis and highlights the failure of existing race relations theory to deal adequately with that situation.

Geertz, C. (1973) *The Interpretation of Culture*. New York: Basic Books. This book comprises a collection of essays on culture by an eminent US anthropologist.

Gordon, M. M. (1964) *Assimilation in American Life: The Role of Race, Religion and National Origins*. New York: Oxford University Press. This is a seminal theoretical book which has been deeply influential in the United States and abroad on the consideration of the multiethnic society.

Green, R. L. (1977) *The Urban Challenge: Poverty and Race*. Chicago: Follett Publishing Company. Areas of urban life such as housing, education and welfare are covered in this collection of material by a well-known academic in the field of race relations.

Habermas, J. (1976) *Legitimation Crisis*. London: Heinemann. In this landmark study, Habermas draws on both systems theory and sociology to identify four major levels of crisis in modern society which may be considered major theoretical inputs into a consideration of multicultural education.

Katz, J. H. (1978) *White Awareness: Handbook for Anti-Racism Training*. Norman, Oklahoma: University of Oklahoma. This book not only seeks to argue the case for racism being a white problem, but also presents a six-part programme to change attitudes and actions.

Lynch, J. (1983) *The Multicultural Curriculum*. London: Batsford. This book seeks to construct a curricular structure for multicultural education based on ethical and social evidence and arguments about the nature of a multicultural society.

Lynch, J. (1986) *Multicultural Education: Principles and Practice*. London: Routledge and Kegan Paul. This book seeks to provide a coherent strategy for teachers adopting policies of multicultural education in their own schools. It includes extensive references to the international literature.

Milner, D. (1983) *Children and Race: Ten Years On*. London: Ward Lock Educational. This successor volume to Milner's earlier book on children and race contains a wide selection of material on the most recent developments in Britain and the United States concerning multicultural education policies and the continuities and changes in racism.

Ogbu, J. U. (1978) *Minority Education and Caste: The American System in Cross-Cultural Perspective*. New York: Academic Press. The concept of caste is used in this book as a comparative basis for minority education in the United States and the education of ethnic groups in Britain, India, New Zealand and Japan.

Rose, P. I. (1974) *They and We: Racial and Ethnic Relations in the United States*. New York: Random House. An indispensable and well-written introduction to major concepts in race relations such as race, ethnicity, prejudice and discrimination.

Sowell, T. (1975) *Race and Economics*. New York: David McKay. This highly readable book discusses the relationship between ethnicity, race and economic achievement.

Verma, G. K. & Bagley, C. (ed.) (1975) *Race and Education Across Cultures*. London: Heinemann. This collection of essays examines race and education in the United States, Australia and Britain.

Glossary

ACCOMMODATION

Accommodation takes place when groups with different cultures, values and ethos maintain their separate identities but live in peaceful interaction. When accommodation occurs, potential conflicts between culturally different groups are minimised because the groups adjust their relationships to each other in order to resolve competition and disagreements.

ACCULTURATION

Acculturation takes place when the culture of an individual or group is modified as it comes into contact with another culture. When cultures come into contact, they influence each other and an exchange of cultural elements occurs. Even when a group is conquered, it influences the culture of its conquerors. The Greeks, even though conquered by the Romans, influenced Roman culture. The Aztec Indians in the Americas also influenced the culture of their conquerors, the Spaniards. The migrant groups that have settled in Western European nations since the Second World War have influenced and are influencing the cultures of their host nations.

ANTI-RACIST EDUCATION

This concept, which is primarily British but is to some extent Canadian, describes a process used by teachers and other educators to eliminate institutionalised racism from the school and society and to help individuals to develop non-racist attitudes. In the anti-racist educational reform movement in the United Kingdom, institutionalised racism is a primary focus, although race awareness workshops and training which focus on individual racism are also a part of this concept. When anti-racist educational reform is implemented, curriculum materials, group and streaming practices, hiring policies, teacher attitudes and expectations, and school policy and practices are examined and steps are taken to eliminate racism from these school variables. A related educational movement in the United States, which focuses more on individuals than on institutions, is known as **prejudice reduction**.

196

ASSIMILATIONIST IDEOLOGY

The assimilationist ideology is a set of beliefs and assumptions which envisages one dominant culture within a society (monism) that all ethnic and cultural groups are expected to acquire. The newer Western immigrant nations, such as the United States and Australia, have historically had strong assimilationist ideologies which have often resulted in cultural dominance and the destruction of the cultures of indigenous ethnic and cultural groups. The tenacious assimilationist ideology in most Western nations has been seriously challenged by the cultural pluralist ideology and ethnic revitalisation movements since the 1960s. Individuals and groups that embrace the cultural assimilationist ideology are called **cultural assimilationists**.

CULTURAL ASSIMILATION

Cultural assimilation takes place when one ethnic or cultural group acquires the behaviour, values, perspectives, ethos and characteristics of another cultural or ethnic group and sheds its own cultural characteristics. **Assimilation** differs from **acculturation**. When acculturation takes place, the group acquires some of the characteristics of another ethnic or cultural group but maintains the essence of its own culture. When assimilation takes place, the group completely loses its original culture. An individual as well as a group can experience the process of assimilation.

In the history of most of the Western nations, policy related to ethnic and immigrant groups has most often been assimilationist oriented. The assimilation of ethnic and immigrant groups in nations such as the United States and Australia has often been harsh and not infrequently resulted in the cultural dominance over and genocide of indigenous ethnic and cultural groups. One of the ironies of the assimilationist policies in the Western democratic nations is that non-white ethnic groups were often denied the opportunity to attain the characteristics needed to assimilate into the society at the same time as they were described as being unassimilable. See also **structural assimilation**.

CULTURAL PLURALISM

Cultural pluralism exists when various cultures, ethnic and religious groups within a nation-state maintain separate group identities and important aspects of their cultures. Cultural pluralism is also an ideology based on the assumption that various cultural and ethnic groups have a right within a democratic pluralistic nation-state to maintain their cultures and group identities as long as these do not conflict with the overarching values and goals of the nation-state. **Cultural pluralists** also believe that the cultures of various groups enrich a nation and provide it with alternative ways to view the world and to solve complex human problems.

Implementing cultural pluralism within a modernised, democratic nation-state is problematic because of the inherent conflicts between the needs, goals and aspirations of cultural and ethnic groups and the values and goals of democratic nation-states.

DEMOCRATIC PLURALISM

Democratic pluralism exists within a society that has an overarching set of egalitarian values and goals that are shared by all subgroups within it. However, groups are allowed to maintain cultural differences that do not conflict with the overarching values of the nation-state. Groups can also organise politically in order to promote their economic, social and cultural interests.

ETHNIC GROUP

An ethnic group is a collectivity that shares a common history and culture, and common values, behaviours and other characteristics that cause members of the group to have a shared identity. A sense of peoplehood is one of the most important characteristics of an ethnic group. An ethnic group also shares economic and political interests. Cultural characteristics, rather than biological traits, are the essential characteristics of an ethnic group. An ethnic group is not the same as a racial group. Some ethnic groups, such as Puerto Ricans in the United States, are made up of individuals who belong to several different racial groups.

An ethnic group may be a majority or a minority within a society. Ethnic minority groups are usually distinguished from an ethnic majority group by unique physical and/or cultural characteristics – which make them convenient targets of racism and discrimination – and by having little political or economic power within society. Ethnic minority groups are usually a numerical minority within their societies. However, the blacks in South Africa, who are a numerical majority within their nation-state, are often considered a sociological minority group by social scientists because they are politically and economically powerless.

Majority groups within a society, such as the Anglos in the United States and Canada, usually resist being called an ethnic group. These groups usually prefer to limit their use of this term to subordinate groups that have distinctive cultural and/or physical characteristics. Many social scientists, however, consider all groups within a society that have distinctive cultural characteristics and a group identity to be ethnic groups.

ETHNIC REVITALISATION MOVEMENT

An ethnic revitalisation movement consists of collective action by an oppressed or victimised racial, ethnic or cultural group to attain inclusion and structural equality within its society and/or nation-state. Ethnic revitalisation movements usually have political, social, cultural and economic goals and characteristics. In the ethnic revitalisation movements that have developed within the Western democratic nations since the 1960s, a major goal has been to change educational institutions so that they reflect the cultures, languages and ethos of marginalised racial, ethnic and cultural groups. Ethnic revitalisation movements usually arise when racial or ethnic groups have internalised a democratic ideology and yet are the victims of institutionalised racism and discrimination.

Ethnic revitalisation movements usually develop within pluralistic democratic nation-states that have not fulfilled their democratic ideals but that permit interest groups to mobilise to promote the group's needs and interests. Ethnic revitalisation movements usually experience different phases that have identifiable characteristics (see Table 1.1, p. 7).

IDEOLOGY

An ideology is an interrelated set of beliefs, ideas and assumptions held by a group or society that reflects, justifies, defends and rationalises its institutions, practices and policies. The ideology of a particular group or society both justifies and reflects its economic and class interests. The curriculum within the schools usually reflects and perpetuates the ideology of the dominant group or groups within a society. Individuals and groups in power usually resist attempts to implement educational programmes and practices that undercut and do not reinforce their ideology.

There has been a great deal of debate within the Western nations about whether the educational reform movement known as multicultural education reinforces or undercuts the dominant assimilationist ideologies extant in Western democratic societies. Assimilationists and radical theorists differ in their assessments of multicultural education (Banks, 1984a). Assimilationist theorists believe that multi-cultural education is a threat to the dominant ideologies within their nation-states. However, radical scholars view multicultural education as a movement that reinforces the dominant assimilationist ideologies in the Western nations because it gives the illusion of change and yet does not promote the restructuring of the institutions that keep powerless groups oppressed. The divergent assessments of multicultural education may result in part from the many different ways in which it is conceptualised in various nations, states, school districts and schools.

INTERACTIONISM

Interactionism is genuine *two-way* interchange between members of two or more ethnic groups where both sides actively participate and share in the process of interaction. It differs from integration, which usually only makes allowance for the retention of selected innocuous features of ethnic cultures, and implies a limited degree of their diffusion to the dominant ethnic group in a pluralist society.

LIBERAL ASSIMILATIONIST

This concept, also known as the liberal expectancy, was developed largely by social scientists in the United States. It views the ideal society as one in which individuals from diverse racial, ethnic and cultural groups participate fully in the society and have equality. However, in order for this kind of open, modernised society to be created, individuals must be freed of their ethnic and cultural attachments and characteristics. This is essential because ethnic attachments and affiliations are inconsistent with a modernised, democratic society. Ethnic cultures and attachments promote conflict and tensions, and promote group rights over the rights of the individual. In a modernised, democratic society, individual rights must be paramount.

Liberal assimilationists believed that Western societies were becoming increasingly less ethnic and more modern when the ethnic revitalisation movements emerged in the 1960s. These movements caught them completely by surprise because they were inconsistent with their concepts and assumptions about the continuing march toward modernisation and progress in the Western nations.

MODERNISATION

Politically and socially modernised societies are characterised by a democratic pluralistic political system, social-class mobility, and an ideology that envisages a society in which individuals from diverse racial, ethnic and cultural groups experience equality and full participation. However, as this concept was formulated by Western social scientists, individuals must be freed of their ethnic and traditional cultures in order to participate fully in and to acquire equality in a modernised nation-state. Modernists view ethnic affiliations and cultures as antithetical to the development of a modernised, democratic nation-state. They view traditionalism and modernity as inherently conflicting.

The concepts **modernisation** and **modernity** have been criticised in recent years as being Western-centric concepts that view development from a biased Western perspective and that fail to envisage diverse ways in which nations – particularly those in the Third World – can experience development and formulate a democratic infrastructure.

MULTICULTURAL EDUCATION

Multicultural education emerged as a response to the ethnic revitalisation movements that arose in the Western democratic nations during the 1960s and 1970s. A major goal of these movements was educational reform so that students from diverse racial, ethnic and social-class groups would experience educational equity. In its first phase of development, multicultural education was primarily **ethnic studies**, the scientific and humanistic study of the history and cultures of ethnic groups. In time, **multiethnic education** was developed, a reform movement designed to change the total school environment so that students from various ethnic and racial groups would attain educational parity with students from majority groups.

The development of the broader concept of multiethnic education was significant because with it came the realisation by ethnic studies advocates that the inclusion of ethnic content in the curriculum was necessary but not sufficient to help students from diverse groups to attain academic success. When multiethnic education is implemented, the total school environment is reformed, including the hidden curriculum, institutional norms, school policy, teaching methods and materials, and assessment and testing procedures.

Multicultural education is a broad concept that encompasses *ethnic studies, multiethnic education* and *anti-racist education*. It consists of educational reform that is designed to reform the school environment so that many different kinds of groups, including ethnic groups, women, and students with special needs (e.g. the handicapped and the gifted), will experience educational equality and academic parity. A debate is taking place in several nations about how far the boundaries of multicultural education can and should be expanded and exactly what groups and issues should be encompassed within the concept.

PARADIGM

A paradigm is a model or schema that describes an interrelated set of facts, concepts, generalisations and theories that attempt to explain human behaviour or a social phenomenon and that imply policy and action. A paradigm, which is also a set of explanations, has specific goals, assumptions and values that can be described. Paradigms compete with each other in the arena of ideas and public policy. When one paradigm replaces another, what Kuhn (1970) has described as a scientific revolution occurs. However, what happens more frequently is that new paradigms coexist with older ones and provide alternative explanations for human behaviour and justify different public policies. In recent years, for example, the theory of multiple intelligences (Gardner, 1983) has challenged the traditional conception that views human intelligence as fixed and related primarily to genetic characteristics (Jensen, 1969). However, both the old and the new paradigms exist side by side, with the old paradigm having more influence in educational theory and school practice.

RACISM

Racism is a belief that human groups can be validly grouped on the basis of their biological traits and that these identifiable groups inherit certain mental, personality and cultural characteristics that determine their behaviour. Racism, however, is not merely a set of beliefs but is practised when a group has the power to enforce laws, institutions and norms, based on its beliefs, which oppress and dehumanise another group (Banks, 1984b). Racism exists in various forms; it can be personal, overt or institutional. Institutional racism occurs when structures exist within institutions that suppress and subordinate individuals and groups with particular physical characteristics.

STRUCTURAL ASSIMILATION

Structural assimilation, according to Gordon (1964), takes place when an ethnic group gains entry into the cliques, clubs and institutions of the host society on a primary group level. Gordon points out that a group can attain cultural assimilation but be denied structural assimilation or inclusion. When this happens an ethnic group such as blacks in the United States acquires the cultural characteristics of the dominant cultural group, Anglo-Americans, but is denied entry into its cliques, clubs and other institutions on a primary group level. Gordon maintains that this describes the relationship of ethnic minority groups to the majority ethnic groups in the United States. He concludes that the United States is characterised by high levels of cultural assimilation but by structural pluralism because culturally assimilated members of ethnic groups such as blacks, Jews and Italians maintain their own ethnic institutions because they are often denied entry into those of the majority group.

STRUCTURAL INTEGRATION

Individuals and groups are structurally integrated into a society or nation-state when they are able to participate fully in its social, economic, political and educational institutions. When they are denied these opportunities, they are **structurally excluded**. When individuals and groups are structurally integrated into a society, they not only participate within its major institutions, but experience equality and exercise power within them. Individuals and groups can be **structurally assimilated** within a society or institution and yet experience inequality and exercise little power within it.

STRUCTURAL PLURALISM

This is a form of pluralism in which there are separate and distinct sets of structures and institutions, each controlled by an ethnocultural, racial or other group, and extending from the local, through regional, up to the nation-state levels of influence, e.g. several separate legal systems, languages, social welfare bureaucracies, public (state) education systems, etc.

TRADITIONALISM

Traditionalism is a belief that a group's culture (including its behaviour, values and languages), which has been handed down from the past, should be valued and perpetuated. In this book, traditionalism is used to describe original cultures and is contrasted with ethnic cultures that have been mediated or changed by modernisation and technological societies.

REFERENCES

Banks, J. A. (1984a) Multicultural education and its critics: Britain and the United States. *The New Era,* **65**(3), 58–65.

Banks, J. A. (1984b) *Teaching Strategies for Ethnic Studies*, third edition. Boston: Allyn and Bacon.

Gardner, H. (1983) *Frames of Mind: The Theory of Multiple Intelligences*. New York: Basic Books.

Gordon, M. M. (1964) *Assimilation in American Life*. New York: Oxford University Press.

Jensen, A. R. (1969) How much can we boost IQ and scholastic achievement? *Harvard Educational Review,* **39**, 1–123.

Kuhn, T. S. (1970) *The Structure of Scientific Revolutions*, second edition, enlarged. Chicago: University of Chicago Press.

Index